STRUCTURED FORTRAN WITH WATFIV-S

Paul Cress

Systems Dimensions Limited, Ottawa, Ontario

Paul Dirksen

University of Manitoba, Winnipeg, Manitoba

J. Wesley Graham

University of Waterloo, Waterloo, Ontario

PRENTICE-HALL, INC., Englewood Cliffs, N.J. 07632

Library of Congress Cataloging in Publication Data

Cress, Paul.
    Structured FORTRAN with WATFIV-S.

    Includes index.
    1. FORTRAN (Computer program language) 2. Struc-
tured programming. I. Dirksen, Paul, joint author.
II. Graham, James Wesley, 1932-   joint author.
III. Title.
QA76.73.F25C73   001.64'24   80-14310
ISBN 0-13-854752-1

© 1980 by Prentice-Hall, Inc., Englewood Cliffs, N.J. 07632

Printed in the United States of America

10 9 8 7 6 5 4 3 2 1

Prentice-Hall International, Inc., *London*
Prentice-Hall of Australia Pty. Limited, *Sydney*
Prentice-Hall of Canada, Ltd., *Toronto*
Prentice-Hall of India Private Limited, *New Delhi*
Prentice-Hall of Japan, Inc., *Tokyo*
Prentice-Hall of Southeast Asia Pte. Ltd., *Singapore*
Whitehall Books Limited, *Wellington, New Zealand*

CONTENTS

PREFACE

WATFIV-S, Version 2, is the latest in a series of FORTRAN compilers developed at the University of Waterloo. WATFOR was developed in 1967, and was basically a FORTRAN-IV compiler with a few important extensions such as format-free input-output. At that time the SHARE FORTRAN Committee was considering extensions to the FORTRAN language. As a result of ideas obtained from the work of this Committee and others the WATFIV compiler was written in 1968. This incorporated many new features into WATFOR; two of the most important were character variables and direct-access input-output.

In the early 1970's structured programming was becoming the accepted style in which to write programs. To write structured programs in FORTRAN required the addition of several new control statements. This was done in 1974, and the resulting compiler was called WATFIV-S.

During the past few years much experience has been gained writing structured programs. In particular, countless people have used the WATFIV-S compiler. Some have suggested a number of additional control constructs which would make the language more powerful. These constructs have been added to WATFIV-S, and the resulting compiler is called WATFIV-S, Version 2.

This text is written specifically to describe this latest WATFIV-S dialect of FORTRAN. Since the emphasis is on the structured programming style, and FORTRAN does not have the required statements, the programs reflect a considerable departure from the language known as FORTRAN. Thus this text is intended to satisfy the specific needs of those users of WATFIV-S, rather than the general user community. Having said that, it is important to add that WATFIV-S contains FORTRAN-IV as a proper subset, and consequently this text includes a comprehensive treatment of FORTRAN-IV. However, for readers who prefer to program using FORTRAN-IV without the structured statements, we should point out that another text written by the same authors and published by Prentice-Hall is probably more appropriate. The title is FORTRAN IV WITH WATFOR AND WATFIV.

The material has been collected from notes and problems that have been in use at the University of Waterloo during the past 20 years. We have attempted to present the material in a manner which has received majority acceptance from students over the years.

The reader will note that the book begins with the imme-diate introduction of a program. We have found that it is important to begin work with the computer as soon as possible - preferably immediately after the first lecture. The interest of the student is then usually so strong that he is motivated to proceed with his work as quickly as possible.

We have chosen to use a rather informal style. Each new concept is introduced by considering an example and then discussing it. Usually the concepts are not tied together formally until a number of examples have been considered. This use of examples is consistent with our belief that "an example is worth a thousand words" and this belief has been justified many times by the responses of our own students.

The book is concerned exclusively with a description of the WATFIV-S language. It does not have an introduction to the digital computer, a discussion of input-output devices, or a dissertation upon number systems. It is assumed that the reader either has already learned such material, or else is learning it concurrently by using one of the many other available reference books. We assume that teachers are well-versed in this other material, and are fully capable of presenting it to their students.

We would like to thank Mrs. Kay Harrison for her careful typing of successive forms of the manuscript. We would also like to acknowledge the work of Ian McPhee and Bruce Hay who are largely responsible for adding the structured statements to the original WATFIV.

Finally, this text was printed on a Multiwriter terminal using the SCRIPT processor. We would like to thank Roger Watt and Bruce Uttley for their invaluable advice concerning the setup and format of the material.

Waterloo, Ontario, Canada   P. H. Cress
                                   P. H. Dirksen
                                   J. W. Graham

Chapter 1

INTRODUCTION TO FORTRAN

This chapter will serve as a general introduction to the WATFIV-S dialect of the FORTRAN language. No attempt will be made to be rigorous, since rigor at this stage tends to introduce details which are unnecessarily confusing to the beginner. The object of this chapter is to introduce the novice to many of the ideas in the FORTRAN language and to put him in a position to solve problems as quickly as possible. The remainder of the book expands upon this introduction and considers the various aspects of the language in more detail.

1.1   BASIC PRINCIPLES

FORTRAN is a language which is useful for expressing many common problems in a form suitable for computer processing. It seems reasonable, therefore, to begin a discussion of FORTRAN by considering a number of problems and examining their formulation using the language.

Example 1.1 illustrates how one could calculate the square of 4 and print the result. This, of course, is too trivial a problem to be considered for solution using a computer, but nevertheless it serves to illustrate a number of important points. More challenging problems will follow!

This example consists of seven statements, the first two of which are comments describing the problem. Comment statements are recognizable by the letter C to the left and will appear in most examples for identification purposes; they serve no other useful purpose. The third statement assigns the value 4 to the real variable X. The fourth statement assigns to Y the value of X multiplied by itself. Note that multiplication is denoted by the symbol *. The fifth statement prints the values of X and Y side by side. The sixth statement brings the process to a halt. The END statement has a special purpose which will be explained in Section 1.2.

```
C EXAMPLE 1.1
C THIS PROGRAM CALCULATES THE SQUARE OF 4
      X = 4.
      Y = X * X
      PRINT, X, Y
      STOP
      END
```

It is important to note that the statements are interpreted sequentially, beginning with X=4. and proceeding until the process is halted. The seven statements, taken collectively, are referred to as a program.

The problem can be further extended by requesting that the squares of 4, 5, 6, 7, etc., be calculated and printed. The solution is illustrated in Example 1.2.

```
C EXAMPLE 1.2
C CALCULATE SQUARES OF 4, 5, 6, 7,  ETC.
      X = 4.
      LOOP
          Y = X * X
          PRINT, X, Y
          X = X + 1.
      ENDLOOP
      END
```

In this case, the statements

```
      Y = X * X
      PRINT, X, Y
      X = X + 1.
```

are to be repeated an indefinite number of times for increasing values of X. This is accomplished by inserting the LOOP statement at the beginning of the statements to be repeated. Y is calculated and the result is printed. Then X is increased by 1. The ENDLOOP statement then causes <u>control</u> to transfer to the beginning of the <u>loop</u>. Once control is transferred, Y is recomputed, this time using the current value of X which is 5. Control resumes sequentially; the results are printed and X is incremented. Then control is transferred once again. It is obvious that the process will continue in a loop endlessly, but will calculate squares of integers beginning at 4 as required. A means of halting the process will be considered in Example 1.3.

The statement X=X+1. is worthy of comment. This is obviously not an equation, which underlines the fact that "=" is not used in its usual arithmetic sense. In FORTRAN, "=" means "is assigned the value". As a result, the statement is properly interpreted to mean "X is assigned the value X+1".

Note that the three statements contained in the <u>range</u> of the loop have been indented 4 spaces. This is done to improve readability so the loop can be readily identified. Later in this chapter we will point out that blank columns in FORTRAN are usually ignored by the computer; thus the number of spaces could just as easily have been 5 or 3, and this is a matter of style chosen by the authors.

In Example 1.3 below, a condition has been placed upon the transfer of control out of the loop. After X is incremented, control proceeds to the IF statement. If X is greater than 9, control transfers out of the loop by means of the QUIT statement. This means that the statement following the ENDLOOP is executed - in this case the STOP. If X is less than or equal to 9, control passes to the ENDLOOP statement. This, of course, causes the loop to be repeated. Note that "greater than" is written as .GT. in FORTRAN.

```
C EXAMPLE 1.3
C CALCULATE SQUARES OF 4, 5, 6, ..., 9
      X = 4.
      LOOP
          Y = X * X
          PRINT, X, Y
          X = X + 1.
          IF (X .GT. 9.) QUIT
      ENDLOOP
      STOP
      END
```

The word IF is followed by an expression in parentheses which, when evaluated, gives the answer "true" or "false". This is referred to as a logical-valued expression or, more briefly, a logical expression. If the logical expression is true, the statement that follows it (in the same line) is carried out; if it is false, the next sequential statement is taken.

All constants used to date contain the decimal point, even though they are integers. In a later chapter we will find that this is not always necessary, but for the time being the programmer should use the decimal point in all constants.

1.2 PREPARATION FOR THE COMPUTER

Once a program has been written, it is necessary to put it into machine-readable form so that it can be processed by a computer. One way of doing this is to punch the program into cards using a special machine called a key-punch. Normally we punch one statement per card, beginning in column 7 or beyond. No statement should use columns 73 to 80 of the card. Comment statements are an exception, as they are identified by a "C" in column 1 followed by whatever message is required. As in other statements, columns 73 to 80 should not be used.

When punching cards the user will notice that only upper case is available for the letters. He is allowed to leave blank columns whenever he feels it will make the program more readable. For example, ENDLOOP could be written and key-punched as END LOOP, and either form is acceptable to the computer. The rule is to insert blanks at will; the computer will ignore them.

Figure 1.1 shows an interpreted card deck containing the program for Example 1.3.

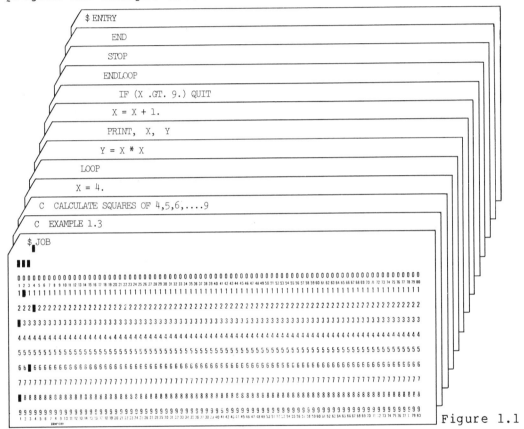

Figure 1.1

Note that two special cards are required, one at each end of the deck. These cards ($JOB and $ENTRY) are called <u>control cards</u>, and are not part of the FORTRAN language. They are necessary to instruct the <u>supervisor</u> or <u>monitor</u> and may vary from computer to computer. The reader should consult his installation's operating manual for the precise format of these special control cards.

- 5 -

The reader will notice that the special FORTRAN statement END has been used as the last statement of every program. In fact, every FORTRAN program must have the END statement as its last statement. When the card deck is read into the computer, this is a signal that the program has been completely read in. Execution can then begin with the first executable statement in the program. Execution is terminated when the STOP statement is encountered. It is important to understand this difference between the STOP and END statements; END signals the physical end of the program, whereas STOP terminates the processing. The END statement is always the last statement, but the STOP statement can appear anywhere in a program. It is also important to note that END is a non-executable statement as are comment statements.

There are ways other than keypunches that can be used to prepare programs. One such way is to use a terminal. In this case, one does not have a deck of cards; instead the program is entered directly into the computer's memory. However the same column rules and control "cards" must be used because the computer functions as if it were reading cards. The method of preparing programs varies from installation to installation and the reader should check for the specific means available.

We will now consider how answers are communicated to us by the computer. When the program deck, as illustrated in Figure 1.1, is submitted to the computer, the results appear on the printer as illustrated in Figure 1.2.

4.0000000	16.0000000
5.0000000	25.0000000
6.0000000	36.0000000
7.0000000	49.0000000
8.0000000	64.0000000
9.0000000	81.0000000

Figure 1.2

When dealing with very large or very small numbers, the values printed will appear in a different format, namely

0.xxxxxxxE yy

which is a computer notation meaning .xxxxxxx times 10 to the power yy. Thus the constants .000006255 and 1,234,000,000 would print out as 0.6255000E-05 and 0.1234000E 10 respectively.

The reader is now in a position to attempt the first set of exercises which are merely extensions of the ideas in Example 1.3.

1.3 EXERCISES

1.1 Calculate a table of squares for the integers ranging from -10 to 10 inclusive.

1.2 Compute a table of squares for the even integers from 2 to 40 inclusive.

1.3 Compute a table of cubes for the odd integers ranging from 1 to 20 inclusive. Note that the statement

Y=X*X*X

can be used.

1.4 Tabulate the function

$$y=x^3+x+2$$

for x = -1, 0, 1, 2, ..., 8.

1.4   COMPILERS

Programs written in FORTRAN cannot be processed directly on any computer. They must be translated into the language of the computer by a compiler. A compiler is a special program read into the computer when the monitor encounters the $JOB control card. This special program is capable of translating FORTRAN statements into what is referred to as machine language. The compiler which is the subject of this book is called WATFIV-S.

WATFIV-S not only compiles the FORTRAN program, but detects errors in syntax while doing so. For example,

$$I+J = K*K$$

is meaningless in FORTRAN. The WATFIV-S compiler would detect this and inform the programmer by printing an error message. A list of all WATFIV-S error messages is given in Appendix B.

1.5   TIMING

It is important to note that every program processed on a computer using WATFIV-S goes through two distinct phases, one following the other in time. First the program is compiled, and then it is executed. We refer to these two phases as compile time and execution time.

WATFIV-S detects errors, not only at compile time, but at execution time as well. For example, the consecutive statements

$$X=0.$$
$$Y=3./X$$

would be compiled, but of course Y cannot be computed, since division by zero is undefined. This would be detected by WATFIV-S at execution time, and an appropriate error message would be printed.

1.6　MORE EXAMPLES

Example 1.4 evaluates the function

$$b = \frac{a^2 + 3a - 2.3}{a + 4.1}$$

for a = 1.25, 1.50, 1.75, ..., 3.00.　(Note that the dot in 2.3 is, as always in this book, a decimal point.)

```
C EXAMPLE 1.4
C EVALUATE FUNCTION
      A = 1.25
      LOOP
         B = (A*A + 3.*A - 2.3) / (A + 4.1)
         PRINT, A, B
         A = A +  .25
         IF (A .GT. 3.) QUIT
      ENDLOOP
      STOP
      END
```

Here we have introduced two new real variables, A and B. This begs the question: "What real variable names can be used in FORTRAN?"　Before answering this question, we must define the term FORTRAN symbolic name.　A FORTRAN symbolic name is any sequence of up to six characters chosen from the letters, the digits, and the character $; it must not begin with a digit.　Thus CAT, $12, MABLE, and J12 are examples of symbolic names, whereas CHARLIE and 2P are not.

A FORTRAN real variable can be any FORTRAN symbolic name not beginning with any of the letters I to N inclusive.　Thus MABLE and J12 are not real variables.　In a later chapter we will see how to use symbolic names beginning with the letters I to N inclusive.

Every statement in which a variable is assigned a value is referred to as an assignment statement.　Assignment statements which are used in this example are

(a)   A = 1.25

(b)   B = (A*A + 3.*A - 2.3) / (A. + 4.1)

(c)   A = A + .25

Note that a single variable always appears to the left of the equals sign and an _expression_ to the right of it. An expression can be a simple constant as in (a), or can be quite involved as in (b). In (b), we see that / is used for division, and that parentheses are used as in algebra to group sub-expressions which are to be considered as single units. In (c), we see that the variable to the left of the equals sign can also appear in the expression to the right of it.

The statement PRINT,A,B is referred to as an _input-output statement_ or, more briefly, an I/O statement. Using this statement, we can print the _values_ of any of the variables which have been assigned by the program. It is important to recognize that the values represented by the variables are printed, not the variables themselves.

The IF, LOOP, ENDLOOP, QUIT, and STOP statements are known as _control statements_ because they control the sequence in which the statements are executed.

Example 1.5 illustrates a FORTRAN program for computing the cubes, squares, square roots, and cube roots of all the integers from 1 to 10 inclusive.

```
C EXAMPLE 1.5
C CALCULATE CUBES, SQUARES, AND ROOTS
      X = 1.
      LOOP
          A = X**3.
          B = X**2.
          C = SQRT(X)
          D = X**(1./3.)
          PRINT, X, A, B, C, D
          X = X + 1.
          IF (X .GT. 10.) QUIT
      ENDLOOP
      STOP
      END
```

Here the exponentiation operator ** is illustrated. The expression X**3. means X^3 and the expression X**(1./3.) means $X^{1/3}$.

The FORTRAN function SQRT is introduced for computation of the square root. The letters SQRT are always followed by an expression contained in parentheses. The computer first evaluates the expression, then its square root. If the value for the expression is negative, the WATFIV-S compiler will produce an execution-time error diagnostic.

A few of the many other functions available are SIN, COS, ABS, ALOG, and EXP; these are used to calculate sine, cosine, absolute value, natural logarithm, and exponential respectively. Each of these evaluates the appropriate function of the parenthesized expression immediately following it. In the case of SIN and COS, the real expression represents radians, rather than degrees.

These functions are referred to as built-in functions, since they are a part of the FORTRAN language. In later chapters we will see how the user can define his own functions.

Example 1.6 calculates the sum of squares of the first 50 integers and prints the results.

```
C EXAMPLE 1.6
C CALCULATE SUM OF SQUARES
      SUM = 0.
      X = 1.
      LOOP
          SUM = SUM + X**2.
          X = X + 1.
          IF (X .GT. 50.) QUIT
      ENDLOOP
      PRINT, SUM
      STOP
      END
```

This example illustrates the use of <u>initialization</u>. The statements

```
SUM = 0.
X = 1.
```

are executed only <u>once</u> and are said to <u>initialize</u> the values of X and SUM prior to entering the loop. SUM is used to accumulate the total, while X is incremented by 1 each time through the loop. When X reaches 51, the process drops out of the loop and proceeds to print the computed sum of squares.

Examples 1.7 and 1.8 point out common errors committed by FORTRAN programmers.

```
C EXAMPLE 1.7
      X = 3.
      Y = X**2 + A
      PRINT, X, Y
      STOP
      END
```

When the computer attempts to calculate the expression X**2+A it cannot do so, since A has not previously been assigned a value. The variable A is referred to as an <u>undefined</u> <u>variable</u>, and WATFIV-S would cause an error message to be printed.

```
C EXAMPLE 1.8
      X = 3.
      Y**2. = X
      PRINT, X, Y
      STOP
      END
```

The statement Y**2.=X is invalid, since a variable must be used to the left of the equals sign in an assignment statement; here the expression Y**2. appears to the left.

1.7 READING DATA AT EXECUTION TIME

It is often necessary to perform computations upon data which are read into the computer at execution time. Values are normally punched into data cards, which are subsequently read by the program as it is being executed by the computer. Example 1.9 is a simple program to introduce the READ statement.

```
C EXAMPLE 1.9
      READ, X
      Y = X + 2.0
      PRINT, Y
      STOP
      END
```

In the example, notice that the variable X is not assigned a value in an assignment statement, but is used in an arithmetic expression. The statement READ,X causes a value, obtained from a data card, to be assigned to the variable X at execution time. Thus the READ statement is another way of assigning values to variables.

A suitable data card for this example might have the integer constant 25.0 punched in the first four columns of the card. In this case, the value printed for Y would be 27.0.

Many problems will require more than one data card, and it is important to note the position of the data cards relative to the FORTRAN program. They always follow the $ENTRY control card, as illustrated in Figure 1.3.

```
$JOB
  ━━━━
  ━━━━        FORTRAN PROGRAM
  ━━━━
$ENTRY
  ━━━━
  ━━━━        DATA CARDS
  ━━━━
```

Figure 1.3

Example 1.10 illustrates how a program can be written to find the average of 50 real numbers punched on 50 separate data cards.

```
C EXAMPLE 1.10 - AVERAGE OF 50 NUMBERS
        CARD = 1.0
        SUM = 0.0
        LOOP
            READ, X
            SUM = SUM + X
            CARD = CARD + 1.0
            IF( CARD .GT. 50.0) QUIT
        ENDLOOP
        AVG = SUM / 50.
        PRINT, AVG
        STOP
        END
```

Each time the READ statement is executed, another card is read from the set of data cards. Since the READ statement will be executed 50 times, there must be 50 data cards present. What happens if there are more than or fewer than 50 data cards? If there are more, only the first 50 will be used, and the rest will be ignored. If there are fewer, an error message is issued when the data are depleted; it indicates that insufficient data cards are present.

1.8   OUTPUT OF CHARACTER DATA

We have seen that a PRINT statement can be used to print the current value of any variable used in a program. As well, it can be used to print a literal string of character data. The statement

PRINT, 'THIS IS A MESSAGE'

when executed would cause the information between the quotation marks to be printed. This can be used to provide headings for output to make it more readable.

As an illustration of this, the reader should replace the PRINT statement in Example 1.10 with the following two PRINT statements:

> PRINT, 'THE AVERAGE IS'
> PRINT, AVG

Run the program and take note of the output. The reader should then replace the above two statements with the following statement

> PRINT, 'THE AVERAGE IS',AVG

When the program is executed the literal string is printed on the same line with the value of AVG. In general, the PRINT statement can print any combination of literal strings and values of variables on one line, provided there is room on the line.

1.9   EXERCISES

In Example 1.3, we introduced .GT. which means "greater than". In the course of solving these and other problems, the reader may find it useful to know the complete list of such operators. It is as follows:

> .EQ.   equal to
> .NE.   not equal to
> .LT.   less than
> .LE.   less than or equal to
> .GT.   greater than
> .GE.   greater than or equal to

These are discussed in detail in Chapter 15.

1.5 Write a FORTRAN program to tabulate the function

$$z = \frac{w^2 + w + 3}{w - 2}$$

for w = 3, 3.5, 4, 4.5, ..., 9.5, 10.

1.6 Compute the sum of squares of the even integers between 10 and 40 inclusive.

1.7 Compute the average of the integers between 15 and 49 inclusive.

1.8 Consider the n terms of the geometric progression

$$a, \ ar, \ ar^2, \ ..., \ ar^{n-1}.$$

Compute these terms for values 3, 4, 8, of a, r, and n.

1.9 Using the built-in functions SIN and COS, tabulate the function

$$y = \sin^2 x + \cos^2 x$$

for x = 0., .1, .2, ..., 1.0. Recall that the value of x represents radians.

1.10 Punch ten real constants into ten cards to form a data deck. Use this data deck as input for the following problems.

(a) Write a program which reads the data deck and prints the 10 numbers on separate lines.

(b) Modify the program to print the numbers in pairs on five lines, that is, the first two numbers will print on line 1, the second two on line 2, etc.

1.11 (a) Modify your program for Exercise 1.5 to produce
          headings over the two columns of numbers. You
          will have to experiment somewhat with the
          spacing by placing blank characters in the
          alphabetic strings.

     (b) Further modify your program so there is a blank
          line between the heading and the column of
          numbers. (This can be done by printing a string
          of blank characters.)

Chapter 2

REPETITION

In Chapter 1 we introduced a number of examples which used the LOOP-ENDLOOP combination of statements to cause repetition to occur. This chapter discusses this mechanism in more detail to provide a basis for many of the examples that will appear in subsequent chapters. As well, the WHILE-ENDWHILE combination is introduced as an alternative means of achieving the controlled repetition of groups of FORTRAN statements.

2.1 DEFINITION OF TERMS

Suppose we have a data deck which contains exactly 5 cards. Each card contains one positive real number punched beginning in column 1. A typical data deck might be:

        12.6
        14.72
        0.0009
        +6.429
        182.03

The problem is to find the sum of the 5 numbers and print it. Example 2.1 is a program which will accomplish the required goal. The reader should study the program, and, if necessary, run it on the computer, to verify that it works.

```
C EXAMPLE 2.1
      CARD = 1.0
      SUM = 0.0
      LOOP
           READ, X
           SUM = SUM + X
           CARD = CARD + 1.0
           IF (CARD .GT. 5.0) QUIT
      ENDLOOP
      PRINT, SUM
      STOP
      END
```

The group of statements between the LOOP and ENDLOOP statements is written further to the right, and is said to be indented. The program contains statements which are written with two levels of indentation; the group of statements farthest right is said to be at a lower level. Moreover, this lower-level group of statements is defined as being a block which is repeated under control of the LOOP-ENDLOOP pair of statements. This block of statements will be repeated endlessly unless a QUIT statement is executed. The QUIT statement is conditionally executed by the IF, and the loop will be repeated until the logical expression

CARD .GT. 5.0

attains the value "true". Note that if this does not happen the repetition will not end, and the program is said to be in an "endless loop". This is almost always an undesirable situation.

When the QUIT statement is executed the repetition ends and there is an immediate transfer of control out of the indented block of statements. The next statement executed will be the one following the ENDLOOP statement; in our example this is the statement PRINT, SUM.

The two statements

```
      CARD = CARD + 1.0
      IF (CARD .GT. 5.0) QUIT
```

can be referred to as <u>loop</u> <u>control</u> statements. In this
example they serve no other purpose than to count the number
of times the repetition has taken place, and provide a test to
exit from the loop.

The two statements

$$CARD = 1.0$$
$$SUM = 0.0$$

which immediately precede the LOOP statement are called <u>loop-
initialization</u> statements; they initialize values for variables prior to beginning the repetition process.

Example 2.2 is another program which achieves the same
result.

```
C EXAMPLE 2.2
      CARD = 0.0
      SUM = 0.0
      LOOP
           CARD = CARD + 1.0
           IF (CARD .GT. 5.0) QUIT
           READ, X
           SUM = SUM + X
      ENDLOOP
      PRINT, SUM
      STOP
      END
```

Here the loop control statements are placed at the beginning of the block, rather than at the end. In this case the
block is executed 6 times, rather than 5, as in Example 2.1.
However, on the 6th repetition the block, will terminate after
only two statements have been executed.

2.2   <u>MULTIPLE</u> <u>TERMINATION</u> <u>OF</u> <u>LOOPS</u>

Suppose the problem described in the last section were
changed slightly to print a data deck with fewer than 5 cards.
If there are fewer than 5 numbers to be added, say 3, we will

place a special card containing a negative number as the last
card of the deck. This card is called a _sentinel_ and is used
to signal that fewer than 5 numbers are to be used. Thus, if
the deck contains 5 cards, the last card either contains a
positive number or is the sentinel; if fewer than 5 cards are
present, the last will be the sentinel card. Example 2.3 is a
program which will accomplish the required result.

```
C EXAMPLE 2.3
      CARD = 0.0
      SUM = 0.0
      LOOP
          CARD = CARD + 1.0
          IF (CARD .GT. 5.0) QUIT
          READ, X
          IF (X .LT. 0.0) QUIT
          SUM = SUM + X
      ENDLOOP
      PRINT, SUM
      STOP
      END
```

Note there are two QUIT statements in the loop block.
Either statement could cause termination of the repetition,
depending upon the nature of the data. The first causes
termination when five items of data are to be included in the
sum; the second causes termination if the sentinel data card
is read.

2.3   LOOPS WITHIN LOOPS

Let us expand upon the original problem in another way.
Suppose we call our 5 numbers a "set" of data. Further,
suppose we have 3 such sets, and the data deck therefore
contains 15 cards arranged as follows:

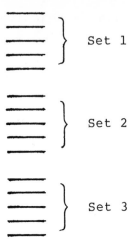

Set 1

Set 2

Set 3

It is required to find the sum of the 5 numbers in each set, and thus print 3 results.

A program to accomplish the task could be written by repeating the function of the former program 3 times. In other words, the body of the program in Example 2.1 could become the block of statements contained within another loop. Example 2.4 illustrates this approach.

```
C EXAMPLE 2.4
      SET = 1.0
      LOOP
          CARD = 1.0
          SUM = 0.0
          LOOP
              READ, X
              SUM = SUM + X
              CARD = CARD + 1.0
              IF (CARD .GT. 5.0) QUIT
          ENDLOOP
          PRINT, SUM
          SET = SET + 1.0
          IF (SET .GT. 3.0) QUIT
      ENDLOOP
      STOP
      END
```

This program is said to contain a "loop within a loop", or more formally it contains <u>nested</u> loops. The two loops are referred to as the <u>outside</u> loop and the <u>inside</u> loop; the block of statements in the latter have the most indentation.

The outside loop has one initialization statement, namely,

$$SET = 1.0$$

and two loop control statements, namely,

$$SET = SET + 1.0$$
$$IF (SET .GT. 3.0) QUIT$$

Thus each loop has its own initialization and loop control which determines the number of times the block of statements it contains is repeated.

In Example 2.4 there are two QUIT statements. When the QUIT statement in the inside loop is executed it causes termination of execution of the block of statements in the <u>inside</u> loop, and control is transferred to the statement immediately following the ENDLOOP associated with the inside loop, namely PRINT, SUM. This "inner" QUIT statement has no effect on the outside loop which has a QUIT statement at its own level; when executed, it terminates the outside loop. In this example when the "outer" QUIT is executed, control is transferred to the STOP statement.

This example has illustrated the application of nested loops at two levels and the use of QUIT at each level. Clearly the ideas can be extended to apply to loops which are nested to many levels. Most large programs will contain several instances of loops nested to various levels.

2.4   THE WHILE-ENDWHILE COMBINATION

WATFIV-S includes another loop control mechanism which can be used as an alternative to the LOOP-QUIT-ENDLOOP combination. Two new statements, namely, WHILE and ENDWHILE are used to define a <u>WHILE loop</u>, as illustrated in Example 2.5 which is an alternative version of Example 2.1

```
C EXAMPLE 2.5
      CARD = 1.0
      SUM = 0.0
      WHILE (CARD .LT. 6.0)
          READ, X
          SUM = SUM + X
          CARD = CARD + 1.0
      ENDWHILE
      PRINT, SUM
      STOP
      END
```

The indented statements between the WHILE and ENDWHILE constitute the block which is to be repeated. The repetition takes place as long as the logical expression following WHILE has the value "true". There is no QUIT statement in the example. Instead the logical expression is evaluated prior to each repetition of the loop; if the result is "false" the looping action is automatically terminated, and control is transferred to the statement immediately following the ENDWHILE.

It should be noted that the WHILE-ENDWHILE combination can always be replaced by the LOOP-QUIT-ENDLOOP combination; therefore, the latter is more general in nature. The former always performs a loop control test _prior_ to each repetition, whereas the latter may perform this test anywhere within the loop. The WHILE-ENDWHILE is a specialized loop control mechanism which has many applications. When it is appropriate to use it, the program is usually more readable.

Some general rules associated with WHILE loops are as follows:

(a) One or more QUIT statements can appear among the statements in a WHILE loop. If executed, they cause termination of the repetition. Example 2.6 is another version of Example 2.3 which illustrates this point

```
C EXAMPLE 2.6
        CARD = 0.0
        SUM = 0.0
        WHILE (CARD .LT. 5.0)
            READ, X
            IF (X .LT. 0.0) QUIT
            SUM = SUM + X
            CARD = CARD + 1.0
        ENDWHILE
        PRINT, SUM
        STOP
        END
```

(b) WHILE loops can be nested to any level. Example
     2.7 is another version of Example 2.4 which illus-
     trates nested WHILE's.

```
C EXAMPLE 2.7
        SET = 1.0
        WHILE (SET .LT. 4.0)
            CARD = 1.0
            SUM = 0.0
            WHILE (CARD .LT. 6.0)
                READ, X
                SUM = SUM + X
                CARD = CARD + 1.0
            ENDWHILE
            PRINT, SUM
            SET = SET + 1.0
        ENDWHILE
        STOP
        END
```

(c) LOOP-QUIT-ENDLOOP's can be contained within a block
     controlled by a WHILE-ENDWHILE, and vice-versa.
     Thus any combination of nested loops containing the
     two types can be used.

2.5 A NOTE ABOUT INDENTATION

     As mentioned in Chapter 1, it is not absolutely necessary
to indent the various statements. This is done to make the
program more readable by clearly identifying the block struc-

- 25 -

ture of the program. It is a highly desirable practice insisted upon by professional programmers.

The reader has probably observed that the ENDLOOP and ENDWHILE statements are not logically necessary to understand the program, provided indentation is used. They are, however, required by WATFIV-S, simply because the indentation is not mandatory.

2.6   EXERCISES

2.1   Suppose a student has written several tests, and each mark is recorded in a single punched card. This data deck therefore consists of a set of real numbers, each of which is between 0.0 and 100.0. However, there are an indefinite number of cards, so a sentinel data card is added at the end. This card contains the student's identification number which is 5 digits in length, and begins with the last two digits of the year in which the student first enrolled. Thus a student who has enrolled in 1979 could have the number 79426, which would be punched in the card as 79426.0.

Write a program which computes the average mark, and prints it on a line beside the student number. You should prepare two versions of the program, one using LOOP-ENDLOOP and the other using WHILE-ENDWHILE.

2.2   With reference to Exercise 2.1, suppose the data decks for several students were appended to each other to form a large data deck. The problem should how a report which has a line for each student, and which shows the student's average beside his student number. A new difficulty is that of determining the end of the entire data deck. To signal this, an additional sentinel data card must be added to the end of the deck. This contains the special constant -1.0.

Write programs to accomplish the job using both LOOP-ENDLOOP and WHILE-ENDWHILE control statements.

2.3 (a) Run the following program to observe the effect.

```
X = 2.6
LOOP
    PRINT, X
    PRINT, 'HELLO'
    Y = X + X
    PRINT, Y
    QUIT
ENDLOOP
STOP
END
```

(b) Move the QUIT statement to other locations within the block and observe the effect when the program is run.

(c) As a result of the above experiments, write a short paragraph to explain why the QUIT statement is more useful when used in conjunction with an IF statement.

2.4 Tabulate the function

$$s = a^2 + \sin b$$

for a = 1, 2, 3, 4, 5, 6;
and b = 0, .125, .25, .375, .5.

Chapter 3

SELECTION

In previous chapters the IF statement has been used in
loops to cause conditional execution of a QUIT statement in
order to terminate repetitions. There are many other uses for
IF's, and some are introduced in this chapter. Extensions to
the IF construct are introduced to permit selective execution
of whole blocks of statements.

3.1   A SIMPLE EXAMPLE

In this section we introduce a simple problem which will
serve as a basis of discussion and illustration in the various
other sections of this chapter.

Suppose a class of exactly 50 students has written a test
which has been marked out of 100. Each mark is recorded
rounded to one decimal place, and so will range between 0.0
and 100.0. The 50 marks are punched into 50 data cards,
beginning at column one in each card. This will be referred
to as the data deck.

Example 3.1 is a program which reads the entire data deck
and prints all 50 marks, one per line.

```
C EXAMPLE 3.1
      CARD = 1.0
      WHILE (CARD .LT. 51.0)
          READ, X
          PRINT, X
          CARD = CARD + 1.0
      ENDWHILE
      STOP
      END
```

3.2   THE LOGICAL IF STATEMENT

Suppose it is required to print only those marks which are 80.0 or higher. Example 3.2 is a program which would accomplish this.

```
C EXAMPLE 3.2
      CARD = 1.0
      WHILE (CARD .LT. 51.0)
          READ, X
          IF (X .GE. 80.0) PRINT, X
          CARD = CARD + 1.0
      ENDWHILE
      STOP
      END
```

When the IF statement

IF (X .GE. 80.0) PRINT, X

is executed it will cause the required marks to be printed. It accomplishes this by evaluating the logical expression which follows the IF. If this evaluates as "true", the single statement following the logical expression is executed. Then control proceeds to the statement following the IF statement.

This type of IF statement is called a logical IF, or, sometimes, a simple IF.

The effect of the logical IF is to selectively execute the statement PRINT, X. Thus each time a card is read in the loop, its mark is printed only if it equals or exceeds 80.

The general form of the logical IF statement is:

IF (logical expression) statement

The statement following the logical expression can be any executable FORTRAN statement that seems appropriate. For example, it could be a READ, PRINT, or an assignment statement such as X=X+3.0. We have already used the QUIT statement in this context to end repetitions. However, it makes no sense to use control statements such as LOOP, ENDLOOP, WHILE, or ENDWHILE, as these are used in combinations with one another. As well, another logical IF statement cannot be used.

Example 3.3 shows the logical IF being used to selectively execute an assignment statement.

```
C EXAMPLE 3.3
      CARD = 1.0
      TOTAL = 0.0
      WHILE (CARD .LT. 51.0)
          READ, X
          IF (X .GE. 80.0) TOTAL = TOTAL + 1.0
          CARD = CARD + 1.0
      ENDWHILE
      PRINT, TOTAL
      STOP
      END
```

Here the data deck is read and a count of the number of students obtaining a mark of 80 or more is accumulated in the variable TOTAL. After all the cards are read, the value of TOTAL is printed.

3.3   THE IF-THEN-ENDIF STRUCTURE

The logical IF statement allows us to conditionally execute one statement. Sometimes it is desirable to select a group of statements for execution under certain conditions. Consider Example 3.4 which computes and prints the average mark for all students who receive 80 or more.

```
C EXAMPLE 3.4
      CARD = 1.0
      TOTAL = 0.0
      SUM = 0.0
      WHILE (CARD .LT. 51.0)
          READ, X
          IF (X .GE. 80.0) THEN
              TOTAL = TOTAL + 1.0
              SUM = SUM + X
          ENDIF
          CARD = CARD + 1.0
      ENDWHILE
      AVG = SUM / TOTAL
      PRINT, AVG
      STOP
      END
```

Here the logical expression in the IF statement is followed by the word THEN. This signals that the block of statements between the IF and the ENDIF statement (indented) is to be executed when the logical expression evaluates as "true". If the logical expression is "false", the entire block of statements is skipped and control proceeds to the statement following the ENDIF statement.

3.4   THE IF-THEN-ELSE-ENDIF STRUCTURE

Now suppose it is required to compute the number of students who achieved a mark of 80 or more and also the number who did not. Two totals must be accumulated and printed, and Example 3.5 contains a program which will accomplish the task.

The reader will note the new statement ELSE. This divides the group of statements contained between the IF and ENDIF into two blocks. The first block is executed when the logical expression evaluates as "true"; the second block is executed when the logical expression evaluates as "false". Only the appropriate block is selected and executed, and control then proceeds to the statement following the ENDIF.

```
C EXAMPLE 3.5
      CARD = 1.0
      TOTAL1 = 0.0
      TOTAL2 = 0.0
      WHILE (CARD .LT. 51.0)
          READ, X
          IF (X .GE. 80.0) THEN
              TOTAL1 = TOTAL1 + 1.0
          ELSE
              TOTAL2 = TOTAL2 + 1.0
          ENDIF
          CARD = CARD + 1.0
      ENDWHILE
      PRINT, TOTAL1, TOTAL2
      STOP
      END
```

Thus, when the mark is 80 or over, TOTAL1 is increased by one; otherwise TOTAL2 is increased by one. After all cards are read by the WHILE loop, the final values of the two totals are printed.

3.5   THE CASE CONSTRUCT

Suppose the problem were extended as follows. The number of students in each of 5 categories is to be counted using 5 totals:

TOTALA	marks of 80 or over
TOTALB	marks of 70 or over but less than 80
TOTALC	marks of 60 or over but less than 70
TOTALD	marks of 50 or over but less than 60
TOTALF	marks of less than 50

Example 3.6 is a program which uses the case construct to accomplish the desired result.

Here the group of statements between the IF and ENDIF has been separated into five blocks. The first block is preceded by an IF statement with its associated logical expression. If this expression evaluates as "true", the statements in this first block are executed and control transfers to the statement following the concluding ENDIF. If it is "false", control transfers to the first ELSEIF statement. Its logical expression is evaluated and if "true", the statements in the second block are executed with control then transferring to the statement following the ENDIF. If "false", the second ELSEIF statement is executed and the third block is selected and executed if its logical expression evaluates as "true". Similarly if the expression is "false", the third ELSEIF test is made to see if the fourth block is to be executed. If not, the fifth block, following the ELSE, is executed.

```
C EXAMPLE 3.6
      CARD = 1.0
      TOTALA = 0.0
      TOTALB = 0.0
      TOTALC = 0.0
      TOTALD = 0.0
      TOTALF = 0.0
      WHILE (CARD .LT. 51)
          READ, X
          IF (X .GE. 80.0) THEN
              TOTALA = TOTALA + 1.0
          ELSEIF (X .GE. 70.0) THEN
              TOTALB = TOTALB + 1.0
          ELSEIF (X .GE. 60.0) THEN
              TOTALC = TOTALC + 1.0
          ELSEIF (X .GE. 50.0) THEN
              TOTALD = TOTALD + 1.0
          ELSE
              TOTALF = TOTALF + 1.0
          ENDIF
          CARD = CARD + 1.0
      ENDWHILE
      PRINT, TOTALA, TOTALB, TOTALC, TOTALD, TOTALF
      STOP
      END
```

The effect of the case construct is to select one of many alternatives. Only one of these alternatives is chosen, its associated block of statements is executed, and control is transferred to the statement following the ENDIF.

Note that the logical expressions are executed in turn from top to bottom in an attempt to find one which evaluates as "true". The first one which evaluates as "true" causes its associated block of statements to be executed, and the remainder of the statements in the case structure is skipped.

The ELSE statement can, in fact, be omitted; if so, there is a possibility that none of the blocks of statements will be selected, which in some program situations could be the desired effect. When it is used, the ELSE statement must be at the beginning of the last block in the case structure.

In the current example, each block contains only one statement. However, the block may contain as many statements as required. Similarly the programmer can use any desired number of blocks or "cases" depending on the problem at hand.

3.6   REMARKS ON INDENTATION

All indentation of statements in IF structures is optional, as was the case with repetition structures. However, by using indentation the natural block structure of the program shows up graphically. This is especially important when using nested IF's as described in the next section.

3.7   NESTED IF STRUCTURES

Just as we could have loops within loops to any level, we can use IF structures within any of the blocks of statements controlled by another IF structure. Example 3.7 is a simple example of an "IF within an IF".

The entire data deck is read under control of the WHILE loop. Each mark is tested to determine if it is 80.0 or over. If so, the mark is increased to 100.0 if it is 95.0 or over; otherwise it is increased by 5.0 marks. Then the adjusted mark is printed. All marks less than 80.0 are ignored.

```
C EXAMPLE 3.7
      CARD = 1.0
      WHILE (CARD .LT. 51.0)
          READ, X
          IF (X .GE. 80.0) THEN
              IF (X .GE. 95.0) THEN
                  X = 100.0
              ELSE
                  X = X + 5.0
              ENDIF
              PRINT, X
          ENDIF
          CARD = CARD + 1.0
      ENDWHILE
      STOP
      END
```

Each level of indentation clearly identifies a block of statements. These blocks are selected appropriately by the logical expressions associated with the IF structure being used. Each IF structure is contained between an IF and the nearest ENDIF which follows at the <u>same</u> level.

Nested IF's are often difficult to follow when reading a program. It is therefore desirable to avoid them if possible. Example 3.8 is an alternative means of programming Example 3.7 which does not use a nested IF. It also illustrates the use of the case construct without an ELSE.

```
C EXAMPLE 3.8
      CARD = 1.0
      WHILE (CARD .LT. 51.0)
          READ, X
          IF (X .GE. 95.0) THEN
              X = 100.0
              PRINT, X
          ELSEIF (X .GE. 80.0) THEN
              X = X + 5.0
              PRINT, X
          ENDIF
          CARD = CARD + 1.0
      ENDWHILE
      STOP
      END
```

3.8 THE QUIT STATEMENT WITH IF STRUCTURES

The QUIT statement can be used in any of the blocks associated with IF structures. When executed, it terminates the entire IF-ENDIF structure, and control proceeds to the statement following the ENDIF. In the case of nested IF's, the QUIT will cause an exit only from the IF structure which locally contains it.

3.9 NESTED COMBINATIONS OF REPETITION AND IF STRUCTURES

A combination of nesting of repetition structures with IF structures can be used to any level. Hopefully, the indentation will make the program readable but sometimes, even with indentation, large programs can become difficult to read and understand. It turns out that large programs can be made more readable by using remote blocks which are described in a later chapter.

3.10 EXERCISES

NOTE:
The following exercises use the data deck which has been described at the beginning of this chapter. The reader is advised to prepare such cards to be used when running the various exercises.

3.1 Calculate the average of all marks which are 50.0 or more.

3.2 Calculate the average of all marks which are greater than 70.0 but less than 80.0.

3.3 Write a program which will print only those marks which are above average. Note you will have to determine the overall average by writing a preliminary program. Then this average will have to be punched into a special data card which is placed at the beginning of the data deck, and read by your program before the main calculations begin.

3.4 Write a program which prints each of the 50 marks, but places an asterisk beside those marks which are above average.

3.5 Write a program which reads the data deck and prints a letter grade beside each mark on the same line. Letter grades are determined as follows:

A	marks of 80 or over
B	marks of 70 or over but below 80
C	marks of 60 or over but below 70
D	marks of 50 or over but below 60
F	marks below 50

NOTE:
The following exercises do not use the data deck described at the beginning of the chapter.

3.6 Tabulate the function

$$y = f(x) + g(x)$$

for x = 1, 2, 3, ..., 10,
where $f(x) = x^2 - 16$

and $g(x) = \begin{cases} 1 & \text{if } f(x) < 0 \\ x^2 + 16 & \text{if } f(x) = 0 \\ 0 & \text{if } f(x) > 0 \end{cases}$

- 37 -

3.7 Write a FORTRAN program which reads three numbers and prints one of the following codes:

- 0 if the numbers do not represent the sides of a triangle.

- 1 if they represent the sides of a triangle which is neither isosceles nor equilateral

- 2 if they represent the sides of an isosceles triangle

- 3 if they represent the sides of an equilateral triangle

Write the program so that it will process an arbitrary number of sets of three numbers, and will terminate upon reading a set of three numbers, all of which are 0.

3.8 Write a program which reads 4 numbers and prints them in ascending numerical sequence on 4 lines.

3.9 Modify your solution for Exercise 3.8 so the 4 numbers are printed in ascending numerical sequence, left to right on the same line.

3.10 Modify Exercise 1.5 so that the denominator is w-5 rather than w-2. Note that you must arrange to skip over the value w = 5.

3.11 Write a program to tabulate the function

$$y = \frac{x3 + 7x - 5}{x^3 - 3x^2 - 4x + 12}$$

for x = -4, -3, -2, ..., 7, 8, 9. Note that, prior to each division, one must test to see whether the denominator is zero.

3.12 With reference to exercise 2.2, some students do not write any tests because of absence or sickness. In these cases the data for a student consists of only the sentinel data which contains the student's number. The report should show an average mark of zero for such a student.

Make whatever program modifications are necessary to accomodate this special situation. Run your program with various types of data to ensure it works properly.

Chapter 4

REAL ARITHMETIC

A number of examples of FORTRAN programs using real arithmetic were discussed in Chapters 1 to 3. The purpose of this chapter is to formalize and extend some of the ideas already introduced.

4.1   REAL CONSTANTS

Probably the best way to describe FORTRAN real constants is to give a number of examples, followed by a discussion of each. The following is a selection which consists of most of the possible variations of real constants.

A)
      (a) 12.34   (e) 1234.567
      (b) -12.34   (f) .0001234
      (c) +12.34   (g) 670000.0
      (d) 0.   (h) 1234567.

B)
      (a) 12.34E3   (f) 12.34E+03
      (b) +12.34E3   (g) 12.34E0
      (c) -12.34E3   (h) 12.34E50
      (d) 12.34E-3   (i) 1234567.E6
      (e) 12.34E+3   (j) 0.E0

Every real constant contains a decimal point explicitly as part of it. This is the case even if the constant happens to be an integer as in A) (h). Each constant can have a plus or minus sign to the left, and if no sign is present, the constant is assumed to be positive. No constant can contain more than seven digits, including non-significant zeros. The greatest precision possible is seven significant decimal digits as indicated in Examples A) (e), A) (h), B) (i).

Group B) has real constants which use FORTRAN exponent notation. The constant 12.34E3 means 12.34×10^3. In all cases, the signed integer following the E indicates the power of ten which is used to multiply the number which precedes it. This notation is generally used to handle very large or very small real constants. Thus the number -0.123×10^{-60} would be written as -0.123E-60 in FORTRAN. As is the case for group A), the greatest precision possible is seven significant decimal digits.

The largest real constant which can be used is .7237005E+76 and the smallest in magnitude (except for zero) is .5397605E-78. These unusual appearing limits are a characteristic of the IBM computer hardware. Under normal circumstances, the programmer need only be aware of their approximate magnitudes, namely 10^{76} and 10^{-78}. More details on IBM computer hardware will follow in a subsequent chapter.

The following are examples of errors frequently made when using real constants.

12.34E6.	No decimal allowed after the E.
123,456.7	No comma allowed.
-123456	No decimal point.
+123.456E90	Too large.
123.456789	Too many digits.
123.450000	Too many digits (zeros count).

4.2 REAL VARIABLES

Variables capable of being assigned values which are real constants are said to be real variables. A real variable can be any valid FORTRAN symbolic name which is declared in a REAL declaration statement. For example, the statement

REAL X, T, MABLE, NUMBER

declares each of X, T, MABLE, and NUMBER to be real variables. This is a non-executable statement and is placed prior to the first executable statement in a program. The reason we have such a statement is because there are other types of variables and constants in FORTRAN. These will be outlined in subsequent chapters.

The reader may be wondering how we managed to get by without the REAL statement in Chapter 1. The answer is that, in the absence of any other declaration, symbolic names are real variables provided they do not begin with the letters I to N inclusive. This is often referred to as the FORTRAN default declaration or implicit declaration.

4.3 REAL-VALUED EXPRESSIONS

Any expression which, when evaluated, produces a real result is said to be a real-valued expression or, more briefly, a real expression. Some examples are:

(a)	(X+3.64)/2.3	(g)	A/B*C
(b)	(X+Y)*(2.1-A)	(h)	-8.2**2
(c)	6.892	(i)	A**B**C
(d)	A	(j)	3.2E50 * 7.0E40
(e)	-A	(k)	3.2E-50 * 7.9E-40
(f)	A*B**2		

The conventions for evaluating expressions are similar to those encountered in algebra. In Example (a), the sum X+3.64

is evaluated first because it is contained in parentheses; then the division by 2.3 is performed.

In Example (b), both quantities in parentheses are evaluated separately, and then multiplied. Note that the * must be used; the expression (X+Y)(2.1-A), while legal in algebra, is not valid in FORTRAN.

Examples (c) and (d) indicate that a real constant or a real variable is a trivial example of a real expression.

Example (e) illustrates the use of the unary minus. Example (h) also contains a unary minus.

In Example (f), B**2 is evaluated, and the result is subsequently multiplied by A. This is because of the priority of operators. The operators in order of decreasing priority are

$$**$$
$$* \text{ and } /$$
$$+ \text{ and } - \text{ (including unary + and -)}$$

Example (g) may seem to be ambiguous, as it is not obvious whether ac/b or a/bc would be calculated. The rule is that the expression is evaluated from left to right, unless the priority of operators dictates otherwise. Thus A/B is calculated and the result is subsequently multiplied by C.

In Example (h), the result is $-(8.2)^2$. A unary minus in an expression is always treated as if there were a zero preceding it. Thus, -8.2**2 produces the same result as 0.-8.2**2.

Example (i) illustrates the only exception to the rules as stated to this point. When successive unparenthesized exponentiations are involved, the computation proceeds from right to left. Thus A**B**C would be equivalent to A**(B**C).

You may always use parentheses in expressions to improve their readability - for yourself or for others who might read your programs. For example, if (A/B)*C seems more meaningful to you than A/B*C, use the former. In particular, it is a good idea to use parentheses always with A**(B**C) since A**B**C depends on an exception to the usual left-to-right evaluation rule.

Examples (j) and (k) show situations which give rise to computed results which are out of the range of magnitude for real constants. In the first case, the result is too large and an error message would be printed indicating an <u>overflow</u> condition. In the second case, the result is too small and an error message would indicate an <u>underflow</u> condition.

It is not possible to have two consecutive operators in FORTRAN. Thus the expression X*-8.2 is illegal and must be written as X*(-8.2). However, recall that **, denoting exponentiation, is a single operator.

4.4   <u>REAL</u> <u>ASSIGNMENT</u> <u>STATEMENTS</u>

The general form of a <u>real</u> <u>assignment</u> <u>statement</u> is

real variable = real expression

Examples are:

Y = (A*B-3.2) / 7.6E-8
SUM = SUM + 3.0

The computer first evaluates the real expression, then assigns the result to the real variable on the left of the equals sign.

4.5 SOME EXAMPLES

The following examples will serve to further illustrate some of the rules and, in certain cases, will point out interesting difficulties encountered when using real arithmetic.

Example 4.1 indicates how we could compute an approximation to π using thirty-one terms of the series

$$\frac{\pi^3}{32} = \frac{1}{1^3} - \frac{1}{3^3} + \frac{1}{5^3} - \frac{1}{7^3} + \ldots$$

```
C EXAMPLE 4.1
      SUM = 0.
      X = 1.
      S = 1.
      LOOP
          SUM = SUM + (1./X**3.)*S
          S = -S
          X = X + 2.
          IF (X  .GT.  61.) QUIT
      ENDLOOP
      PI = (SUM*32.)**(1./3.)
      PRINT, PI
      STOP
      END
```

The variable S alternates between +1 and -1 in order to add or subtract a new term each time through a loop. There is no particular reason why the example is set up to go through the loop thirty-one times. As an exercise, the reader may wish to compute and print the approximation each time through the loop to observe how the accuracy increases as each term is added.

```
C EXAMPLE 4.2
      X = 3.1
      Y = 3.1E20
      Z = Y - Y + X
      T = Y + X - Y
      PRINT, Z, T
      STOP
      END
```

In Example 4.2, we would expect Z and T to be assigned identical values. In actual fact, Z becomes 3.1 and T becomes zero! This happens because computation of expressions proceeds from left to right, and real constants retain only seven digits of precision. When computing Z, the quantity Y-Y is evaluated first, yielding zero; then X is added to produce the result 3.1. When computing T, the quantity Y+X is evaluated first. Since the computer retains only seven significant digits, the result is 3.1E20 because X is insignificant relative to Y. Then Y is subtracted, producing the zero result for T. This points out that operations which are associative in ordinary algebra are not necessarily associative in FORTRAN.

In Example 4.3, we would expect the result for Y to be 1.0. However, when the program is run on the computer, the output produced is 0.9999999, which is slightly in error. This happens because the IBM computer records its real constants using hexadecimal, rather than decimal, arithmetic. It is impossible to convert .2 to a hexadecimal equivalent using a finite number of hexadecimal digits. The computer truncates the hexadecimal number, and thus ends up with only an approximation to .2. When this is added to itself four times, as in the example, the error is increased by a factor of 5, with the result that Y is not exactly as expected.

```
C EXAMPLE 4.3
      X = .2
      Y = X + X + X + X + X
      PRINT, Y
      STOP
      END
```

As a further explanation of this problem, suppose the IBM computer recorded its real constants using decimal rather than hexadecimal arithmetic. Then one-third would be approximated by the decimal fraction .3333333. If this were added together three times the result would be .9999999 rather than 1.

This example illustrates a point which needs to be kept in mind when one is doing computations in real arithmetic. The actual numbers used are frequently only good approximations, and hence may contain errors. These errors can increase during the course of a computation. Thus it is likely that the final result is not accurate to seven significant digits. Unfortunately, there is no general rule for predicting the accuracy of the results.

4.6   REAL BUILT-IN FUNCTIONS

In Chapter 1 we introduced the real function SQRT, and mentioned some others such as SIN, COS, EXP, etc. A complete list of available functions and their characteristics can be found in Appendix A. However, a number of observations are useful.

Every FORTRAN function has a name such as SIN, COS, or SQRT, and this is always a FORTRAN symbolic name. The fact that SIN begins with an S is consistent with the fact that its value is a real constant. The function name is always accompanied on the right by an argument list enclosed in parentheses. Often this list has only one argument. For example, X is the argument in SIN(X) whereas A and B are the arguments in SIGN(A,B). These arguments can be any expressions, provided they are of the proper type. For example, SIN(X**2+2.3*X-8.4) is legal provided that the argument within the parentheses, when evaluated, produces a real constant. On the other hand, SIN(3) is illegal since the constant 3 is not a valid real constant (3. would be valid).

All functions are treated as if they were variables and

can be used as components of expressions. The following are
all legal real expressions.

$$(X + COS(X**2)) / (A + 2.0)$$
$$SIN(A)*SIN(B) + 2*(A + B)$$
$$SIN(A + COS(X))$$
$$SQRT(SQRT(X))$$

The last example shows how a function can have, in its
argument list, an expression which contains the function
itself.

Example 4.4 shows how the ABS function can be used to
terminate the loop when approximating π (see Example 4.1).
Here, the statement

IF (ABS(SUM-SUMOLD) .LT. .00001) QUIT

will cause a transfer out of the loop when the absolute value
of the difference between two consecutive values of SUM is
less than .00001.

```
C EXAMPLE 4.4
      SUM = 0.
      SUMOLD = 0.
      X = 1.
      S = 1.
      LOOP
          SUM = SUM + (1./X**3)*S
          IF (ABS(SUM-SUMOLD) .LT. .00001) QUIT
          SUMOLD = SUM
          S = -S
          X = X + 2.
      ENDLOOP
      PI = (SUM*32.)**(1./3.)
      PRINT, PI
      STOP
      END
```

Example 4.5 computes tables of sine, cosine, square root,
and exponential for X ranging from 1 to 2 at increments of .1.
Note that the argument is considered to be in radians when SIN
and COS are used. Note also that when this program is run,

the values printed for X are 1.0000000, 1.0999990, 1.1999980, ..., 1.9999940. In each case the value of X is slightly smaller than the value expected and possibly not different enough to matter. Before describing why this occurs let us consider another example.

```
C EXAMPLE 4.5
C CALCULATE TABLES
      X = 1.
      LOOP
          A = SIN(X)
          B = COS(X)
          C = SQRT(X)
          D = EXP(X)
          PRINT, X, A, B, C, D
          X = X + .1
          IF (X .GT. 2.) QUIT
      ENDLOOP
      STOP
      END
```

Example 4.6 shows how we could tabulate the function

$$y = e^x + \sin(x+.1) + x|x|$$

for x = 0, .5, 1.0, 1.5, ..., 5.0.

```
C EXAMPLE 4.6
      X = 0.
      LOOP
          Y = EXP(X) + SIN(X+.1) + X*ABS(X)
          PRINT, X, Y
          X = X + .5
          IF (X .GT. 5.) QUIT
      ENDLOOP
      STOP
      END
```

In this example, when the program is run the values of X are 0.0000000 0.5000000, 1.0000000, 1.5000000, ..., 5.0000000. The difference between the values printed in these two examples occurs because, in converting X to hexadecimal (the number base used by the computer), .1 cannot be converted accurately while .5 can be converted accurately. While more

will be said about this in future chapters, the reader can
broaden his understanding of such matters by studying the
properties of hexadecimal arithmetic and observing computer
output in specific instances.

4.7   EXERCISES

4.1   Given that A=2, B=3, C=4, and D=2 evaluate the
      following FORTRAN expressions by hand and also by
      using the computer, to compare the results.

      (a)   A*B/C**D   (d)   A**B**D
      (b)   A*(B/C)**D-7.   (e)   -B**A-C**D
      (c)   C/A/B*D

4.2   (a)   Write a program which tabulates the function x^{-3}
            for x = 1, 3, 5, 7, ..., 51

      (b)   Make the necessary changes to the program in (a)
            to tabulate the function

            $$(-1)^{(x-1)/2} x^{-3}$$

            over the same range.

4.3   Define S_n as the sum of the first n terms of the
      series

      $$\frac{1}{1^3} - \frac{1}{3^3} + \frac{1}{5^3} - \frac{1}{7^3} + \ldots$$

      Note that the nth term can be written as

            $t_n = (-1)^{n-1}(2n-1)^{-3}$.

      Write a program which tabulates S_n and t_n for n = 1,
      2, 3, ..., 50.

4.4 The program written for Exercise 4.3 calculates S_{50} by adding the terms in the order t_1, t_2, t_3, ..., t_{50}. Modify the program so the addition is done in the reverse order. Are the computed answers for S_{50} identical? Which result would you expect to be more accurate? Why?

4.5 (a) Compute a table of the sine, cosine, and tangent for the angles from 0 degrees to 45 degrees at intervals of 1 degree. Verify your results by consulting published tables.

(b) Modify the program in (a) to compute the tables at intervals of 5 minutes. To conserve computer time, do the tabulation up to 5 degrees only.

4.6 Tabulate the function

$$f(x) = e^{\sin x} + |x|$$

for $x = -5, -4, -3, ..., 5$.

4.7 Write a program to evaluate the expression

$$y = \frac{\pi}{2} \sin^2 (3\theta + \frac{\pi}{4})$$

for

$$\theta = 0, \frac{\pi}{8}, \frac{2\pi}{8}, \frac{3\pi}{8}, \frac{4\pi}{8}, ..., \pi$$

where $\pi = 3.141593$

4.8   The roots of the quadratic equation

$$ax^2 + bx + c = 0$$

can be calculated using the formula

$$x = \frac{-b \pm \sqrt{b^2 - 4ac}}{2a}$$

provided a is not equal 0 and $b^2 - 4ac$ is not negative.
Write a program which computes the roots and prints
them together with one of the following messages,
according to circumstances:

- not a quadratic or linear equation, no roots
- not a quadratic, one root only
- equal real roots
- distinct real roots
- complex roots.

Test your program with various values for a, b, and
c.

Chapter 5

INTEGER ARITHMETIC

The FORTRAN language has a completely separate set of
facilities for handling computations with <u>integers</u>. These
facilities may seem redundant since real arithmetic (Chapter
4) encompasses operations upon integers, which are a subset of
the real numbers. However, the separate facilities provide
certain advantages to the programmer. Proper use of the
integer feature can enable the programmer to obtain more accurate results for certain types of problems; often he will use
less computer time in the process.

5.1   INTEGER CONSTANTS

Examples of valid FORTRAN <u>integer</u> <u>constants</u> are:

(a)	1234	(d)	0
(b)	-1234	(e)	987654321
(c)	+1234	(f)	+0003

The common characteristic of all integer constants is the
absence of a decimal point; it is always assumed to be immediately to the right of the farthest-right digit.

Examples (b) and (c) illustrate the use of the sign. If
the sign is absent, the constant is assumed to be positive.

Integer constants can be any integer n in the range

$$-2147483648 \leq n \leq 2147483647$$

These unusual-looking limits are a function of the IBM hardware. Under normal circumstances the programmer need only be aware of their approximate magnitude, namely, 10^9. In other words, integer constants are capable of having any nine-digit integer as their value.

The following are examples of invalid integer constants.

(a)   1,234   Comma not allowed.
(b)   13E12   Exponent not allowed.
(c)   18.0   Contains a decimal point.
(d)   111222333444   Too large.

5.2   INTEGER VARIABLES

Variables capable of being assigned values which are integer constants are said to be integer variables. An integer variable can be any valid FORTRAN symbolic name which is declared in an INTEGER type statement. The statement

INTEGER A, B, SUM, TOTAL

declares each of A, B, SUM, and TOTAL to be integer variables. This statement is non-executable and is placed prior to the first executable statement in a program.

In the absence of any other declaration, FORTRAN symbolic names which begin with the letters I to N inclusive are declared as integer variables by default.

5.3   INTEGER-VALUED EXPRESSIONS

Any expression which yields an integer constant when evaluated is said to be an integer-valued expression or, more briefly, an integer expression. Some examples are:

(a)　(I + 3)*20

(b)　(I + J) / (3 - K) + I**4

(c)　6

(d)　MABLE

(e)　-MABLE + 3

(f)　14/3

(g)　1234*1234*1234*1234

Examples (a) and (b) illustrate that all the arithmetic operators used in real expressions can also be used in integer expressions. The operators follow the same rules of priority, and parentheses can be used. Examples (c) and (d) show the simplest possible integer expressions, and Example (e) uses the operator unary minus.

Example (f) is worthy of discussion. Since 14/3 is an integer expression, it yields the integer result 4; the remainder is ignored. Similarly (-14)/3 yields -4 and 2/3 yields zero. Note that 9/2*2 yields 8 but 9/3*3 yields 9.

Example (g) is a legal integer expression which would produce unexpected results. Since $(1234)^4$ is too large to be an integer constant, the computer would produce a result which is incorrect. No warning message is given, and it is the programmer's responsibility to ensure that this type of thing does not occur. The unexpected results are related to the way in which integer constants and integer arithmetic are handled by the computer hardware.

5.4　INTEGER ASSIGNMENT STATEMENTS

The general form of an integer assignment is

integer variable = integer expression

Examples are

$$I = (J + 3) / K$$
$$I = J + 1$$

The computer first evaluates the integer expression, then assigns the result to the integer variable to the left of the equals sign.

5.5   SOME EXAMPLES

Example 5.1 computes a table of the squares and cubes of the integers from -2 to 5 inclusive.

```
C EXAMPLE 5.1
      INTEGER SQUARE, CUBE
      I = -2
      LOOP
          SQUARE = I**2
          CUBE = I**3
          PRINT, I, SQUARE, CUBE
          I = I + 1
          IF (I .GT. 5) QUIT
      ENDLOOP
      STOP
      END
```

When the reader runs this example on the computer, he will notice that the computer output of integer constants is different than is the case for real constants. Output for Example 5.1 is shown in Figure 5.1.

-2	4	-8
-1	1	-1
0	0	0
1	1	1
2	4	8
3	9	27
4	16	64
5	25	125

Figure 5.1

Example 5.2 determines whether or not 31 is a prime number. The essence of the method is to find a prime factor of J by successively dividing by 2, 3, 4, etc., until a remainder of zero is encountered. This test is made in the statement

IF (J/TEST*TEST .EQ. J) QUIT

Because of the nature of integer arithmetic, the expression J/TEST*TEST will be equal to J only when the division is exact. This is bound to happen when TEST=31, but will happen earlier if 31 is not a prime number. Thus the values of J and TEST are printed when the loop terminates. They are both 31 which confirms that 31 is a prime number.

```
C EXAMPLE 5.2
      INTEGER TEST
      J = 31
      TEST = 2
      LOOP
          IF (J/TEST*TEST .EQ. J) QUIT
          TEST = TEST + 1
      ENDLOOP
      PRINT, J, TEST
      STOP
      END
```

Note the operator .EQ. (equal to) has been introduced in this example.

5.6   INTEGER BUILT-IN FUNCTIONS

Only a few built-in functions are available for use in integer arithmetic. There are no integer functions for sine, cosine, square root, exponential, logarithm, etc., because these functions would not be much use in a world restricted to integers. One useful function which is available is IABS. It computes the absolute value of an integer expression. Others can be found in the table in Appendix A. Note that all integer functions begin with one of the letters I to N inclusive.

5.7   EXERCISES

5.1 Given that I=2, J=3, K=4, and L=2, evaluate the following FORTRAN expressions by hand, and also by using the computer; compare your results.

    (a) I*L/K**J   (d) K**J/I/J/L

    (b) I**K/L*J   (e) K**J**I

    (c) J/I*I

5.2 Write a program to determine which of the positive integers from 1 to 25 inclusive are perfect squares. For each of these integers, the output is to be 1 if the integer is a perfect square; otherwise, the output is to be 0.

5.3 Tabulate the function

$$k = 2^n$$

for n = 1, 2, 3, ..., 50. Notice that, after n=30, unexpected results are printed for the required function.

5.4 Write a computer program to compute n! (n factorial) for n = 0, 1, 2, ..., 10. Note that n! can be defined as follows

$$0! = 1$$
$$n! = n\,(n-1)!$$

5.5 (a) Write a program to produce all the right-angled triangles which have sides of integral lengths (each hypotenuse is to have length less than 100.)

(b) Modify the program in (a) to produce all right-angled triangles which have sides of integral lengths, and which have perimeters of less than 100.

5.6 (a) Write a program that converts a quantity expressed in millimeters to a corresponding quantity expressed in metres, centimetres, and millimetres. For example, 3821 millimetres equals 3 metres, 82 centimetres and 1 millimetre.

(b) Repeat (a), converting seconds into days, hours, minutes, and seconds.

(c) Write a program to convert a positive decimal integer to a sequence of zeros and ones which represent the binary equivalent.

5.7 A positive integer is said to be prime if it has no integer factors other than one and itself (1 is not considered prime).

(a) Run Example 5.2 which tests a given positive integer greater than 2 to determine whether or not it is prime.

(b) Note that it is not necessary to divide by all integers between one and the number itself. For example, only odd integers are necessary if the trial divisor two has already been used. Also, it is only necessary to test divisors whose squares are less than or equal to the integer being tested. Write a new program incorporating these improvements.

(c) Modify the program in part (b) so that it can be used to compute all prime numbers greater than two and less than 200.

5.8 Find all twin primes in the set of prime numbers less than 200. Twin primes are consecutive odd numbers such as 11 and 13.

5.9 From the set of prime numbers less than 200, find all pairs of primes such that the larger is just one more than twice the smaller, i.e., pairs of primes of the form j, 2j+1 (e.g., 2 and 5; 3 and 7; 5 and 11).

5.10 Write a program which takes a positive four-digit integer, reverses the order of the digits, and prints the resulting integer. For example, 1289 would become 9821.

5.11 It is generally not possible to multiply a six-digit integer p by another six-digit integer q and obtain accurate results. This is because the result pq can have twelve digits, which exceeds the precision of an integer constant. However, an accurate result can be obtained by segmenting the problem.

First express p and q as

$$p = a \times 10^3 + b$$
$$q = c \times 10^3 + d$$

where a, b, c, and d each have 3 digits. Then use the formula

$$pq = (a \times 10^3 + b)(c \times 10^3 + d)$$

The computation can proceed using a, b, c, and d, and recording the result in two integers, one containing the first six digits, and the other containing the last six digits.

(a) Write a program to perform this extended-precision integer arithmetic, and try it for several values of p and q. Your program should work for negative as well as positive values of p and q.

(b) Modify the program in (a) so it works properly
if p and q have up to 9 decimal digits. Can you
explain why it is difficult to go beyond 9
decimal digits?

Chapter 6

MIXED-MODE ARITHMETIC

In each of Chapters 4 and 5, a particular mode of operations has been discussed. In the former, computation with
real variables and constants was considered; in the latter,
computation involved integer variables and integer constants.
The FORTRAN language allows complete freedom to mix both types
of computations in arithmetic expressions and assignment
statements. Such expressions are referred to as mixed-mode
expressions. In actual fact, the computer stores and handles
the two types of constants quite differently. Thus, although
mixed-mode is legal, it is important to study the details of
how the computations are done so that the programmer can
achieve predictable results.

6.1   EVALUATION OF EXPRESSIONS

The following are examples of mixed-mode expressions:

(a)   A + I

(b)   SIN(A + I)

(c)   I - 1.3 + J

(d)   2/3*6.2

(e)   3 + SIN(X)

(f)   123456789 + B

(g)   X**5

In Example (a) the computer will convert the integer constant, which is the current value of I, to a real constant. Then the result will be added to the real constant which is the current value of A. The final result is a real constant. Since the result of the expression is a real constant, the expression is, by definition, a real-valued expression. Thus it is possible to use it as the argument of a built-in function such as SIN, as illustrated in Example (b).

The general rule is that when a binary operation takes place between two expressions, one of which is real-valued and the other integer-valued, the integer value is automatically converted to a real value before the operation takes place; the final result is a real constant. There is one exception to this rule; it will be illustrated in Example (g).

The usual rules of priority are observed, as is the convention that evaluation of expression proceeds from left to right. Thus the expression in (d) gives rise to the result zero, represented as a real constant. This is because 2/3 is evaluated first, yielding the integer constant 0. Then this integer constant is converted to a real constant because it must enter into multiplication with the real constant 6.2. The final result is zero, represented as a real constant.

In Example (e) the sine would be evaluated first. Then the integer constant 3 would be converted to the real constant 3.0; the addition is then performed.

Example (f) illustrates how accuracy can be lost. The integer constant 123456789 must be converted to a real constant before computation can proceed. But this cannot be done accurately, since real constants can represent a precision of at most seven digits. Thus the conversion produces the real constant 1234567.E2, which is subsequently added to the current value of B.

Example (g), although a mixed-mode expression, is handled differently. The integer-valued exponent is used to instruct the computer to multiply the current value of X by itself 5 times. The rule is that, whenever an integer-valued expression appears as an exponent, it is never converted; its integer value is merely used to indicate the number of multiplications that must be done.

The expression X**5.0 is not a mixed mode expression but it is appropriate to discuss it at this point. Whenever the exponent is a real-valued expression, and X is different from 0, the exponentiation is evaluated using logarithms. Thus the expression X**5.0 could not be evaluated if X happened to have a negative value. This suggests the rule that integer-valued expressions should be used in exponents whenever possible. However, if the calculation $X^{1/5}$ must be done, the exponent is, of necessity, a real-valued expression, namely (1./5.). Under these conditions, if X has a negative value an error message will be printed.

As has been pointed out in the chapter on real arithmetic, expressions such as SIN(3) or SQRT(4) are illegal. This is because the arguments of such built-in functions must be real-valued expressions. It is interesting to note that while SQRT(4) is illegal, SQRT(4+0.) would be legal, since 4+0. is a mixed-mode expression producing a real-valued result.

6.2   MIXED-MODE ASSIGNMENT STATEMENTS

Two general types of mixed-mode assignment statements will be discussed.

    (a)   real variable = integer expression

    (b)   integer variable = real expression

In case (a), the integer constant which is the computed value of the integer expression is converted to a real constant, and is assigned to the real variable. Note that this could result in reduced accuracy, since integer constants can have greater precision than real constants.

In case (b), the real constant which is the computed value of the real expression must be converted to an integer constant prior to assignment to the integer variable. This is done by truncating any fraction which is a part of the real constant. For example, 123.76 becomes 123, -86.98 becomes -86 and .0042 becomes zero. Large real constants such as 12.3E20 cannot be accurately converted to integer constants. In cases like this, inaccurate assignment will occur, and it is the programmer's responsibility to see that this situation does not arise.

6.3   MIXED-MODE BUILT-IN FUNCTIONS

The FORTRAN language provides built-in functions which facilitate the conversion of real-valued expressions to integer-valued expressions and vice-versa. They are IFIX and FLOAT respectively. For example,

IFIX(X + 2.4)

would evaluate the real expression X+2.4 and convert the result to an integer constant using the same rule as outlined for mixed-mode assignment statements. On the other hand,

FLOAT(I + 2)

would evaluate the integer expression I+2 and convert the result to a real constant, subject to the same restrictions already discussed for mixed-mode assignment statements. This suggests another method of computing the illegal expression SIN(3); it can be written as SIN(FLOAT(3)), which is legal.

6.4   EXTENDED ASSIGNMENT STATEMENT

The WATFIV-S compiler allows extended assignment state-ments as a useful extension to the FORTRAN language.   Examples are:

(a)   X = Y = 2.4

(b)   X = Y = Z = A = B = -3.56 + SIN(T)

(c)   I = J = 9

(d)   I = X = J = 123456789

In case (a) the real variables X and Y are both assigned the value 2.4; in case (b), all five of X, Y, Z, A, and B are assigned the real value of the computed expression -3.56+SIN(T).   In case (c) we see that assignments can be made to integer variables as well.

When using mixed-mode assignments, as in case (d), it is important to know the exact way in which the extended assign-ment statement is implemented in WATFIV-S.   The general form is

$$v_1 = v_2 = v_3 = \ldots = v_n = \text{expression}$$

This is equivalent to

$$v_n = \text{expression}$$
$$v_{n-1} = v_n$$
$$\cdot$$
$$\cdot$$
$$\cdot$$
$$v_2 = v_3$$
$$v_1 = v_2$$

Example (d) is therefore equivalent to the three statements

$$J = 123456789$$
$$X = J$$
$$I = X$$

When X is assigned in the second statement, accuracy is lost. This means that, when I is assigned in the third statement, it ends up with a value different from that of J. This could have been avoided by arranging the original statement as follows:

$$X = I = J = 123456789$$

Note that, in each example of the extended assignment statement, the only expression involved is to the right of the farthest-right equals sign. The item to the left of <u>every</u> equals sign must be a variable which is to be assigned. It follows therefore, that the statement

$$X = X + Y = Z = T*2.0$$

is invalid.

6.5   EXERCISES

6.1   Given that I=2, J=3, A=4.2, B=2.0, evaluate the following FORTRAN expressions by hand. For verification, also evaluate the expressions using the computer.

      (a)   J/I*A   (c)   J**I+A**B

      (b)   A*J/I   (d)   J**I+A**I

6.2   Tabulate the function

$$y = x^5$$

for x = 1, 2, 3, ..., 25, using the two expressions X**5. and X**5; compare your results.

6.3 Find

$$\sum_{n=0}^{10} \frac{x^n}{n!}$$

for x = .1, .2, .3, ..., 1.0

6.4 A program is required to convert inches to metres, centimetres, and millimetres (recall that there are 2.54001 centimetres in 1 inch).

(a) Write the program without using any built-in functions.

(b) Write the program using the built-in function IFIX.

Chapter 7

SIMPLE INPUT AND OUTPUT

By now the reader has learned some of the basic concepts of the FORTRAN language. However, one facility has not been described in detail. Most examples presented have used some form of the PRINT statement to output values. This has been the only way available for the computer to communicate results to the user. This chapter will present some of the details and rules for printing values.

As well, the programmer often wishes to introduce new data to the program at execution time. This is accomplished by the READ statement which is also described in this chapter.

The style of input and output which is used in this chapter is called format-free, and is valuable and useful to the reader who is learning to program. In later chapters, other methods of performing I/O will be described.

7.1 OUTPUT DURING EXECUTION

We have seen the PRINT statement used in many examples, but let us review it by considering Example 7.1.

```
C EXAMPLE 7.1
      A = B = C = 20.
      D = E = F = -25.
      I = J = 739
      K = L = -52
      PRINT, I, A, K, D
      STOP
      END
```

The line printed would be

739   20.0000000   -52   -25.0000000

The "PRINT," is followed by a list of variables separated by commas. At execution time the values of these variables are printed across the page with spaces inserted for clarity. Each value is printed to full precision. If the statement

PRINT, I, A, K, D, J, B, L, E, C, F

is executed, the number of values to be printed cannot fit on one line. In this case, the values are printed across the page for the full width of the page; then a new line is started.

The number of values per line depends on the type of variable and the particular printer used. On most standard printers, the first eight values would appear on the first output line, followed by the last two values on the second output line.

Example 7.2 shows that constants as well as variables may appear in the PRINT list.

```
C EXAMPLE 7.2
      X = 30.0
      PRINT, 2, X, 500032
      STOP
      END
```

The resulting line would be

2   30.0000000   500032

This feature is useful when debugging programs. If the programmer is having difficulty in determining why his program will not work, statements of the form PRINT,1 and PRINT,2, etc., can be inserted at appropriate places in the program. The output will then help him trace the order in which the statements are executed.

Finally, Example 7.3 demonstrates that expressions may appear in the PRINT list.

```
C EXAMPLE 7.3
      I = 25
      J = 3
      Z = 92.
      X = 25.
      PRINT, X, X*Z/I, I+I/J, ABS(SIN(X))
      STOP
      END
```

In this case, the expressions are evaluated and the resulting values are printed. Notice that any arithmetic expressions may be used, including those using built-in functions. The type of value printed is determined by the type of expression.

One rule must be kept in mind. No expression in the PRINT statement may start with a left parenthesis. Thus the statement PRINT,(A+B)/C is invalid, while the statement PRINT,+(A+B)/C is valid.

7.2   INPUT DURING EXECUTION

In Chapter 1 we introduced the basic ideas involved when reading real constants from a data deck during execution. We are now also familiar with integer constants, and, of course, these can be processed in a similar manner. As well, more than one constant can be read from a single data card, and they may be of different types. For example, to read more than one constant from one card we could use the statement

                    READ, X, I

which has two items in its READ list. In this case two constants could appear on the card; the first one would be a real constant and the second would be an integer. The constants could be separated by a blank column or comma. It

- 71 -

is important that the type of constant read correspond exactly to the type of variable used in the READ list. Otherwise an error will be signalled and the program will terminate execution. Incidentally, the real constant can take any of the forms available, including E notation.

Consider Example 7.4, which causes four values for X, Y, Z, and N to be read, and calculates $X^N + Y^N + Z^N$. If the value read for X is zero, the program is terminated.

```
C EXAMPLE 7.4
      LOOP
          READ, X, Y, Z, N
          IF (X .EQ. 0.) QUIT
          W = X**N + Y**N + Z**N
          PRINT, X, Y, Z, N, W
      ENDLOOP
      STOP
      END
```

The data for this program can be punched in a number of ways. The first and most logical way is to place the four required constants on one card. The constants are separated by one or more blanks or by a comma. We give three examples of data cards punched in this manner. In each case, the data need not start in column 1 of the data card.

```
3.0    6.2    9.E-2 5
9.2,   6.4,   9.E+2,3
67.            39.              40.6,1
```

Alternatively, we can punch the four required values on four consecutive cards. There are many other possibilities, any of which must satisfy the following two rules.

(a)   Each time a READ statement is encountered in the course of execution of the program, a new card is read.

(b)   If necessary, additional data cards will be read until the list of variables has been satisfied, that is to say, values have been assigned to all the variables in the READ list.

Thus, if there are not sufficient constants on the first data card, further data cards will be read until the list is fully satisfied. Blank cards are ignored, since they contain no constants and may be placed anywhere in the data deck. If the READ list is satisfied and there are still more constants on the current data card, these are ignored.

This brings up an important point. Example 7.4 uses the value 0.0 for X as sentinel data. If the last data card contained only the value 0.0, the program would terminate with an error message. Rule (b) above tells us the reason for this. The variables Y, Z, and N could not be assigned, since the data deck is depleted. Therefore, the last card should contain 0.0, followed by any two real constants and any integer constant.

To emphasize rule (a), consider the following statements:

READ, A   READ, A, B

READ, B

The statements on the left, when executed in succession, require that two data cards be supplied, as each of the statements initiates the reading of a new card; the statement on the right requires only one data card but could have two.

Finally, READ statements such as the following, which contain constants or expressions, are considered invalid.

READ, 1, 3.9

READ, X+Y, SIN(Z)

7.3 THE AT END STATEMENT

In many examples in earlier chapters a data deck was read and processed. In all cases either the exact number of cards was known in advance, or a sentinel data card was used to signal the end of the data deck. The AT END statement provides a more general way to signal that all the cards have been read. Consider Example 7.5 which computes the average of a set of real numbers punched in a data deck. These real numbers must be punched one per card, but the total number of data cards is unknown when the program begins to execute.

```
C EXAMPLE 7.5
      SUM = 0.0
      N = 0
      LOOP
          READ, VALUE
          AT END, QUIT
          SUM = SUM + VALUE
          N = N + 1
      ENDLOOP
      AVG = SUM / N
      PRINT, N, AVG
      STOP
      END
```

Note that the READ statement is immediately followed by an AT END statement. Each time through the loop, if a card is read, the AT END statement is ignored, and VALUE is added to SUM. Eventually the data deck will be completely read. When the computer attempts to read another card it cannot, and the statement AT END then becomes activated. It causes the QUIT statement to be executed, and the loop is terminated.

If used, the AT END statement must always immediately follow the READ statement. Its general form is as follows:

AT END, statement

The statement which follows the comma can be an assignment statement or an input-output statement, but usually the QUIT statement is the appropriate choice. Just as with the logical IF, this statement cannot be any of the statements such as LOOP, ENDLOOP, WHILE, ENDWHILE, ELSE, ELSEIF, ENDIF, or IF, as these would make no sense.

7.4   EXERCISES

7.1   It is required to compute the average of five real
      numbers read in from data cards.   The following
      program will do the job.

                    READ, A, B, C, D, E
                    PRINT,+(A+B+C+D+E)/5.0
                    STOP
                    END

      All of the data could be punched in one card.   Alter-
      natively, five cards, each with one number punched on
      it, will do.   How many other ways are there to punch
      the data?

7.2   A data deck has n values for x.   Write a program
      which reads the values and computes

$$\sqrt{\frac{1}{n-1}\left[\Sigma x^2 - \frac{(\Sigma x)^2}{n}\right]}$$

      where

                    Σx = sum of the values of x
                    Σx^2 = sum of the squares of the value of x.

7.3   A data deck contains 100 integer values.   Write a
      program which reads these data and determines the
      following.

      (a)   The total of all negative integer values.

      (b)   The total number of integers which are negative.

      (c)   The total of all positive integer values.

      (d)   The total number of all even integers.

      (e)   The total number of all odd integers.

      (f)   The total number of all odd negative integers.

Chapter 8

THE DO STATEMENT

Thus far in the text, blocks of statements have been
controlled by IF structures of various types, or if the blocks
formed loops, by LOOP or WHILE structures. We now wish to
introduce the DO statement, which is a specialized but
powerful, loop control statement. It is especially useful
whenever it is desirable to control a loop by means of an
index or counter. It has important applications for computations involving subscripted variables which are discussed in
the next chapter.

8.1 INTRODUCTORY EXAMPLES

Let us see how a DO statement works by comparing two
sample programs which perform a repetitive calculation.
Example 8.1 prints a table of the integers 1 to 100 and their
squares.

```
C EXAMPLE 8.1 - SQUARES OF INTEGERS
      I = 1
      LOOP
          ISQ = I*I
          PRINT, I, ISQ
          I = I + 1
          IF (I .GT. 100) QUIT
      ENDLOOP
      STOP
      END
```

Example 8.2 achieves the same result but uses a DO statement.

```
C EXAMPLE 8.2 - SAME PROBLEM USING DO
      DO 13 I=1,100
         ISQ = I*I
         PRINT, I, ISQ
13    CONTINUE
      STOP
      END
```

The action of the DO statement

DO 13 I=1,100

might be paraphrased as: "Perform repetitively all the statements following the DO, up to and including the statement numbered 13, for I starting at 1 and increasing by 1 for each repetition as long as I is less than or equal to 100. Then continue on in the program." It can be seen that the DO statement has control over a set of the statements that immediately follow it in the program. Thus in Example 8.2, the two statements

ISQ = I*I

PRINT, I, ISQ

would be executed one hundred times with I ranging in value from 1 to 100.

The CONTINUE statement has been introduced to specify the end of a block of statements controlled by the DO, and its purpose is similar to the ENDLOOP statement. This statement contains a statement number, namely 13, which was referenced in the DO statement. This number is a means of identifying a particular statement, and it has nothing to do with the position of the statement in the program. For example, the statement with statement number 13 is actually the fifth statement in the program, including the comment statement. There are other reasons to use statement numbers in FORTRAN, and these will be covered later in the text. In particular we will see that they play an important role in the topic of format control.

A statement number is any positive integer up to 99999. It is punched in columns 1 to 5 inclusive, and need not be right-justified.

Example 8.3 shows that it is, in fact, not necessary to use the CONTINUE statement. The statement number has been placed on the last executable statement in the set of statements controlled by the DO. Many FORTRAN programs are written this way, but as a matter of good programming style, the authors encourage the reader to use the CONTINUE statement, even though it is usually redundant.

```
C EXAMPLE 8.3 - OMIT CONTINUE
      DO 13 I=1,100
          ISQ = I*I
13        PRINT, I, ISQ
      STOP
      END
```

Before proceeding to other examples, let us introduce some jargon that is usually associated with the DO statement by referring to Example 8.2. The statement numbered 13, i.e., CONTINUE, is called the object of the DO statement. The object is always the statement whose number is referenced in the DO. The set of statements following the DO, up to and including the object, is called the range of the DO. Thus the range of the DO statement in Example 8.2 is the three statements

```
      ISQ = I*I
      PRINT, I, ISQ
      CONTINUE
```

The values of I, 1, 100 used in the DO statement are called the DO-parameters, with the variable I also called the index of the DO. A loop in a program controlled by a DO statement is commonly called a DO-loop.

Example 8.4 illustrates that the index of the DO need not be employed in any statements within the range, since its primary purpose is to count the number of times the loop is repeated.

```
C EXAMPLE 8.4 - TABULATION USING A DO
      X = 0.
      DO 4 J=1,25
          Y = (X*X-3.*X+2.) / (X+5.)
          PRINT, X, Y
          X = X + 1.
4     CONTINUE
      STOP
      END
```

Example 8.5 shows that the value by which the index is incremented after each passage through the range may be specified to be different from 1, and the initial value may be greater than 1. The example sums all the odd integers from 27 to 99. The final constant 2 in the DO statement specifies the increment to be applied.

```
C EXAMPLE 8.5 - SUM OF ODD INTEGERS
      INTEGER SUM, COUNT
      SUM = 0
      DO 43 COUNT=27,99,2
          SUM = SUM + COUNT
43    CONTINUE
      PRINT, SUM
      STOP
      END
```

Example 8.6 shows that the DO-parameters may be integer variables as well as integer constants. The program prints a table of the first M integers and their squares, where the value of M is read from a data card.

```
C EXAMPLE 8.6 - SQUARES OF INTEGERS
      READ, M
      DO 93 J=1,M
          PRINT, J, J*J
93    CONTINUE
      STOP
      END
```

8.2 GENERAL FORM OF DO STATEMENT

The general form of the DO statement is specified as follows:

$$DO \ n \ i = m_1, m_2, m_3$$

Here n stands for the statement number that identifies the object of the DO. The DO-parameters are i, m_1, m_2, and m_3, with i also being called the index. The value m_1 is called the _initial_ value, m_2 is called the _test_ value, and m_3 is called the _increment_.

The DO statement exercises control over the statements in its range by first setting the index to the initial value m_1 when the DO statement itself is executed; then the statements of the range are executed in turn. After the object has been executed, the increment m_3 is added to the index i and, if the resulting value is less than or equal to the test value m_2, control is automatically transferred back to the first statement in the range for repetition of all statements in the range. This looping action continues each time the object statement is executed, as long as the incremented value of i is less than or equal to the test value m_2. When the test value is exceeded, control passes to the next executable statement following the object; the DO-loop is then said to be _satisfied_.

It is unfortunate that the DO statement is encumbered with a relatively large number of rules. These do not detract from its power, and are very easily learned and mastered. At any rate, the WATFIV-S compiler will give an error message if these rules are violated; this fact makes it easy to correct the program.

Rule 1: The DO index must be an integer variable and the other DO-parameters must be unsigned integer constants greater than zero or integer variables whose values are greater than zero. Furthermore, if the increment value is not explicitly stated, it is assumed to be 1. Thus DO 3 I=1,10 is the same as DO 3 I=1,10,1. The following are valid DO statements:

```
        DO 14 JACK=KEN,LEN,MEL
        DO 38 IGNATZ=3,MX3,2
        DO 12345 I=J,510,L
        DO 627 KB3=K,J,62
```

The following are not valid DO statements because they violate Rule 1.

```
        DO 6 K=-5,+15,+3
        DO 53 X=.1,2.8,.2
        DO 143 K=J,2*M+3,L+5
        DO 652 A=0,10
        DO 19 J=14
```

Rule 2: Because the testing of the incremented value of the index is done following execution of the object of the DO, the range of the DO is always performed at least once, even if the initial value is greater than the test value when the DO loop is entered.

Thus the range of the following DO statement will be performed once:

```
        DO 175 I=17,3
```

Rule 3: The DO-parameters may not be modified by statements within the range of the DO. (It is perfectly legal to modify them outside the range.) For example, the following DO-loop violates this rule:

```
        DO 12 I=J,K,L
        L = 3
        READ, I
12      J = I + 2
```

Rule 4: As has been suggested, the object of the DO is normally a CONTINUE statement. However it could be any other executable statement, but not LOOP, WHILE, QUIT, STOP, ELSE, ENDLOOP, ENDIF, ENDWHILE, ELSE, another DO, or a logical IF containing any of the previously named.

Rule 5: The QUIT statement can be used to exit from a DO-loop before it is satisfied.

Rule 6: If control passes from the DO-loop because it is satisfied, the value of the index is to be considered indefinite, that is, it may have the last value it had while in the loop, or that value plus the increment, or some value completely different. Because this is a compiler implementation feature, it is not safe to use the index in this situation if the program is expected to produce the same results with different compilers. However, if control passes from the loop by means of a QUIT, the value of the index is usable outside the loop, and is the value the index had when control passed from the loop.

A few words should be said about what happens if the index never actually equals the test value, as would be the case for a statement such as DO 17 I=1,6,2. The range would be performed for I equal to 1, 3, and 5, since a further increment of 2 to I would increase it beyond 6. This is easily determined from the definition of the DO statement. The following examples are given as further illustrations of this rule.

(a)	DO 2 I=1,9,3	3 times
(b)	DO 65 JACK=2,9,5	2 times
(c)	DO 9 J12K=2,9,11	1 time
(d)	DO 721 KB3=3,25,3	8 times
(e)	DO 16 L=11,1000,37	27 times

8.3   USE OF CONTINUE

Let us consider a few more examples which illustrate points arising from Rules 1 to 6. Example 8.7 shows where the use of a CONTINUE statement is absolutely necessary. The problem is this: A collection of data cards has been punched, each containing two real numbers. A program is to be created which reads, the data cards in turn, and prints out each pair of values in the order: larger, smaller. It does this until the data cards are exhausted or a data card is found with the two values equal. The first data card will contain an integer value which is the count of the number of data cards with pairs. Before terminating, the program is to print out the number of data cards read, exclusive of the first data card.

```
C EXAMPLE 8.7 - PRINTS LARGEST, SMALLEST  .
C N IS THE NUMBER OF DATA CARDS
      READ, N
      DO 4 I=1,N
          READ, X, Y
          NUM = I
          IF (X .EQ. Y) QUIT
          IF (X .GT. Y) THEN
              PRINT, X, Y
          ELSE
              PRINT, Y, X
          ENDIF
4         CONTINUE
      PRINT, NUM
      STOP
      END
```

There are several points to note about this example. Probably the most important is the mandatory use of the

CONTINUE statement as the object of the DO. This is necessary here since, following any executions of the IF structure, the object of a DO must be reached in order to increment and test the index for further repetitions of the loop. (Recall that ENDIF cannot be the object of a DO.) Thus the use of the CONTINUE statement solves the problem.

Also note that the program illustrates that it is perfectly legal to transfer control out of the range of a DO using a QUIT. It is also legal to transfer within the range of a DO using an IF statement as long as its corresponding ENDIF is within the range of the DO.

The program also shows how to get around the difficulty imposed by Rule 6. The extra statement NUM=I is within the DO range to ensure that the value of I is defined properly for the last PRINT statement in case control reaches the PRINT statement by satisfying the DO-loop.

Consider the following problem: Read a data card containing an integer value n. Then read n more data cards each containing a positive real value. Find the largest real value, and print it before terminating. (Here n might be the number of students in a class, and the real values might be the marks in a particular course. The program would find the highest mark.) Basically, the program works like this: Initialize a variable BIG to zero. Then read n followed by the n values in turn, each time checking whether the value just read is larger than the current value of the variable BIG and replacing BIG with it, if so. (This will certainly be true the first time, since BIG is zero and all the values are positive.) Finally, after all the cards have been checked using a DO-loop, the final value of BIG is printed out.

Example 8.8 is one possible program for this problem. As in the last example, the CONTINUE statement must be used as the object of the DO. However, CONTINUE is also used in the "true" range of the IF to indicate that no computation is to be done. This application of the CONTINUE statement can be thought of as "no operation", and has no relationship to the use of the CONTINUE as the object of a DO statement.

```
C EXAMPLE 8.8 - FIND LARGEST NUMBER
      BIG = 0.
      READ, N
      DO 2 I=1,N
          READ, X
          IF (X .LE. BIG) THEN
              CONTINUE
          ELSE
              BIG = X
          ENDIF
2         CONTINUE
      PRINT, BIG
      STOP
      END
```

8.4   NESTED DO-LOOPS

The final topic to discuss is what happens when a DO statement appears within the range of another DO. This is as simple as the previous topics, and only one rule need be added to handle it.

Rule 7: All statements in the range of the inner DO must also be in the range of the outer DO.

DO statements satisfying this rule are said to be nested.

In essence, Rule 7 states that the object of the inner DO of a nest must appear physically no later in the program than the object of the outer DO. Example 8.9 illustrates improperly nested DO-loops.

```
C EXAMPLE 8.9 - IMPROPER NESTING
      DO 1 I=1,5
          DO 2 J=1,5
1             L = I + 5
2             PRINT, L
      STOP
      END
```

8.5 EXERCISES

8.1 Tabulate the following functions using DO statements to control any loops.

(a) $k = i^2 + i + 1$
for $i = 0, 1, 2, \ldots, 10$

(b) $y = (x^2 + 10)/(x + 3)$
for $x = 5, 6, 7, \ldots, 15$

(c) $f(x) = (x^3 + 3x + 16)/(x^2 - 4)$
for $x = -5, -4, -3, \ldots, 10$

(d) $f(x,y) = (x^2 - y^2)/(x^2 + y^2)$
for $x = 0, 1, 2, \ldots, 5$
and $y = 3, 5, 7, \ldots, 15$ for each value of x

(e) $f(x,y) = (x^2 + 3x + y^2)/(xy - 5y - 3x + 15)$
for $x = 2, 3, 4, \ldots, 7$
and $y = 0, 1, 2, \ldots, 5$, for each value of x

8.2 Compute the number of points with integer valued co-ordinates that are contained within the ellipse

$$\frac{x^2}{16} + \frac{y^2}{25} = 1$$

8.3 A rectangular area is defined by the relationships

$$N1 \leq x \leq N2$$
$$N3 \leq y \leq N4$$

where N1, N2, N3, and N4 are integers greater than zero. In this area, there are $(N2-N1+1)(N4-N3+1)$ points which have integer-valued co-ordinates. Call these points the set A. Suppose the following data were read by a program:

(a) N1, N2, N3, N4

(b) the co-ordinates of a point, P, taken at random.

Write a program which uses DO-loops to compute the
distance from the point P to each point in set A.
The printed output should have a separate line for
each of the distances. Each line should contain the
co-ordinates of the point in A, together with the
computed distance.

Chapter 9

SUBSCRIPTED VARIABLES

Subscripted variables are an extremely useful feature of the FORTRAN language since they allow flexible and general programs to be written. Indeed, they are so useful and important that it is rare to find a FORTRAN program of any size which does not use at least one of them. This is partly because they facilitate programming the repetitive calculations that are so common in computation and, in this respect, are often used with DO-loops. Also, they allow the programmer to refer to whole collections of values using one name much in the same way a mathematician refers to a set, e.g., the set of marks for a class or the set of prime numbers less than 100.

The notation used with subscripted variables is similar to the mathematical notation for vectors and matrices and facilitates the programmming of problems that use these concepts.

9.1   NOTATION AND USE

Consider the problem of calculating the average mark in a certain course for a class of five students. Each student's mark is to be printed along with the class average. Example 9.1 is a simple program to solve this particular problem. Note that a different real variable name is given to the mark of each student, and each mark is punched on a separate data card.

This approach to the problem is obviously inflexible in that a great deal of modification would have to be made to the program if there were a different number of students in the class, say 12 or 30. Indeed, it would be impossible to use the approach if the number of students was not known beforehand, but was to be read in as data to the program.

```
C EXAMPLE 9.1 - AVERAGE MARK
      READ, A
      READ, B
      READ, C
      READ, D
      READ, E
      TOTAL = A + B + C + D + E
      AVRGE = TOTAL / 5.
      PRINT, A, AVRGE
      PRINT, B, AVRGE
      PRINT, C, AVRGE
      PRINT, D, AVRGE
      PRINT, E, AVRGE
      STOP
      END
```

Let us approach this problem again, and introduce the idea of a <u>subscripted variable</u>. Suppose we consider all the students' marks as a set named, say, m. Then we could refer to a particular student's mark by writing the name of the set, m, with a subscript which identifies the student. Thus m_1 refers to the mark of student number one, m_2 to the mark of student number two, and so on. (Of course, we would have to agree upon some method for numbering the students.) In general, we could call the i'th student's mark m_i, where i would have some value between 1 and the number of students in the class, inclusive. Thus the use of a subscript with the set name allows us to refer to a particular element of the set. This notation has been found to be useful in mathematics and engineering, and is carried over into FORTRAN in the following way: the subscript is written inside parentheses following the set name.

Eg. M(1), M(2), M(16), M(I)

- 89 -

The variable M is referred to as a subscripted variable.

Since a particular element of the set has a value, this element can be used in a program in exactly the same way that other variables have been used in the programs seen so far.

Example 9.2 uses a subscripted variable to find the average mark for a class of 30 students.

```
C EXAMPLE 9.2 - CLASS AVERAGE
      DIMENSION MARK(30)
      INTEGER SUM
      SUM = 0
      DO 22 I=1,30
          READ, MARK(I)
          SUM = SUM + MARK(I)
22    CONTINUE
      AVE = SUM / 30.
      DO 222 I=1,30
          PRINT, MARK(I), AVE
222   CONTINUE
      STOP
      END
```

Aside from the DIMENSION statement, which will be explained later, the program looks much like many of the examples seen before. There is a DO-loop which causes successive data cards to be read, each containing a mark. The first time through the loop, I has the value 1, and is used as a subscript for variable MARK in the READ statement. Thus the value of MARK(1) is read in and accumulated into SUM. Since I is incremented each time through the loop, successive repetitions of the loop read in values for MARK(2), MARK(3), MARK(4), ..., MARK(30). Thus it is an easy matter to read in any number of marks, and the program could be modified quite simply to do this if the class contained, for example, 25 students. In fact, this will be done in the next section.

9.2   ONE-DIMENSIONAL ARRAYS

What is the purpose of the DIMENSION statement? It is another example of a declaration statement and, as such, has no effect at execution time. It is used strictly at compile time to provide the compiler with certain information about the variable named in it.

With reference to Example 9.2, the information it provides is this:

(a)   It identifies MARK as the name of a set of values; a particular member of the set will be referenced in the program by the use of the name MARK followed by a subscript enclosed in parentheses.

(b)   It informs the compiler that there are at most 30 elements in the set, and that enough memory must be allocated to store values corresponding to these elements.

(c)   It contains a tacit promise that the value of any subscript used with MARK will never be less than 1 or greater than 30. Thus it would be impossible to refer to MARK(-5) or MARK(79).

The value 30 used in the DIMENSION statement is called the dimension of MARK. Any variables that are to be used with subscripts must have their dimensions declared before they are used in the program. Subscripted variables are also referred to as dimensioned variables or arrays.

The names for arrays follow the usual rules of FORTRAN. Thus, each element of MARK is an integer value, and will be treated as such by the compiler. It is possible to have arrays of other than integer type, as subsequent examples will show.

Example 9.3 is a modification of 9.2, and illustrates the flexibility of programs which use subscripted variables. This new version declares MARK to have 30 elements, but does not assume that 30 student marks will be read. Instead, the first data card contains an integer constant which specifies the actual number of student marks which follow it on cards. Thus the program is general, in the sense that it can be used with a class of any size up to a maximum of 30. The program simply reads in the particular class size at execution time; no modifications are required to the program itself.

```
C EXAMPLE 9.3 - GENERAL PROGRAM FOR AVERAGE
      DIMENSION MARK(30)
      INTEGER TOTAL
      TOTAL = 0
      READ, N
      DO 26 I=1,N
          READ, MARK(I)
          TOTAL = TOTAL + MARK(I)
26    CONTINUE
      AVRGE = TOTAL / N
      DO 4 I=1,N
          PRINT, MARK(I), AVRGE
4     CONTINUE
      STOP
      END
```

Note that the program does not necessarily use all 30 locations reserved for MARK; in fact only the first N are used. Also the answers printed for Example 9.2 differ from those of Example 9.3; the former program uses mixed-mode arithmetic to calculate the average, whereas the latter uses integer arithmetic for this calculation. In both cases, the average is a real number.

It should be apparent by now that a subscripted variable may be used in the same ways that a simple variable may be used, that is, in READ statements, assignment statements, IF statements, etc. Example 9.4 shows the use of a subscripted variable on the left side of an assignment statement and in a

PRINT statement. The program prints the first ten Fibonacci numbers which are defined by the following rules:

$$f_1 = 1$$
$$f_2 = 1$$
$$f_{i+2} = f_{i+1} + f_i \quad i > 0$$

Thus, each Fibonacci number after the second is obtained by adding together the previous two. Hence,

$$f_3 = f_2 + f_1 = 2$$
$$f_4 = f_3 + f_2 = 3$$
$$f_5 = 5, \quad f_6 = 8, \quad \text{etc.}$$

Note that all Fibonacci numbers have integer values.

```
C EXAMPLE 9.4 - FIBONACCI NUMBERS
      INTEGER F(10)
      F(1) = 1
      F(2) = 1
      DO 1 I=1,8
         F(I+2) = F(I+1) + F(I)
1     CONTINUE
      DO 43 J=1,10
         PRINT, F(J)
43    CONTINUE
      STOP
      END
```

The program illustrates some other features about subscripted variables. Since we want the array F to represent integer values, we declare its name in an INTEGER statement. It is also possible to declare the dimensions of arrays in type-declaration statements, and hence the single statement

        INTEGER F(10)

serves both purposes. It would be perfectly legal to use a DIMENSION statement to declare the dimension of F, for example,

        DIMENSION F(10)   or   INTEGER F
        INTEGER F   DIMENSION F(10)

However, using one statement saves extra key-punching, and localizes all the information about F. The dimension must be declared only once; for example, the following pair of statements is invalid.

$$\text{DIMENSION } F(10)$$
$$\text{INTEGER } F(10)$$

The assignment statement

$$F(I+2) = F(I+1) + F(I)$$

shows that subscripts may be expressions and not just simple values as in previous examples. The statement is within the range of the DO, and hence is repeated eight times. The first time, I has value 1 and the statement is equivalent to $F(3)=F(2)+F(1)$. Next time through the loop, I has value 2, and the calculation performed is $F(4)=F(3)+F(2)$. Thus, going eight times through the loop computes the third to tenth Fibonacci numbers - the desired result.

A subscript may, in fact, be <u>any</u> integer-valued or real-valued expression; if real, the value is converted to an integer by truncating any fractional part. For example, $X(17.88)$ is taken as $X(17)$ if X is an array. Although this feature is occasionally convenient, the programmer is cautioned against using real-valued subscripts because the necessary conversion can be costly in computing time.

Example 9.5 contains one modification to the previous example.

```
      C EXAMPLE 9.5 - USE OF IMPLIED DO
            INTEGER F(10)
            F(1) = 1
            F(2) = 1
            DO 1 I=1,8
               F(I+2) = F(I+1) + F(I)
      1     CONTINUE
            PRINT, (F(I), I=1,10)
            STOP
            END
```

The PRINT statement contains a new feature not seen in previous examples, although the I=1,10 part may look familiar. The construction

$$(F(I), I=1,10)$$

is called an _implied_ _DO_ because it is a means of causing a looping action within the PRINT statement. The statement

$$PRINT, (F(I), I=1,10)$$

means, effectively: "Print values of F(I) for I ranging from 1 to 10". The ten values so printed would be strung out across the printer line as follows:

$$1 \quad 1 \quad 2 \quad 3 \quad 5 \quad 8 \quad 13 \quad 21 \quad 34 \quad 55$$

The same effect could be achieved by the equivalent, though more cumbersome, statement

$$PRINT, F(1),F(2),F(3),F(4),F(5),F(6),F(7),F(8),F(9),F(10)$$

The parameters of the implied DO have the same significance as those of a DO statement; accordingly, an increment may be specified. Thus, to print out the third, fifth, seventh, and ninth Fibonacci numbers, we could use the statement

$$PRINT, (F(I), I=3,9,2)$$

The same effect could be obtained from

$$PRINT, (F(2*I+1), I=1,4)$$

but the former method is superior since its execution involves fewer computations and hence is faster.

It is important to note that the outer parentheses and the comma preceding the DO index are always necessary when constructing an implied DO. The only executable statements in which the implied DO is allowed are the input and output statements.

One simplification that could be made to the program is shown by Example 9.6.

```
C EXAMPLE 9.6 - OUTPUT OF WHOLE ARRAY
      INTEGER F(10)
      F(1) = 1
      F(2) = 1
      DO 1 I=1,8
         F(I+2) = F(I+1) + F(I)
1     CONTINUE
      PRINT, F
      STOP
      END
```

In this example, the PRINT statement contains only the name of the array F. This is one of the few places an array name may appear in a program without subscripts; the effect of the statement is to print out <u>all</u> the elements of the array, i.e., as many elements as are reserved by the dimension. For this example, the two statements

```
PRINT, F
PRINT, (F(I), I=1,N)
```

would produce the same result only if N were equal to 10. Thus, if it is desired that a whole array be printed, we need mention only its name; if part is to be printed, we use an implied DO. The same remarks are true for READ statements which operate on subscripted variables.

Example 9.7 is a program which computes a grocery bill using two arrays. The first array, COST, will contain the cost per item for one hundred different items. The second array, ITEM, will contain the number of units of each item purchased on a trip to the grocery store. The program first reads in the cost for each of the one hundred items, then reads in the corresponding one hundred values for elements of array ITEM and proceeds to compute the bill.

It is important to understand how the data cards for this program could be punched. Obviously more than one data card will have to be punched to contain the two hundred values which are to be read in. The question is: Will the single READ statement read all the cards? The answer to this is yes; enough data cards will be read until values have been assigned to the one hundred elements of COST and the one hundred elements of ITEM. The successive elements of COST could be punched one after the other on a data card, with an intervening comma or blank to separate the values; a new data card would be started if the next value would not fit into the remaining columns of the current card. The values of ITEM would be punched next, with ITEM(1) following COST(100) or starting a new data card. Note that the values of COST must be punched as real constants, and the values of ITEM as integer constants.

```
C EXAMPLE 9.7 - GROCERY BILL
      DIMENSION COST(100), ITEM(100)
      READ, COST, ITEM
      BILL = 0.
      DO 2 I=1,100
          BILL = BILL + COST(I)*ITEM(I)
2     CONTINUE
      PRINT, BILL
      STOP
      END
```

As can be seen, more than one array may be declared in a single DIMENSION statement, with a comma between the various array declarations.

The program would be more efficient if both COST and ITEM were real arrays, since the present version uses mixed-mode arithmetic. This is time consuming, particularly when used in a loop such as is contained in the example. The improved version is Example 9.8.

```
C EXAMPLE 9.8 - IMPROVEMENT OF 9.7
      DIMENSION COST(100)
      REAL ITEM(100)
      BILL = 0.
      READ, COST, ITEM
      DO 2 I=1,100
          BILL = BILL + COST(I)*ITEM(I)
2     CONTINUE
      PRINT, BILL
      STOP
      END
```

Alternatively, the first two statements could be replaced by

```
      REAL COST(100), ITEM(100)
```

or

```
      DIMENSION COST(100), ITEM(100)
      REAL ITEM
```

or, for that matter,

```
      REAL ITEM
      DIMENSION COST(100)
      DIMENSION ITEM(100)
```

One-dimensional arrays are sometimes called <u>vectors</u>. Mathematicians will note that the DO-loops in Examples 9.7 and 9.8 calculate the scalar or inner product of two vectors.

The following example is a program to evaluate the polynomial expression

$$a_1 x^{n-1} + a_2 x^{n-2} + a_3 x^{n-3} + \ldots + a_n$$

for given values of n, a_1, a_2, ..., a_n using various values of x which are read in. The program terminates when a zero value for x is read.

An efficient way to organize the polynomial for evaluation using a computer is as follows:

$$(\ldots((a_1 x + a_2) x + a_3) x + \ldots + a_{n-1}) x + a_n$$

To be specific, we will assume n to be less than or equal to
25.

```
      C EXAMPLE 9.9 - POLYNOMIAL EVALUATION
            DIMENSION A(25)
            READ, N, (A(J), J=1,N)
            LOOP
                READ, X
                IF (X .EQ. 0.) QUIT
                POLY = A(1)
                DO 12 I=2,N
                    POLY = POLY*X + A(I)
         12     CONTINUE
                PRINT, X, POLY
            ENDLOOP
            STOP
            END
```

The data deck consists of a value of n followed by the n
coefficients a_i on one or more data cards. These are followed
by successive data cards, each with a value of x; the final
card contains the value zero.

9.3   TWO-DIMENSIONAL ARRAYS

The previous section shows that it is convenient to have
variable names which may be used with a subscript. This
section introduces the idea of two-dimensional arrays; these
involve variables having two subscripts. Their principal use
in programs is for working with tables of values. The mathematical equivalent is a matrix, and a similar notation is
used.

Consider Figure 9.1, where a table of values is shown.
The table consists of the number of various items that are
stocked at several warehouses belonging to a company.

	Item 1	Item 2	Item 3	Item 4
Warehouse 1	50	0	16	2
Warehouse 2	3	4	0	98
Warehouse 3	0	1	4	220

Figure 9.1

Using this table, it is easy to answer many questions
concerning the company's inventory. What is the total stock
of item 4 on hand? What is the total number of items stored
at warehouse 2? Are there any items completely out of stock?
Are there any items out of stock at a particular warehouse?
How many of the fourth item are in stock at warehouse 2?

Notice that the data in the table are organized in three
rows and four columns. The last question above could be
paraphrased as: What is the value in row 2 and column 4? Or,
more generally, what is the value in row i and column j?

In order to use such a table in FORTRAN, we need only
give it a name, say, for this example, STOCK; then, to refer
to a particular element of the table we append two subscripts,
in parentheses, to the name. Thus STOCK(2,4) is the stock of
item 4 on hand in warehouse 2, i.e., 98. Similarly,
STOCK(3,2) is the stock of item 2 on hand at warehouse 3,
i.e., 1. The first subscript always refers to the row number
in the table; the second always refers to the column number;
a comma always separates the two subscripts. Thus STOCK(I,J)
refers to the entry in row I and column J of the table (or
matrix or two-dimensional array) named STOCK.

Let us proceed to write programs which answer some of the questions mentioned above. Example 9.10 is a program to compute the total stock of item 4. It reads in the table, sums down column 4, and prints out the resulting sum.

Again we use a DIMENSION statement to declare the array for the same reasons given under one-dimensional arrays. However, the particular DIMENSION statement in the example supplies one additional piece of information. It informs the compiler that the variable named STOCK has two dimensions and will be used with two subscripts throughout the program. Note that 12 locations are set aside for STOCK, since it has 3 rows and 4 columns.

```
C EXAMPLE 9.10 - STOCK ON HAND OF ITEM 4
      DIMENSION STOCK(3,4)
      INTEGER STOCK
      DO 2 I=1,3
         READ, (STOCK(I,J), J=1,4)
2     CONTINUE
      NUMBER = 0
      DO 25 I=1,3
         NUMBER = NUMBER + STOCK(I,4)
25    CONTINUE
      PRINT, NUMBER
      STOP
      END
```

The method of reading in the table requires a brief explanation. A DO statement controls a READ statement containing an implied DO. Since I, the index of the DO statement, is used as row designator for STOCK in the READ statement, the implied DO has the effect of reading in the values across a row of the table. The looping action of the DO statement causes all three rows to be read in. The data could consist of three cards, each containing the four values in a row of the table.

The foregoing remarks virtually explain the action of the second DO statement as well. Since the column designator for

STOCK in the statement numbered 25 is the constant 4, computation within the DO loop is confined to values in that column. Thus the sum of all values in column 4 is calculated.

As before, the two declaration statements at the start of the program could be replaced by the single statement

INTEGER STOCK(3,4)

Example 9.11 is a program which determines the total number of articles in stock at each warehouse, and stores these values in the vector AMOUNT.

```
C EXAMPLE 9.11 - AMOUNT IN WAREHOUSES
      INTEGER STOCK(3,4), AMOUNT(3)
      READ, ((STOCK(I,J), J=1,4), I=1,3)
C ZERO OUT VECTOR AMOUNT FOR SUMMING
      DO 1 I=1,3
         AMOUNT(I) = 0
1     CONTINUE
C SUM ACROSS ROWS OF STOCK
      DO 2 I=1,3
         DO 20 J=1,4
            AMOUNT(I) = AMOUNT(I) + STOCK(I,J)
20       CONTINUE
2     CONTINUE
      PRINT, AMOUNT
      STOP
      END
```

The READ statement

READ, ((STOCK(I,J), J=1,4), I=1,3)

introduces the concept of nested implied DO's; the inner implied DO is performed for each application of the outer DO. Thus, one statement reads in the twelve values of STOCK, by rows; they could be punched on one card as:

50,0,16,2,3,4,0,98,0,1,4,220

The READ statement above could read the data cards for Example 9.10, since any trailing blanks on a card are skipped over by the READ mechanism in its search for enough values to satisfy the READ.

Note that comment statements may be included anywhere in a program; they can serve a valuable documentary purpose.

Although the double DO-loop ending on statement 2 performs the proper row summations for each row, a slightly more efficient program could be obtained by writing the loops in the following fashion:

```
      DO 26 I=1,3
         NUMBER = 0
         DO 2 J=1,4
            NUMBER = NUMBER + STOCK(I,J)
   2     CONTINUE
         AMOUNT(I) = NUMBER
  26  CONTINUE
```

Notice that this modification reduces the number of array references from 36 to 15, a saving which could mean a significant difference in execution time, since array referencing, although convenient, involves many hidden computations of which the programmer may not be aware.

The PRINT statement in Example 9.11 outputs the entire vector AMOUNT by mentioning its name only. Could we have read the entire array STOCK by mentioning only its name in the READ statement? The answer to this question is yes, but, before giving an example, a few details concerning storage of arrays in FORTRAN must be explained.

A one-dimensional array or vector is stored in the computer's memory with successively numbered elements in successively higher numbered adjacent storage locations. The linear ordering of vector elements is well adapted to the conventional linear ordering of computer memory elements.

Two-dimensional arrays present some problem of storage in a linearly-ordered memory but this problem is easily overcome by the convention that matrices are to be stored by columns, that is, column 1 is stored linearly, followed by column 2 linearly, etc., for as many columns as the array possesses. Thus the elements of a table T, declared by DIMENSION T(3,2), would be stored in ascending memory locations as follows:

$$T(1,1) \quad T(2,1) \quad T(3,1) \quad T(1,2) \quad T(2,2) \quad T(3,2)$$

Ordinarily the programmer need not be aware of this storage order but it allows a very simple rule for describing what happens when input or output is done on an array mentioned by name only. The rule is this: All elements of the array are read or printed in storage order.

Thus the statement

READ, STOCK

causes elements of STOCK to be read by columns. This statement is used in Example 9.12 which is merely a modification of 9.11.

```
C EXAMPLE 9.12
C READING AN ENTIRE MATRIX COLUMNWISE
        INTEGER STOCK(3,4), AMOUNT(3)
        DO 6 I=1,3
            AMOUNT(I) = 0
6       CONTINUE
        READ, STOCK
        DO 2 I=1,3
            DO 20 J=1,4
                AMOUNT(I) = AMOUNT(I) + STOCK(I,J)
20          CONTINUE
2       CONTINUE
        PRINT, AMOUNT
        STOP
        END
```

This time, the data would be punched as:

50,3,0,0,4,1,16,0,4,2,98,220

Thus, it can be seen that there are several ways to read or print an array. All or part of the array can be read or printed by rows or by columns, using implied DO's. Or the whole array can be read or printed in storage order merely by using its name without subscripts.

It is a company policy to send a shipment of an item to restock a warehouse if the quantity on hand drops below 10. Example 9.13 is a program that scans the entries in the stock table to detect such items and prints the warehouse, item, and quantity on hand for shipment planning purposes.

```
C EXAMPLE 9.13 - SCAN FOR SHIPMENT LEVEL
      INTEGER STOCK(3,4), W
      READ, STOCK
      DO 1 W=1,3
          DO 10 I=1,4
              IF (STOCK(W,I) .LT. 10) THEN
                  PRINT, W, I, STOCK(W,I)
              ENDIF
10            CONTINUE
1     CONTINUE
      STOP
      END
```

The final example on two-dimensional arrays is a program which reads in an n by k matrix A, a k by m matrix B, forms the matrix product A x B, and prints the result. For this example the values of n, k, m, will be read in from a separate data card with the data for A, and B following. To be specific, let us assume that each of k, m, n, will be less than or equal to 25.

```
C EXAMPLE 9.14 - MATRIX MULTIPLICATION
      DIMENSION A(25,25), B(25,25), C(25,25)
      READ, N, K, M, ((A(I,J), I=1,N), J=1,K)
      READ, ((B(J,I), J=1,K), I=1,M)
      DO 1 I=1,N
          DO 10 J=1,M
              C(I,J) = 0.
              DO 100 L=1,K
                  C(I,J) = C(I,J) + A(I,L)*B(L,J)
100           CONTINUE
10        CONTINUE
1     CONTINUE
      PRINT, ((I, J, C(I,J), J=1,M), I=1,N)
      STOP
      END
```

Note that both A and B are read by columns, but that C is printed by rows. The row and column designators are printed for each matrix element, since they are also within the parentheses of the implied DO's.

If n, k, and m are, in fact, less than 25, only part of the storage reserved for the arrays is used during execution of the program. This is indicated by the shaded portion of Figure 9.2.

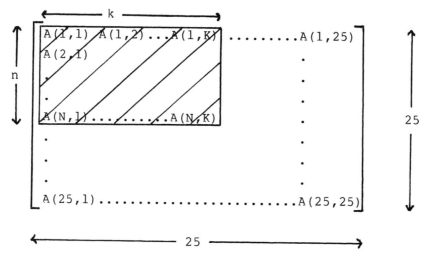

Figure 9.2

Storage Used for Array A, Example 9.14, if n,k<25.

9.4   HIGHER-DIMENSIONAL ARRAYS

FORTRAN allows arrays with more than two dimensions, and essentially the same rules carry over. For example,

DIMENSION X(5,4,7), M(3,3,5,2)

declares a three-dimensional array X and a four-dimensional array M. Storage reserved is 140 elements for X and 90 elements for M. The array X so declared may be imagined as a collection of 7 parallel blackboards, each containing a matrix of 5 rows and 4 columns. Thus, the element X(3,2,4) refers to the element in row 3, column 2, of the fourth blackboard.

Arrays with up to seven dimensions may be declared in FORTRAN programs, but those with more than three dimensions are difficult to depict physically.

The storage order for arrays is defined as follows. Arrays are stored in ascending memory locations with the value of the first subscript increasing most rapidly and the value of the last subscript increasing least rapidly. The range of each subscript is from one to the declared dimension corresponding to that subscript.

The reader should verify that the simple rules given in Section 9.3 for vectors and matrices are particular applications of this general rule.

The concept of storage order is important for an understanding of COMMON and EQUIVALENCE statements, which are discussed in later chapters.

9.5   SUMMARY

This section summarizes in point form most of the important rules about the use of subscripted variables.

(a)   An array must be declared by including its dimension in a DIMENSION or type declaration statement before it is used in a program. The dimensions of an array are declared only once. Programmers commonly place all array declarations near the beginning of a program for convenience.

(b)   An array may have from one to seven subscripts, but the number of subscripts must remain the same within a program. Thus, if a variable is declared to be two-dimensional, when that variable is used with subscripts, two subscripts must be given - no more, no fewer.

(c) A subscript may be any integer-valued or real-valued expression always in the range from one to the value of the dimension declared for the subscript position. If the subscript value is real, it is converted to an integer by truncating any fractional part.

(d) Array names may appear without subscripts in I/O statements. The I/O operation is performed on the elements of the array in storage order.

9.6   EXERCISES

9.1   Write a program that inputs 15 positive real values and stores them in a vector. Determine the largest and smallest value. Print the entire vector and the two computed values. Use the implied DO in any input and output statements.

9.2   Consider a set of 41 data cards, each of which contains a student's number and his mark in a certain course: Write a program to do the following:

(a) The 41 cards are to be read. The student numbers are to be stored in a vector, and the corresponding marks are to be stored in another vector.

(b) The marks are to be scanned to determine the maximum mark. This is to be printed, together with the corresponding student number. Then this mark is set equal to a negative quantity.

(c) Step (b) is then repeated for each student. Thus the second-highest, third-highest, etc., marks are located and printed.

The effect of the overall program is to print the class record as a descending sequence of examination marks.

9.3 Modify the program for Exercise 9.2 so that the results are not printed, but are stored in two new vectors, one for the student numbers and one for associated marks. These new vectors reflect the rank of the student in the subject.

Further modify the program in order to compute the class average and the class median. The median is defined as the mark obtained by the student who is in the middle-ranking position of the class, in this case, the 21st. (If the class had an even number of students, the median would be the average of the two marks at the half-way point.)

Print the class record in ascending sequence, with the class average and the class median adjacent to each student mark.

9.4 Suppose the 41 data cards for Exercise 9.2 were each to contain a student's number and his marks for each of six subjects.

Write a program which reads these data into an integer array of 41 rows and seven columns. The first column contains the student numbers. The program is to do the following:

(a) Compute the average for each student, and store it in a new vector of 41 elements.

(b) Compute the average for each course, and store it in a new vector of 6 elements.

(c) Compute the class average in two ways - by averaging the student marks, and by averaging the course marks.

(d)   Finally, print all computed results.

9.5   With reference to Exercise 9.4, arrange to print the examination results, in descending order by average, for each student. The final line of output contains the average for each course.

9.6   Modify the programs for Exercises 9.4 and 9.5 in the following way. The average for each student is to be computed by using only his five best marks. Thus, the minimum mark must be determined, and be eliminated from the averaging process.

9.7   Using the table described in Figure 9.1, write programs to answer the following questions concerning the company's inventory.

(a)   Which items are completely out of stock at warehouse i? (The value of i is to be read in as data.)

(b)   Which of the items are completely out of stock at any of the warehouses? Your output should be the warehouse numbers and item numbers.

(c)   What is the total number of items on hand in all the warehouses?

9.8   Consider Example 9.11 which is concerned with the total numbers of various items in various warehouses. Suppose the cost of each item is recorded in a real vector named COST. Write a program which computes and prints the following quantities:

(a)   the total cost of each item in each warehouse

(b)   the total cost of inventory in each warehouse

(c)   the total cost of each item for all warehouses

(d)   the grand total cost of inventory.

9.9 When a customer places an order for a particular item from the company, an order card is punched containing the item number and the quantity ordered. Write a program which uses the information in Figure 9.1, and which reads in the order card and checks if there is enough of the item in stock at any warehouse. If there is enough, the table should be updated to reflect the order. If there is not enough in any single warehouse, the order has to be filled by taking the items from a number of warehouses. Again, the table should be updated. If the total number of items at all warehouses is insufficient to fill the order, this should be indicated.

9.10 Write separate programs to perform the following operations upon vectors. The data consist of the dimensions of the vectors and the values of the vector elements. Read the data from cards, and check the dimensions to ensure they are appropriate before calculation takes place.

(a) Compute the length of any vector.

(b) Compute the inner product of any two vectors.

(c) Compute the angle between any two vectors.

9.11 Write separate programs to perform the following matrix operations. Where necessary, read the data from cards, and check the dimensions to ensure they are appropriate before calculation takes place. The data consist of the matrix dimensions and values for the matrix elements.

(a) Add two matrices.

(b) Multiply two matrices.

(c) Invert a matrix.

(d) Compute the largest element in a matrix.

(e) Initialize a square matrix to be the identity matrix.

(f) Initialize any matrix of given dimensions to be the zero matrix.

(g) Find the sum of the squares of the diagonal elements in any square matrix.

9.12 Write a program which:

(a) reads the coefficients of a polynomial and stores them in an array. (The program should handle polynomials of degrees up to and including 20.)

(b) evaluates the polynomial for any values of the independent variable that are read in from cards.

9.13 Write a program which:

(a) reads the coefficients of a polynomial, as in Exercise 9.12

(b) evaluates the first derivative of the polynomial for any values of the independent variable that are read in from cards.

9.14 Write a program which determines prime numbers in the following way.

(a) Set up a vector M which has 200 elements, and initialize these elements so that $M(I)=I$ for $I=1, 2, 3, \ldots, 200$.

(b) Print out the contents of $M(2)$. This is the first prime, namely, the integer 2.

(c) Then proceed through the vector, and replace all multiples of 2 by zero.

(d) Beginning at the position of the last prime that has been printed, scan along the vector until the first non zero element is found. Print this as the next prime. Then proceed through the vector, replacing by zero all multiples of this prime.

(e) Repeat step (d) as long as there are non-zero elements remaining in the vector.

9.15 Table 9.1 consists of the quantities of various items that are stocked at several warehouses belonging to a company. As has been seen, this form of table is useful for answering questions about the company's inventory. However, a company would probably like to insert other information about its inventory in the table. For example, the number of items sold to date from each warehouse in the current year - the current-year total - might be a requirement. These additional data could be inserted by changing the table from a two-dimensional array to a three-dimensional array. The first row of the following diagram is the first row of the STOCK table. A second row is added to contain the current-year totals.

In the previous examples, the value 50 was referred to as STOCK(1,1), and the value 16 as STOCK(1,3). If we use a three-dimensional array, the value 50 will be referred to as STOCK(1,1,1) and the value 16 as STOCK(1,3,1). Then, the value 700, representing the current number of the first item shipped from warehouse 1, would be referred to as STOCK(1,1,2), and the value 453 as STOCK(1,3,2).

Assume that the price of items 1, 2, 3, and 4 is $5.00, $6.00, $4.26, and $2.42, respectively; furthermore, assume these are stored in a vector called COST. The current-year totals, in storage order, are 700, 3500, 62, 651, 73, 57, 453, 962, 459, 54, 5763, 492.

Write a program which answers the following questions.

(a) What is the total stock and value of item 2 shipped in the current year?

(b) What is the total value of all inventory on hand?

(c) What is the total value of all items shipped in the current year?

Chapter 10

BASIC FORMAT

All examples prior to this chapter have used format-free
input and output. The programmmer has had little or no
ability to control the appearance or precision of information
printed. However, it is desirable for the programmer to have
some means of controlling the manner in which results are
printed and the FORMAT statement provides this facility.

Furthermore, it is desirable to be able to read data
cards which are punched in a manner not suited to format-free
input. Again, the FORMAT statement provides the necessary
flexibility to allow this.

The purpose of this chapter is to introduce some of the
immediately useful features of format. Later chapters will
expand upon the material as the need arises.

10.1   A SIMPLE EXAMPLE

We have already observed that the sequence of statements

$$X = 32.125$$
$$PRINT, X$$

will produce the following printed line.

$$32.1250000$$

The following sequence of statements prints the same value using a FORMAT statement.

```
          X = 32.125
          PRINT 27, X
   27     FORMAT('0', F7.3)
```

This time, the printer will double-space, and print the more readable line

                    32.125

The FORMAT statement has a statement number, in this case, 27. This statement number also appears in the PRINT statement immediately following the word PRINT. It serves to associate the FORMAT statement with the PRINT statement.

The word FORMAT is followed by a list of format codes, contained in parentheses. In this case, the list is

                '0', F7.3

The first code, '0', causes the printer to double-space, and prepares it to print a new line; this code is referred to as the printer control character. The second code, F7.3, specifies that (a) a real number, in this case X, is to be printed using the first available 7 print positions; these positions are referred to as a field, in this case, of width 7; (b) the real number is to be printed with 3 decimal places; (c) the value printed is to be right-justified in the 7-position field.

Thus the FORMAT statement is a coded set of rules indicating the precise form in which information is to be printed. Many format codes are available, and these are described in detail in this and later chapters.

10.2 CONTROL CHARACTERS

The control character is used to determine line spacing on the printer. It appears as the first entry in the format list, and is required only when printing. The following table gives the valid control characters and their associated actions:

'b' single spacing
'0' double spacing
'-' triple spacing
'1' skip to the top of a new page
'+' do not space to a new line

Notice that the letter b is used to denote a blank space.

Examples (a), (b), and (c) below demonstrate single, double, and triple spacing of printer output.

Should the programmmer want output to start at the top of a new printer page, the control character '1' may be used.

(a) 123456789
     123456789

(b) 123456789

     123456789

(c) 123456789

     123456789

10.3 PRINTING REAL VALUES

The F format code is used to print real values when no exponent is desired. In general, the format code has the form Fw.d, where w refers to the next available w print positions and d refers to the number of decimal positions which are to appear to the right of the decimal point.

```
C EXAMPLE 10.1 - DEMONSTRATE F FORMAT
      X = 7.639
      Y = -66.93745
      PRINT 3, X, Y
3     FORMAT(' ', F11.3, F14.5)
```

In Example 10.1, the printer would single-space and print the following line (the letter b is used to indicate blanks or spaces).

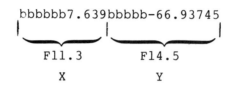

The format code F11.3 informs the computer that X is to be printed in the next available 11 print positions; it is to be printed with 3 decimal places.   Then F14.5 indicates that the next 14 print positions are to be 'used for Y, with 5 decimal places to be printed.   In each case, the value printed is to be placed right-justified in the field.   Notice that there is a one-to-one correspondence between the variables in the PRINT list and the format codes.

$$X \longleftrightarrow F11.3$$
$$Y \longleftrightarrow F14.5$$

Example 10.2 demonstrates the effect of F format in a number of special cases.

```
C EXAMPLE 10.2 - SOME MORE F FORMAT
      A = 6.50
      B = -256.496
      C = 1.03239
      D = 62345.67
      PRINT 9, A, B, C, D
9     FORMAT(' ', F10.5, F7.3, F12.4, F5.2)
```

The following line would be printed

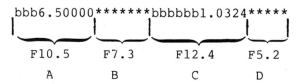

Since the number of digits of A following the decimal is less than the 5 specified by the format F10.5, zeros are supplied on the right.

The value for B requires eight positions (six digits, the sign, and the decimal point), and, since only seven are specified, an error condition is indicated by placing *'s in the field. Similarly, D is too large to fit into five print positions, and again *'s are used to fill the field. When this happens, either the _field_ _width_ w must be increased, or the required number of decimal places, d, must be decreased, if the real number is to be printed using the F format code.

The format code for C specifies four decimal places, but C has five. In this case, the value is rounded before printing.

In some cases, unexpected results can be obtained using F format codes. For example, the sequence of statements

```
        A = 123.665
        PRINT 15, A
15      FORMAT('0', F16.7)
```

would cause the value 123.6649000 to be printed. This is because the computer stores the value 123.665 in hexadecimal notation, and the conversion is not exact. Furthermore, only seven digits are retained by the computer.

The E format code provides another means of printing real numbers. It is generally used when the magnitude of numbers is large or unknown at the time the program is written. The general form is Ew.d, and again w refers to the width of the field to be printed. However, in this case d refers to the total number of significant decimal digits which are to be printed. Example 10.3 demonstrates the use of the E format code.

```
      C EXAMPLE 10.3 - DEMONSTRATE E FORMAT
            X = 725.6975
            Y = -.0005239
            Z = 76.599
            A = -16.5E7
            PRINT 7, X, Y, Z, A
      7     FORMAT(' ', E14.7, E13.5, E14.3, E7.5)
```

The following line would be printed.

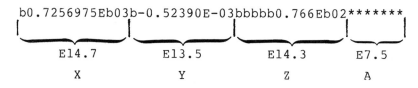

Each field contains a zero, a decimal point, the first d significant digits, an E, and a signed two-digit exponent. The field starts with a minus sign if the number is negative. If the sign of the exponent is plus, the sign is replaced with a blank.

The example shows X printed with seven significant digits, as requested, and Y with five significant digits.

The format code for Z specifies only three significant figures; in this case, rounding occurs.

The value for A cannot fit into the seven-digit field which is specified for it; hence, *'s are used to indicate the format error. Note that every value printed with the E format code starts with s0. and ends with Esnn where s is either the minus sign or a blank. Thus seven print spaces should be available over and above the d significant digits. This means that the relationship $w \geq d+7$ should hold for E format codes.

Finally, the values are always placed right-justified in the fields.

10.4   PRINTING INTEGER VALUES

The I format code is used to output integer values. Since there is no fractional part, a decimal point is not required. The format code is of the form Iw, where w refers to the next w print positions. The value printed is placed right-justified in the field. Example 10.4 illustrates I format.

```
      C EXAMPLE 10.4 - DEMONSTRATE I FORMAT
            L = 39
            M = 72654
            N = -256
            PRINT 17, L, M, N
      17    FORMAT('0', I4, I12, I8)
```

The printer would double-space, and print the following line.

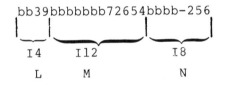

Again there is a one-to-one correspondence between the list to be printed and the list of codes in the FORMAT statement.

$$L \quad <\longrightarrow \quad I4$$
$$M \quad <\longrightarrow \quad I12$$
$$N \quad <\longrightarrow \quad I8$$

If the same example were used with L = 76543, the following line would be printed.

                ****bbbbbbb72654bbbb-256

Note that L requires five print positions; but four positions are the maximum specified by the format code I4. This is

considered an error and, as an indication, *'s are placed in
the field.

10.5   SPACING

Often the programmer wishes to insert blanks between
values printed on one line. The format code nX causes n
spaces or blanks to be printed. Example 10.5 shows how the X
code can be used.

```
      C EXAMPLE 10.5 - DEMONSTRATE X FORMAT CODE
            I = J = 156
            PRINT 6, I, J
      6     FORMAT(' ', I6, 3X, I4)
```

```
          bbb156bbbb156
         |___|  |__|  |
          I6   3X   I4
```

Notice that the statement

      6   FORMAT(' ', I6, I7)

would accomplish the same purpose, since integer values are
always printed right-justified in the field, with blanks
inserted to the left. Many programmers make the field width
larger than required, both for spacing of results and also for
safety, in case numbers become larger than expected.

10.6   HEADINGS

On many occasions, alphabetic information is desirable
for headings and identifications. In previous chapters this
has been done by including the character string as part of the
PRINT statement. Example 10.6 demonstrates how this can also
be accomplished using the FORMAT statement.

```
C EXAMPLE 10.6 - HEADINGS
        PRINT 25
25      FORMAT('1', 'THIS IS A HEADING')
        PRINT 13
13      FORMAT('0', 4X, 'X', 10X, 'F(X)')
```

The printer would skip to a new page, and print the following lines:

THIS IS A HEADING

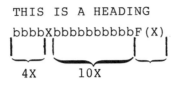

The PRINT statements used in Example 10.6 do not have a list of variables. As will be seen in Section 10.8, it is possible to intersperse strings with values to be printed.

Any character may be placed in a string. A quote which is required as part of the output must be duplicated, i.e., to print IT'S the string 'IT''S' would be used.

The format code nH may be used instead of quotes when constructing strings. (To this point in the text we have referred to character data as strings. They are also called Hollerith strings in honour of Herman Hollerith, an American pioneer in the use of punched card equipment.) Using the format code nH causes the n characters following the H to be printed, for example

        25   FORMAT(' ', 17HTHIS IS A HEADING)

Care should be taken to ensure that the character count n is correct for the particular string. The quote-type Hollerith string is usually more convenient, and requires no counting of characters. Early versions of FORTRAN did not use the quote-type Hollerith string.

It has probably been noted that the control character is a Hollerith string of one character, but it is never printed. The first position of the print line is reserved for printer control. Control characters may be inserted by any permissible format code. The following ways of obtaining the control character blank are valid, and perform the same action.

```
1       FORMAT(' ',...
1       FORMAT(1X,...
1       FORMAT(1H ,...
```

Failure to provide a control character can lead to unexpected results. For example, the sequence of statements

```
        I=12345
        PRINT 3,I
3       FORMAT(I5)
```

would cause the printer to skip to a new page and print the incorrect result 2345. This is because the first character of the first field is used as the control character.

If, under any circumstances, an invalid control character is used, WATFIV-S replaces it with blank, with the result that single spacing occurs.

10.7   CONTINUATION CARDS

When FORMAT statements are punched, or when any FORTRAN statement is punched, it may not be possible to punch the complete statement on one card. FORTRAN permits the programmer to overcome this difficulty by means of a continuation card. If a statement is too long for one card, it may be continued on successive cards by placing any character other than blank or zero in column 6 of each continuation card. The first card of the statement must have a blank or zero in column 6. For example,

```
        IF (STOCK(I,J) .LE. 10) PRINT, W, I, J,
1       ((STOCK(I,J) ,I=1,3) ,J=1,4)
```

The programmer can determine the maximum number of continuation cards allowed by referring to his installation's operating manual, but typically, it is at least five.

10.8   COMBINING CODES

The reader has now seen some of the basic format codes available in FORTRAN. In most examples presented so far, only one type of code was employed.

Any of the types of format codes may be mixed within a FORMAT statement.

```
      C EXAMPLE 10.7 MIXING FORMAT CODES
            X = 14.753
            I = -156
            PRINT 9, X, I
    9       FORMAT(' ', 'X=', F8.3, 3X, 'I=', I5)
```

Example 10.7 would print the following line

```
      X=bb14.753bbbI=b-156
      |_____|  | |  |____|
```
```
        F8.3     3X    I5
```

The variables X and I are matched respectively with the format codes F8.3 and I5. The Hollerith strings and blanks are placed in the required positions in the output line. It is important that the format code be appropriate for the type of the corresponding variable, that is, I format must be used for integer values and E or F format must be used for real values. Violation of this rule will cause an error message and termination of the program at execution time.

10.9   FIELD COUNTS

On many occasions, it is desirable to print several values using the same format code. This is particularly true when dealing with arrays. Example 10.8 reads in ten integer values and seven real values, and prints them on one line.

```
      C EXAMPLE 10.8
            REAL A(7)
            INTEGER N(10)
            READ, (N(I), I=1,10), (A(I), I=1,7)
            PRINT 6, (N(I), I=1,10), (A(I), I=1,7)
      6     FORMAT(' ', 10I6, 7F10.2)
```

The 10 preceding I6 and the 7 preceding F10.2 are called field counts: they specify that the format code I6 is to be used ten times for the ten elements of N, and that F10.2 is to be used seven times for the elements of A. Alternatively, we could have written the FORMAT statement as

```
      6     FORMAT(' ',I6,I6,...,I6,F10.2,F10.2,...,F10.2)
```

            10 times   7 times

If we had wished to print the first four values of N under I4 and the last six values under I6, the following FORMAT statement could have been used.

```
      6     FORMAT(' ', 4I4, 6I6, 7F10.2)
```

Field counts must be positive non-zero constants. Thus, the following example contains an invalid field count.

```
      C INCORRECT USAGE OF A FIELD COUNT
            M = 10
      7     FORMAT('0', MI6)
```

Field counts may be used with I, E, or F format codes, but may not be used with Hollerith and X codes.

10.10   SOME RULES

There are many rules concerning format codes, and some of these have been presented in the previous sections. The following rules apply to the FORMAT statement in general, and should be studied carefully before using this feature.

(a) FORMAT statements are <u>non-executable</u> statements and may only be referred to by input or output statements.

(b) More than one I/O statement may refer to the same FORMAT statement.

(c) FORMAT statements may be placed almost anywhere in a program. Some programmers prefer to place all their FORMAT statements at the beginning or end of the program, while others like to keep I/O and FORMAT statements together.

(d) It must be remembered that a printer has a maximum number of print spaces per line (120, 132, 144, etc. - check with your installation). Since FORMAT is used to print lines, the total number of print positions requested by the list of format codes may not exceed this maximum value. The statement
   FORMAT(' ', 6I10, 4X, 4F10.2, 4E11.3)
   requires 148 print positions; this would be too many for most printers.

(e) The format code must be appropriate for the type of the variable to be printed. If this is not the case, an error message is issued, and the program is terminated.
```
      C THIS IS NOT ALLOWED
            PRINT 256, I
      256   FORMAT(' ', F16.8)
```

(f) Values used for n, w, d, and field counts must be positive non-zero integer constants, and may not exceed 255. Using the FORMAT statement as described to this point, the programmer does not have the ability to change or define these values at execution time. Another feature that allows this flexibility is described in Chapter 21.

(g) Commas which separate format codes may be omitted, unless ambiguity would result. For example, the statement

    FORMAT(' 'I5'ANSWER'F36.2, 2I7)

is equivalent to

    FORMAT(' ', I5, 'ANSWER', F36.2, 2I7)

Note that all commas except the last have been omitted. If the last comma were omitted, the sequence F36.2I7 would be ambiguous (F36.22 instead of F36.2). Note also that two adjacent quote-type Holleriths must be separated by a comma. The statement

    FORMAT('ABC''DEF')

has only one Hollerith string, namely,

    ABC'DEF

It is advisable not to omit commas; their use greatly improves readability of FORMAT statements.

Blanks may be placed in the format list to further improve readability.

10.11   FURTHER FEATURES OF FORMAT

The sequence of statements

                X = 13.25
                Y = -16.3
                PRINT 3, X, Y
        3   FORMAT('0', F7.2, F7.2, F7.2)

would cause the following line to be printed

            bb13.25bb-16.3

Note that the number of format codes is greater than the number of variables to be printed. In this case, the extra format code is not used. However, if the FORMAT statement had been

    3   FORMAT('0', F7.2, F7.2, 6X, 'HELLO', F7.2)

the following line would have been printed

       bb13.25bb-16.3bbbbbbHELLO

The rule is that the computer processes the format codes in sequence from left to right, matching format codes with variables to be printed. If a format code requiring an entry in the print list is encountered after all items in the print list have been processed, the action is terminated.

If the list of variables has not been completely processed when the end of the list of format codes is reached, processing will continue by returning to the beginning of the format list, and a _new_ print line will be started. For example, the statements

          PRINT 12, (X(I), I=1,12)
    12   FORMAT(' ', 5E16.7)

would print three lines; the first two lines would each contain five elements of X, and the third line would contain two elements. This feature is useful when printing arrays, but can cause problems in certain cases. Consider the statements:

          N=6
          PRINT 22, N, (X(I), I=1,N)
    22   FORMAT(' ', I3, 5E16.7)

The above statements attempt to print X(6) using the format code I3; this, of course, is an error. Chapter 21 will introduce a method for handling this type of situation.

A final example is given to demonstrate the flexibility of format. Example 10.9 calculates the squares of the integers from 1 to 15, and prints a table of values.

```
C EXAMPLE 10.9
C CALCULATE SQUARES OF THE NATURAL NUMBERS
C FROM 1-15 AND PRINT RESULTS
        INTEGER N(15)
        DO 1 I=1,15
            N(I) = I**2
1       CONTINUE
        PRINT 13, (J, N(J), J=1,15)
13      FORMAT(' ', 'N(' ,I2, ')=' ,I5)
        STOP
        END
```

The output from this example is

```
N( 1)=    1
N( 2)=    4
N( 3)=    9
N( 4)=   16
N( 5)=   25
N( 6)=   36
N( 7)=   49
N( 8)=   64
N( 9)=   81
N(10)=  100
N(11)=  121
N(12)=  144
N(13)=  169
N(14)=  196
N(15)=  225
```

10.12 FORMAT WITH PUNCHED OUTPUT

Example 10.10 shows how data cards can be produced by a program using the PUNCH statement.

```
C EXAMPLE 10.10 - USE A PUNCH STATEMENT
        A = 924.625
        B = 890625.
        J = 762
        PUNCH 19, A, B, J
19      FORMAT(F7.3, 4X, E14.6, I3)
```

The PUNCH statement is similar to the PRINT statement, with the exceptions that only 80 digits and/or characters may be punched on the output card, and no control character is required. The PUNCH statement may be used with the format-free scheme, or may refer to a FORMAT statement in the conventional manner.

10.13 INPUT WITH FORMAT CODES F, E, I, AND X

Format may also be used with READ statements to input data values. This is useful if a program is to be written to process data decks pre-punched by someone other than the programmer. Furthermore, the use of format allows more data to be punched on one card, since the data item separators are not required.

For example, suppose a questionnaire were given involving 80 questions with answers of a true or false variety. The results could be punched on cards, with zero representing false and one representing true. Using format-free input, at least two data cards would be required for each reply to the questionnaire, i.e., 40 answers per card, each value followed by a blank or comma. However, it would be more convenient to place all 80 answers on one card, and, in this case, a FORMAT statement would be required to read it.

These problems show that on occasion it would be convenient to associate FORMAT with a READ statement in order to define the sizes of the input fields. Example 10.11 shows how this is accomplished.

```
C EXAMPLE 10.11 - READ STATEMENT WITH FORMAT
      READ 47, A, B, J
47    FORMAT(F7.3, 4X, E14.6, I3)
```

The X code can be used to space over columns to be ignored.

If the data card

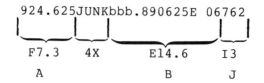

were read, the values 924.625, .890625E+06, and 762 would be assigned to A, B, and J respectively. Notice that no control character is used for input.

To make the preparation of data cards more convenient, certain of the rules have been relaxed, and these are now described.

For the three format codes - I, F, and E - any blanks within the field are interpreted as zeros. A field consisting entirely' of blanks is treated as zero.

    7b5 -> 705
    7.9b -> 7.90
    63.5bEb5 -> 63.50E05
    bbbbb -> 0 or 0.0

Hence, for the I format code, the integer constant should be placed right-justified in the field. Input of the digit 7 using the format code I5 would cause values to be assigned as described in the following table

    bbbb7 -> 7
    bbb7b -> 70
    bb7bb -> 700
    b7bbb -> 7000
    7bbbb -> 70000

With the F format code, the decimal point can be included anywhere in the field, and overrides the position indicated by the d portion of Fw.d. If the decimal point is omitted, the d is used to determine the position of the decimal point. We present several examples using the format code F7.3:

```
b72.76b  -> 72.760
72.76bb  -> 72.7600
bb72.76  -> 72.76
bb7276b  -> 72.760
7276bbb  -> 7276.000
7.0E+05  -> ERROR (invalid characters)
```

In the last example, the field contains an E exponent and a plus sign, which is considered invalid when read using F format.

With the E format code, considerable flexibility is allowed in the exponent part. The exponent may be punched in any one of the following forms:

$$E+06 = E6 = E+6 = E06 = Eb06 = +6 = +06$$
$$E-02 = E-2 = -2 = -02$$

If the E is omitted, the plus or minus sign must be present.

If a decimal point is punched in the fractional portion, it overrides the position indicated by the d portion of Ew.d. If the decimal point is omitted, the d is used to determine the position of the decimal point. Finally, the exponent may be omitted completely, in which case the rules for Fw.d are used instead of Ew.d. The following examples using E12.4 should clarify the use of E format with input.

$$bbb7.345E+01 \rightarrow 7.345 \times 10^1$$
$$bbbbb7.345E1 \rightarrow 7.345 \times 10^1$$
$$-bbbb7.345E1 \rightarrow -7.345 \times 10^1$$
$$bb-7.345E+01 \rightarrow -7.345 \times 10^1$$
$$bbb76522E+02 \rightarrow 7.6522 \times 10^2$$
$$bbbbb76522E2 \rightarrow 7.6522 \times 10^2$$
$$bbbbbb7654-3 \rightarrow .7654 \times 10^{-3}$$
$$bbbb16.75bbb \rightarrow 16.75000$$
$$bbbb1675bbbb \rightarrow 1675.0000$$
$$bbbb1.23E+5b \rightarrow 1.23 \times 10^{50}$$

10.14   HOLLERITH INPUT

An H-type or quote-type Hollerith string in a FORMAT statement can be modified by reading character data. The information read is inserted into the Hollerith string of the FORMAT statement, and can be printed if the FORMAT statement is referenced in a subsequent PRINT statement. The value n of nH or the number of positions between quotes is used to determine how many characters are to be inserted. Example 10.12 uses this feature to read and print the first 21 columns of ten data cards.

```
C EXAMPLE 10.12 - READ HOLLERITH DATA
      DO 1 I=1,10
         READ 7
7        FORMAT('THIS WILL BE REPLACED')
         PRINT 7
1     CONTINUE
```

Notice that the example uses the same FORMAT statement for reading and printing. Note also that the contents of column 1 of the data card will ultimately determine the spacing of the printer.

10.15   EXERCISES

10.1 Write a program which sets up and initializes a vector X of 10 elements so that each element contains the same real value, namely, 3.456789. Then, print this vector by using the statement

```
PRINT 6, (X(I), I=1,10)
```

with each of the following FORMAT statements;

(a) 6 FORMAT('0',6F10.6)

(b) 6 FORMAT('0',F10.5,F10.4,F10.3,F10.2,F10.1,F10.0)

(c) 6 FORMAT(' ',6F10.8)

(d)   6 FORMAT(' ',6F5.4)

(e)   6 FORMAT(' ',F15.3,6X,F15.2)

(f)   6 FORMAT('0',4E15.7)

(g)   6 FORMAT('0',E15.6,E15.5,E15.4,E15.3,E15.2)

(h)   6 FORMAT('0',5E12.8)

(i)   6 FORMAT('0',E17.4,F17.4)

It is instructive for the reader to predict what the results will be, before the program is run on the computer.

10.2   Write a program which sets up and initializes a vector I of 10 elements so that each element contains the same integer value, namely, 123456. Then, print the vector by using the statement

        PRINT 8, (I(J), J=1,10)

with each of the following FORMAT statements.

(a)   8 FORMAT('0',6I10)

(b)   8 FORMAT(' ',I10,I9,I8,I7,I6,I5)

(c)   8 FORMAT(' ',10I6)

(d)   8 FORMAT('0',3I8,3X,2I8)

(e)   8 FORMAT(' ',I20)

(f)   8 FORMAT(' ',10F13.6)

It is instructive for the reader to predict what the results will be before actually running the program on the computer.

10.3   Modify any program in any of the examples or exercises so that it has descriptive headings and acceptable FORMAT statements. Try to use FORMAT statements, as outlined in Example 10.9, for some of the other problems.

10.4 A test is given which involves 10 questions with answers of a true or false variety. The results are punched on cards in columns six to fifteen; zero is used to represent false, and one is used to represent true. Columns one to five are used for the contestant number. The first data card contains the correct answers for the test. Write a program that reads the data and calculates the mark for each contestant. Your output should include, for each contestant, the contestant number, his answers, and his mark out of 10.

10.5 Write a program that reads and prints the contents of columns ten to sixty-five of 35 data cards. Use Example 10.12 as a guide.

10.6 Write a program which prints a calendar for a particular year. The following specifications should be used.

(a) January 1 is a Wednesday.

(b) February has 28 days.

(c) Each month should have its name spelled out in full.

(d) The days of the week should be printed as alphabetic headings in abbreviated form.

(e) Each month should be printed starting on a new page.

10.7 Given that the horizontal spacing on the printer is 10 characters to the inch, and that the vertical spacing is six lines to the inch, write a program which uses asterisks to outline an 8-inch-square checkerboard.

Chapter 11

CHARACTER MANIPULATION

All examples to this point have involved the manipulation of numerical quantities such as real and integer constants and variables. WATFIV-S is also capable of processing alphabetic data, including special characters. This facility considerably broadens the scope of WATFIV-S to include those applications which require the input-output, storage, and comparison of character data.

11.1   CHARACTER CONSTANTS

Examples of valid FORTRAN character constants are:

(a) 'ABCDE'   (d) '1234567'

(b) 'A'   (e) '   '

(c) 'A*B+C'   (f) 'IT''S'

(g) 'THE FOX JUMPED OVER THE FENCE'

(h) 'The fox jumped over the fence'

The common characteristic of all character constants is that each is enclosed within quote symbols. These quote symbols, with the exception of example (f), are not part of the constant itself. Character constants are also referred to as character strings. The reader will recall that this type of constant has been used previously for headings and identification purposes in PRINT statements.

Examples (c) and (d) illustrate that characters other than letters of the alphabet can be used. Example (e) shows that the blank or space is also a valid character. Example (f) demonstrates how the character quote can itself be part of the string. In this case, the constant is IT'S. Whenever a quote must appear as part of a constant, two consecutive quotes must be used. Example (g) shows that the string can have many characters; in fact, with WATFIV-S, strings can contain up to 255 characters. Example (h) shows that lower-case letters can be used if these are available on your data-preparation device.

The following are examples of invalid character constants:

(a) 'DOG   No closing quote.
(b) ''   No character between quotes.
(c) 'DON'T'   Invalid inner quote.

11.2   CHARACTER VARIABLES

Variables capable of being assigned values which are character constants are said to be character variables. A character variable can be any valid FORTRAN symbolic name which is declared in a CHARACTER declaration statement. However, with character variables, the length, or number of characters also has to be specified. For example, the statement

CHARACTER A, T*5, NUMBER*7, SENT*40, TAB*3(40)

declares A, T, NUMBER, and SENT to be character variables with lengths of 1, 5, 7, and 40 respectively. TAB is declared to a character array of 40 elements, each with a length of 3 characters. The length of the character variable is specified by placing an asterisk (*) after the variable name followed by the desired length. Note if no length is specified, it is assumed to be 1. This statement is non-executable and is placed prior to the first executable statement in the program.

All character variables must be declared using the CHARACTER statement as there is no default declaration.

11.3   MANIPULATION OF CHARACTER VARIABLES AND CONSTANTS

It is possible to assign a value to a character variable using an assignment statement. For example

```
          CHARACTER A*3, B*2, C*3, D*5(10)
          A = 'CAT'
          B = 'GO'
          C = 'DOG'
          D(6) = 'HORSE'
```

would cause the strings 'CAT', 'GO', 'DOG', and 'HORSE' be assigned to the character variables A, B, C, and the 6th element of the array D respectively. Subsequently if the statement

```
                PRINT, C, B, A, D(6)
```

were executed, the following line would be printed

```
          CAT GO DOG HORSE
```

Note that the delimiting quotes do not appear on the output, thus making it more readable. The same effect could have been achieved by executing the statement

```
          PRINT, 'CAT', 'GO', 'DOG', 'HORSE'
```

NOTES:

(a)   The statement A='CAT' is called a character assignment statement. The variable A must have been declared as type character. If A is declared to have a length of 2 characters, the assignment would cause the value 'CA' to be given to A, with the T being dropped. On the other hand, if the length of A were 6 characters, it would be assigned the value 'CATbbb', with three blank characters added on the right.

(b) Consider the following sequence of statements

        CHARACTER A*3, B*8
        B = 'HELLO'
        A = B
        PRINT, A

Here B is first assigned the value 'HELLObbb'. In the next statement A is assigned the current value of B. Since A has a length of three, only 'HEL' is assigned to A. This is the value output by the PRINT statement.

(c) None of the arithmetic operators is meaningful when used with character data. For example, expressions such as

        A = A + 'CAT'
        A = A*A
        A = 'BOY' / 'HOUSE'

where A is declared as a character variable are not permitted, and result in a error.

11.4   PRINTING CHARACTER STRINGS

Character strings can be printed using format-free output as seen in the previous section. The values are printed without quotes and are separated by 1 blank character. If formatted output of character strings is desired, the A format code is used. The code is of the form Aw, where w refers to the next w print positions. Example 11.1 illustrates A format.

```
C EXAMPLE 11.1 - DEMONSTRATE A FORMAT
      CHARACTER A*7, B*13, C*13
      A = 'CHARLIE'
      B = 'LOTS OF STUFF'
      C = 'LOTS OF STUFF'
      PRINT 19, A, B, C
19    FORMAT('0', A9, A14, A4)
      STOP
      END
```

The printer would double space and print the follwing line:

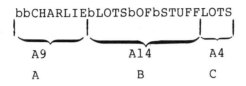

A   B   C

As before there is a one-to-one correspondence between the list to be printed and the list of codes.

$$A \longleftrightarrow A9$$
$$B \longleftrightarrow A14$$
$$C \longleftrightarrow A4$$

Note that in each case the value printed is placed right-justified in the field and is padded on the left with blanks if the length of the string is less then w. The variable C contains 13 characters and is to be printed in a field of width 4; as a result the left-most 4 characters are printed. (Note that this is different from the technique of printing *'s when numerical data is too large for the field to be printed.)

In summary, if the number of characters stored in the string being printed is less than the field width w, the field is padded on the left with blanks. If the number of characters in the string exceeds the field width, only the left-most w characters are printed to fill out the field.

11.5   INPUT OF CHARACTER DATA

Character data can be input with or without format control.   Example 11.2 is a program which reads a number of cards using format-free input and which then prints a line for each card read.   Each card contains a student number followed by the name of the student.   A typical data card might be prepared as follows:

```
              1234  'JONES, JOHN'
```

```
      C EXAMPLE 11.2
            CHARACTER NAME*20
            LOOP
                READ, NUMBER, NAME
                AT END, QUIT
                PRINT, NUMBER, NAME
            ENDLOOP
            STOP
            END
```

Note that with format-free input, the character constant must be enclosed in quotes, and the number is separated from it by at least one blank column (or a comma).   Putting the quotes on strings in the data deck probably strikes the reader as an unfortunate nuisance.   The next example shows how character data can be read without the quotes.

It is usually more convenient to read character data using format control.   Suppose the following sequence of statements was executed.

```
            CHARACTER A*7, B*10, C*4
            READ 4, A, B, C,
      4     FORMAT(A7, A10, A4)
```

In this case, the A format is used with input.   A card would be read, and the first seven columns would be assigned to A as character data, because of the A7 format code.   Similarly, the characters in columns 8 to 17 would be stored in B, and the characters in columns 18 to 21 would be stored in C.

Thus, if the input data card contained the following characters in columns 1 to 21 inclusive,

X$*AB123+9Z'*+-/ADOGS

then the character variables A, B, and C, would have assigned to them the character strings X$*AB12, 3+9Z'*+-/A, and DOGS respectively.

Suppose that the FORMAT statement was replaced by

4   FORMAT(A7, A2, A6)

and the same input data card were read. In this case, the first seven columns are considered as the field associated with the character variable A and A has assigned to it the character string X$*AB12 as before.

The character variable B has its input controlled by the format code A2. Only a two-column field is involved, namely the contents of columns 8 and 9, however, the character variable B is capable of storing ten characters. In this case, the two characters are stored left-justified, and blanks are inserted on the right. Thus, B has assigned to it the character string 3+bbbbbbbb.

The variable C contains only four characters but has its input controlled by the format code A6. Since C can store only four characters, the four farthest-right characters are assigned. Thus C has assigned to it the string '*+-.

In summary, if w exceeds the length specification s of the variable which is to store the string, only the farthest-right characters in the field are stored. If w is less than s, the entire field is stored left-justified in the variable, and blanks are inserted on the right.

Finally, blank columns are treated as blanks or spaces when read using the A format code. Recall blanks are treated as zeroes when read using F, E, or I format codes.

11.6   COMPARISON OF CHARACTER STRINGS

The previous sections were concerned with the assignment, printing, and reading of character strings. It is also important to be able to do comparisons with character strings, as illustrated in Example 11.3.

This example reads a single data card which contains an English sentence, beginning in column one. The individual words in the sentence may have any length, up to a maximum of ten characters. The words are separated by single blanks, with a period terminating the sentence. The program determines the number of words having one letter, the number of words having two letters, and so on up to words having ten letters.

```
C EXAMPLE 11.3
        CHARACTER BLANK, DOT, CHAR(80)
        INTEGER COUNT(10)
        READ 22, CHAR
        BLANK = ' '
        DOT = '.'
        DO 1 I=1,10
            COUNT(I) = 0
1       CONTINUE
        NUMBER = 0
        I = 1
        LOOP
            IF (CHAR(I) .EQ. DOT) QUIT
            IF (CHAR(I) .EQ. BLANK) THEN
                COUNT(NUMBER) = COUNT(NUMBER) + 1
                NUMBER = 0
            ELSE
                NUMBER = NUMBER + 1
            ENDIF
            I = I + 1
        ENDLOOP
        COUNT(NUMBER) = COUNT(NUMBER) + 1
        PRINT 23, CHAR
        PRINT24, (COUNT(I), I, I=1,10)
        STOP
24      FORMAT(' ', I3, 'WORDS OF LENGTH', I3)
23      FORMAT(' ', 80A1)
22      FORMAT(80A1)
        END
```

The program reads the data card, and places each character of the sentence into separate elements of the vector CHAR. The elements of the array COUNT are used as word length counters, and NUMBER is used as the character counter. All these counters are initialized to the value zero. A loop is used to control the scanning of the characters. The scan consists of testing for a period or blank. For each character in a word, unity is added to NUMBER. Each time a blank is encountered, the appropriate element of the array COUNT is increased by one, using the current value of NUMBER as a subscript. When the period is encountered the loop is terminated, and the appropriate element of the array COUNT is increased by one. The original sentence and counts are then printed.

The statements

```
IF (CHAR(I) .EQ. DOT) THEN
IF (CHAR(I) .EQ. BLANK) THEN
```

are used to compare the successive characters of the data sentence for a period or a blank; this shows that the logical expression can contain character variables. As one might suspect, it makes no sense for one variable of the logical expression to be of type character and the other to be real or integer. In fact, this would be an error.

NOTES:

(a) All of the relational operators .EQ., .NE., .LT., .GT., .LE., and .GE., can be used to compare character data.

(b) When a comparison is being made, the two strings are frequently of different lengths. When this occurs, the shorter string is considered as if it were temporarily lengthened by adding sufficient blanks on the right to make the strings of equal length. Then the comparison operation is performed.

(c) In order for two strings to be equal, they must be identical, character by character. For example 'CATb' is not equal to 'bCAT' because of the different position of the blank character.

(d) If an alphabetic character string is "less than" another alphabetic character string, it is implied that the first precedes the second in alphabetical order. Thus 'CAT' is less than 'DOG'. It is important to extend this notion of alphabetic sequence to the other characters by defining a collating sequence which includes all the possible characters. This sequence is as follows when using the IBM computers which support WATFIV-S:

```
blank .  (+$*);-/  ="
abcdefg........z
ABCDEFG........Z
0123456789
```

It follows that '*' is "greater" than '$' because it comes "later" in the collating sequence.

11.7   ALPHABETIC SORTING OF CHARACTER STRINGS

The previous section mentioned that strings can be compared; this feature can be used to arrange character strings into alphabetical order. The program in Example 11.4 reads at most one hundred data cards, each containing a word which consists of ten letters, and stores them in the vector WORD. Then it arranges them into alphabetical sequence.

The method used first reads in the words to be sorted. It then compares successive pairs of ten-letter words. Two

successive words are interchanged in the vector if they are
not in alphabetical order, i.e., the first is "greater than"
the second. After the entire vector has been processed, the
last word in alphabetical order has been "shuffled" to the end
of the vector. The vector is processed again, and, as a
result, the "second-largest" word appears in the second-last
position. This process continues until the words are sorted,
after which they are printed.

```
C EXAMPLE 11.4
      CHARACTER WORD*10(100), SWT*3, TEMP*10
      NUM = 0
      LOOP
          READ 2, WORD(NUM+1)
          AT END, QUIT
          NUM = NUM + 1
      ENDLOOP
      NUMOUT=NUM
      IF (NUM .NE. 0) THEN
          NUM = NUM - 1
          LOOP
              SWT = 'OFF'
              DO 4 J=1,NUM
                  IF (WORD(J) .GT. WORD(J+1)) THEN
                      TEMP = WORD(J)
                      WORD(J) = WORD(J+1)
                      WORD(J+1) = TEMP
                      SWT = 'ON'
                  ENDIF
4             CONTINUE
              IF (SWT .EQ. 'OFF') QUIT
              NUM = NUM - 1
          ENDLOOP
          PRINT 7, (WORD(I),I=1,NUMOUT)
      ENDIF
      STOP
7     FORMAT('0', 10A12)
2     FORMAT(A10)
      END
```

The variable NUM is first used to keep track of the
number of words read. It then is used to control the comparison of successive words. Thus it must be decreased by 1
before entering the loop, i.e., we do one less comparison than
the number of words. At the end of the DO-loop, we again

decrease NUM by 1 since we know the "largest" word is at the end. This is done each time through th loop. When NUM becomes 1, all the necessary comparisons have been made and the words are sorted.

The character variable SWT serves a very useful purpose. If by chance the original data were already in alphabetical order, the logical expression WORD(J).GT.WORD(J+1) would never become "true". Thus SWT would remain 'OFF' and the entire process would terminate. However, as the sort progresses, we are working with a shorter array each time through the loop. At each stage, the remaining data could be in alphabetical sequence and the value of SWT could not become 'ON'. This will cause the looping to terminate as soon as the array is in sequence, thus making the execution time shorter on average.

11.8   EQUIVALENCE

Sometimes in a program that uses character strings, we refer to an entire string by one name; in other situations we wish to refer to the individual characters of a string using a subsripted character name. Often, it would be convenient if we could do both. In order to do this we would like to give the string two names (a normal name and a nickname). One name would be used to refer to the entire string while the second name would be used to refer to the individual characters.

The EQUIVALENCE statement permits us to do this in the following manner:

```
        CHARACTER CARD*80, CHAR*1(80)
        EQUIVALENCE (CARD,CHAR)
```

The CHARACTER statement declares two variables and then the EQUIVALENCE statement says, in effect, that they are the same string with two different names. It should be noted that the EQUIVALENCE statement must follow the declaration statement.

The following example uses this technique. The program reads a message in "coded form" and proceeds to "decode" it. The code used is quite simple; only the vowels have been changed. A's have been replaced with E's, E's with I's, I's with O's, O's with U's, and U's with A's.

The message ends with a period and is read into an array named MSG.

```
C EXAMPLE 11.5 - DECODE A MESSAGE
      CHARACTER MSG*1(80), ALLMSG*80
      EQUIVALENCE (MSG,ALLMSG)
      READ 1, ALLMSG
      DO 2 J=1,78
          NUM = J
          IF (MSG(J) .EQ. '.') QUIT
          IF (MSG(J) .EQ. 'A') THEN
              MSG(J) = 'E'
          ELSEIF (MSG(J) .EQ. 'E') THEN
              MSG(J) = 'I'
          ELSEIF (MSG(J) .EQ. 'I') THEN
              MSG(J) = 'O'
          ELSEIF (MSG(J) .EQ. 'O') THEN
              MSG(J) = 'U'
          ELSEIF (MSG(J) .EQ. 'U') THEN
              MSG(J) = 'A'
          ENDIF
2         CONTINUE
          PRINT 3, ALLMSG
          STOP
1         FORMAT(A80)
3         FORMAT(1X, A80)
          END
```

The program reads the message using the variable ALLMSG. It then uses the array MSG to perform the decoding, and finally prints the message using ALLMSG. Although the use of EQUIVALENCE was not strictly necessary in this example, it was introduced here to show that the EQUIVALENCE feature can simplify some programs with strings.

11.1 Write a program which sets up and initializes a vector C of ten elements of length 5 characters each. Each element should contain the string HELLO. Then, print the vector using the statement

                PRINT 8,(C(J),J=1,10)

with each of the following FORMAT statements.

(a)   8 FORMAT('0',10A8)

(b)   8 FORMAT('0',10A5)

(c)   8 FORMAT(' ',10A4)

(d)   8 FORMAT(' ',10A1)

(e)   8 FORMAT(' ',A1,A2,A3,A4,A5)

(f)   8 FORMAT(1X,A5)

It is instructive for the reader to predict what the results will be.

11.2 Prepare a data deck which contains 40 cards, one for each of 40 students. Each card contains the student's name and his mark for a particular course.

(a) Write a program which reads the data deck and prints the data.

(b) Write a program which reads the data deck, stores the information in the computer, and prints a list of student names and marks in descending sequence according to marks.

11.3 Consider a data deck of eight cards which contain some literary text. (For example, they could contain a poem.) Write a program which reads all of the text and stores it in a one-dimensional array. The array is then to be scanned to determine

(a) the number of non-blank characters

(b)   the number of occurrences of the letter A

(c)   the number of words

(d)   the number of occurrences of the word THE.

11.4   Consider a data deck of twenty cards, each of which
contains a family name of not more than 10 letters,
beginning in column 1.   This deck is in random
sequence.   Write a program which reads the cards,
and stores the names in array form.   As each card is
read, it should be inserted in the array to reflect
alphabetic sequence.   Thus, the position for each
new name must be determined, and all previously
stored data of higher alphabetic order must be shuffled to make room for the new name.   After all data
cards have been read, print the stored data to check
that it is in alphabetic sequence.

11.5   (a)   Write a program which prints all possible
three-letter sequences involving the five
letters A, C, E, T, and W.   Print these
sequences five to a line.

(b)   Modify the program in (a) so that each three-
letter sequence has at least one vowel.

Chapter 12

REMOTE BLOCKS

Most useful programs are quite large, and can contain
hundreds or thousands of statements. Such programs can become
difficult to read and to understand. The REMOTE BLOCK
provides a means of "packaging" a large program in order to
make it more manageable.

12.1 SEGMENTING A PROGRAM USING REMOTE BLOCKS

Example 12.1 is a program that reads a data deck which
contains course marks, stores these marks in a table, finds
their average, and subsequently prints all marks which are
above average.

The program contains three loops, which perform the
following functions:

first loop: The marks are read and stored in the array
MARK. The variable TOTAL is assigned a value which
indicates the number of marks which have been read.

second loop: The marks are added to compute the aggre-
gate. Then the average is computed by dividing by
TOTAL.

third loop: The above average marks are determined and
printed.

These functions could be summarized with the short functional definition "get and store marks", "calculate average", and "print appropriate marks". The program can be viewed as consisting of three shorter programs which perform these functions in the proper order. This "functional packaging" of the program thus permits the reader to study the whole program in smaller segments.

```
C EXAMPLE 12.1
      DIMENSION MARK(100)
      I = 1
      LOOP
          READ, MARK(I)
          AT END, QUIT
          I = I + 1
      ENDLOOP
      TOTAL = I-1
      I = 1
      SUM = 0
      LOOP
          SUM = SUM + MARK(I)
          I = I + 1
          IF (I .GT. TOTAL) QUIT
      ENDLOOP
      AVG = SUM / TOTAL
      I = 1
      LOOP
          IF (MARK(I) .GT. AVG) PRINT, MARK(I)
          I = I + 1
          IF (I .GT. TOTAL) QUIT
      ENDLOOP
      STOP
      END
```

Example 12.2 is an alternative means of writing the program so this packaging becomes explicit. Three remote blocks have been introduced, one to perform each of the three functions. They are called GETMKS (get marks), CALAVG (calculate average), and PRTMKS (print marks). These blocks are each introduced by a header statement such as

REMOTE BLOCK GETMKS

All statements following this header, up to the trailer statement

    END BLOCK

are said to define the function of the remote block, and in the above statements GETMKS is said to be the <u>name</u> of the block.

```
C EXAMPLE 12.2
      DIMENSION MARK(100)
      EXECUTE GETMKS
      EXECUTE CALAVG
      EXECUTE PRTMKS
      STOP

      REMOTE BLOCK GETMKS
      I = 1
      LOOP
          READ, MARK(I)
          AT END, QUIT
          I = I + 1
      ENDLOOP
      TOTAL = I - 1
      END BLOCK

      REMOTE BLOCK CALAVG
      SUM = 0
      I = 1
      LOOP
          SUM = SUM + MARK(I)
          I = I + 1
          IF (I .GT. TOTAL) QUIT
      ENDLOOP
      AVG = SUM / TOTAL
      END BLOCK

      REMOTE BLOCK PRTMKS
      I = 1
      LOOP
          IF (MARK(I) .GT. AVG) PRINT, MARK(I)
          I = I + 1
          IF (I .GT. TOTAL) QUIT
      ENDLOOP
      END BLOCK

      END
```

To execute the statements in a remote block we use the WATFIV-S statement EXECUTE followed by the name of the block. Thus the statements

```
EXECUTE GETMKS
EXECUTE CALAVG
EXECUTE PRTMKS
STOP
```

cause the computer to invoke each of the three remote blocks in turn, and then stop. When a block is invoked by EXECUTE, control is transferred to the first statement in the block. Then the statements in the block are executed in sequence until the END BLOCK statement is encountered. This causes a return of control to the statement immediately following the EXECUTE statement.

The remote block mechanism has been used to divide the original program into four components - the main program plus three remote blocks. The reason for doing this is to make the program more readable by separating its various functions into well-defined segments. The usefulness of this technique will become obvious when the reader applies it to larger programs.

12.2   NESTED REMOTE BLOCKS

Suppose a data deck contains several cards. Each card contains several words, with words being separated by at least one blank space. A typical data deck might be as follows:

```
        CAT     DOG            card 1
     HOUSE FARM                card 2
      BOY     GIRL    SON       card 3
```
column 1

- 155 -

Note that the collection of words in a card is not enclosed between quote symbols; we will use A format to read an entire card and assign it to a single character variable.

It is required to write a program which prints the words and their lengths in the following form:

```
3       CAT
3       DOG
5       HOUSE
4       FARM
3       BOY
4       GIRL
3       SON
```

The entire program could be written using REMOTE BLOCKS as illustrated in Example 12.3.

In the main program two REMOTE BLOCKS are invoked, namely GTCARD and GTWORD.

The GTCARD (get card) block causes the next card to be read, and its contents are stored as a single character constant in the variable CARD. Then an index variable PTR is set to 1 to point at column 1 in subsequent processing. An EQUIVALENCE statement is used to make the variable WORD occupy the same physical memory locations as the subscripted variable COL; this is done to permit character-by-character reference of the input string. Note that when GTCARD is invoked and no cards are in the input data deck, the special string '***' is assigned as the value of CARD.

The GTWORD (get word) block causes the next available word in the input data deck to be assigned to the variable WORD. This is accomplished by invoking two remote blocks, namely SKIPBL (skip blanks) and MKWORD (make word). The SKIPBL routine causes PTR to be increased whenever it points to a blank column, thus having the effect of "scanning" away blanks. Whenever a non-blank column is encountered the block finishes, leaving PTR pointing at the first column of the next word. Whenever required, the block GTCARD is invoked in order to read a new card.

```
C EXAMPLE 12.3
      CHARACTER CARD*80, COL*1(80)
      CHARACTER WORD*80, CHAR*1(80)
      EQUIVALENCE (CARD,COL)
      EQUIVALENCE (WORD,CHAR)
      CHARACTER*3 FOUND
      INTEGER SIZE, PTR
      EXECUTE GTCARD
      LOOP
          EXECUTE GTWORD
          IF (CARD .EQ. '***') QUIT
          PRINT, SIZE, WORD
      ENDLOOP
      STOP

      REMOTE BLOCK GTCARD
      READ 1, CARD
      AT END, CARD='***'
1     FORMAT(A80)
      PTR = 1
      END BLOCK

      REMOTE BLOCK GTWORD
      EXECUTE SKIPBL
      EXECUTE MKWORD
      END BLOCK

      REMOTE BLOCK SKIPBL
      FOUND = 'OFF'
      WHILE (FOUND .EQ. 'OFF')
          IF (PTR .EQ. 81) EXECUTE GTCARD
          IF (COL(PTR) .NE. ' ') THEN
              FOUND = 'ON'
          ELSE
              PTR = PTR + 1
          ENDIF
      ENDWHILE
      END BLOCK

      REMOTE BLOCK MKWORD
      SIZE = 1
      WORD = ' '
      WHILE (PTR .LT. 81)
          CHAR(SIZE) = COL(PTR)
          SIZE = SIZE + 1
          PTR = PTR + 1
          IF (COL(PTR) .EQ. ' ') QUIT
      ENDWHILE
      END BLOCK

      END
```

The MKWORD routine simply assigns all consecutive non-blank characters to the subscripted variable CHAR. As CHAR is EQUIVALENCE'd to WORD, the variable WORD will contain the character constant representing the next word when the block terminates.

This program has illustrated that a remote block can be invoked by another remote block (SKIPBL and MKWORD are invoked from block GTWORD). This process is acceptable provided that a remote block must not invoke itself directly or indirectly i.e. it must not invoke another block which ultimately will re-invoke the original block.

12.3   EXERCISES

    12.1   In previous chapters some of the examples have been
            fairly large, and their readability could probably
            be improved using remote blocks. Some examples
            might include the following:

                        Example 2.7
                        Example 11.4
                        Example 11.5

            Modify each of these examples to use remote blocks
            where appropriate.

    12.2   Example 12.3 can be extended in an important way.
            Instead of printing each word and its size on a
            separate line, the words could be arranged in
            sequence on one printed line as follows:

                CAT DOG HOUSE FARM BOY GIRL SON

            The first word appears to the left, and each word is
            separated from the other by one blank column. Of
            course, if the data deck is large, there will be too
            many words for one line. In this case the rule is

to put as many words on one line as possible, and then begin a new line with the remainder of the words. This procedure would continue, using as many printed lines as necessary, until the data deck has been completely processed. The lines would usually have a few blank spaces on the right, as the next word would often be too large to fit in the space available. The resulting printed output is said to be left-justified and ragged right, much like the pages in this text.

Modify the program to produce the required effect. In order to use a smaller data deck, you can arbitrarily decide that the printed lines have only 30 positions, for example.

Chapter 13

SUBPROGRAMS

Some programs are of such a general nature that they can be used over and over by the same programmer, or indeed by any programmer. Examples are:

(a) determine the largest element in an array

(b) sort a collection of character strings into an ascending sequence

(c) calculate a sine, cosine, etc.

(d) perform a table look-up

(e) do a statistical analysis on some data

(f) solve a system of linear equations.

When such programs have been written and tested, they should be available in a computer library so that all programmers can have access to them. These library programs are usually referred to as subprograms. A program which is not a subprogram is referred to as a main program. FORTRAN has statements such as CALL, SUBROUTINE, COMMON, and RETURN, which make communication possible between a main program and subprograms or among subprograms.

The use of subprograms has other advantages which will be discussed at the end of this chapter. In the meantime, the following sections discuss the details of defining and using subprograms.

The reader will note some similarity in function between remote blocks and subprograms. However, subprograms are much more powerful, have more flexibility, and consequently have many more applications. The major differences between remote blocks and subprograms will be outlined where appropriate.

13.1   SUBROUTINE SUBPROGRAMS

We will begin by describing a main program which will subsequently be converted to a subprogram. Example 13.1 is a program designed to find the arithmetic maximum of N real constants, after they have been read in from N data cards and stored in an array. In addition to determining the maximum, the program uses a pointer J to indicate which of the input data cards actually contains the maximum value. The program will function for any number of data cards up to 100, since the array size has been chosen to be 100.

```
C EXAMPLE 13.1 - MAXIMUM OF N REAL NUMBERS
      REAL X(100), LARGE
      READ, N, (X(I), I=1,N)
      LARGE = X(1)
      J = 1
      DO 1 I=2,N
          IF (X(I) .GT. LARGE) THEN
              LARGE = X(I)
              J = I
          ENDIF
1     CONTINUE
      PRINT, J, LARGE
      STOP
      END
```

The program initializes LARGE to X(1) and the pointer J to 1. Control proceeds through the loop where LARGE is replaced by any one of the X(I) which is greater than the current value of LARGE. At the same time J, the pointer, is updated. When the loop is satisfied, the value of LARGE is the maximum value, and it and the pointer J are printed.

The program accepts a vector X and an integer N as input. It performs the required calculation and ultimately assigns the results to J and LARGE as output. This can be represented schematically, as in Figure 13.1. X and N are referred to as the input; J and LARGE are referred to as the output.

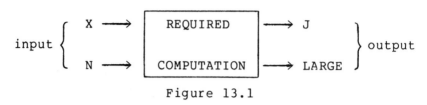

Figure 13.1

Example 13.2 shows how this program can be rewritten as a subroutine subprogram.

```
C EXAMPLE 13.2
      SUBROUTINE MAX (N, X, J, LARGE)
      REAL X(100), LARGE
      LARGE = X(1)
      J = 1
      DO 1 I=2,N
          IF (X(I) .GT. LARGE) THEN
              LARGE = X(I)
              J = I
          ENDIF
1     CONTINUE
      RETURN
      END
```

Note that the following statements, which were in the main program, are no longer present.

        READ, N, (X(I), I=1,N)

        PRINT, J, LARGE

Their input-output function has been assumed by the new statement

        SUBROUTINE MAX(N, X, J, LARGE)

This statement identifies the program as a subroutine subprogram. Furthermore, it assigns the name MAX to this particular subprogram. The name MAX is followed by a list of input-

- 162 -

output parameters, separated by commas and contained in parentheses. There is no explicit designation as to which of the parameters is input and which of them is output. The subprogram clearly requires values for X and N before it can function; hence, they are implicitly assumed to be input parameters. On the other hand, the operation of the subprogram causes assignments to be made to J and LARGE; hence, they are implicitly assumed to be output parameters.

Note also that the STOP statement in Example 13.1 has been replaced by a RETURN statement in the subprogram. It is usual to employ the RETURN statement in a subprogram wherever a STOP statement would occur in a main program.

We will now consider a trivial main program which makes use of the subprogram called MAX.

```
C EXAMPLE 13.3
      REAL X(100), LARGE
      READ, N, (X(I), I=1,N)
      CALL MAX(N, X, J, LARGE)
      PRINT, J, LARGE
      STOP
      END
```

Example 13.3 causes a number of values, determined by the variable N, to be read into an array X. Then the following statement is encountered:

CALL MAX(N, X, J, LARGE)

This causes control to transfer to the first executable statement in the subprogram called MAX. It also defines the input-output arguments using an argument list similar to the parameter list in the subprogram.

The subprogram MAX performs its calculations, and ultimately encounters the RETURN statement. This statement causes control to be transferred back to the statement immediately following the CALL statement in the main program. This happens to be PRINT,J,LARGE and, consequently, the results appear as printed output.

The example, simple though it may be, demonstrates some of the basic ideas common to all subprograms. For example, the subprogram is a <u>separate</u> entity and has a special statement, SUBROUTINE, as its first statement. Furthermore, the subprogram has a distinct name and a list of parameters. As for the main program, it <u>calls</u> the subprogram using the special statement CALL, which names the required subprogram and gives a list of arguments. Control is transferred to the subprogram for it to perform its function. When a RETURN is encountered, control is returned to the first executable statement following the CALL in the main program.

Note the similarities and differences between remote blocks and subprograms. The remote block also has a name which is defined in the REMOTE BLOCK statement. It is invoked using the EXECUTE rather than the CALL, but no parameter list can be used with remote blocks. The return from a remote block is normally accomplished by completing execution of all statements in the block, whereas the subprogram must always be terminated with a RETURN statement. The END statement defines the end of a subprogram, and the END BLOCK statement serves the same function in a remote block.

Figure 13.2 outlines in pictorial form the flow of control between the main program and the subprogram.

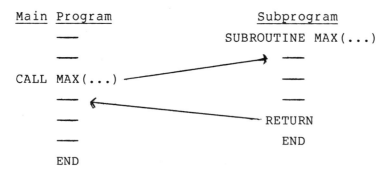

Figure 13.2

The above discussion outlines the basic philosophy concerning subprograms. They possess considerable flexibility, and have many other features. These will be described in the examples which follow.

Example 13.4 is exactly the same as Example 13.3 except that the variable names in the main program have been changed.

```
C EXAMPLE 13.4
      REAL A(100)
      READ, K, (A(I), I=1,K)
      CALL MAX(K, A, N, ANS)
      PRINT, N, ANS
      STOP
      END
```

This illustrates that the names of the entries in the CALL argument list need not be the same as those in the SUBROUTINE parameter list. All that is required is that they correspond _exactly_ in number and type. The parameters in the SUBROUTINE statement are merely _dummies_ which are replaced by their true names when the CALL statement is executed.

$$
\text{CALL argument list} \left\{ \begin{array}{l} K \rightarrow N \\ A \rightarrow X \\ N \rightarrow J \\ ANS \rightarrow LARGE \end{array} \right\} \text{SUBROUTINE parameter list}
$$

Figure 13.3

Figure 13.3 illustrates the relationship between the CALL argument list and the SUBROUTINE parameter list. Thus we see that N takes on the value of K, X is the same array as A, and, when LARGE and J are assigned, it is really ANS and N which are assigned. This points out the fact that arrays declared in subprograms should have the same dimensions as those in the main program, since they are the same arrays. It is a common error to assign different array sizes in the main program and in the subprograms.

It should be further pointed out that all variable names used in a subprogram are local to that subprogram. In other words, these names are defined only in the subprogram, and are not known outside the subprogram. This means that it is perfectly acceptable, and in fact common practice, to use the same variable names in a subprogram as those in other subprograms or in the main program, even though they may have a completely different use. This is illustrated in Example 13.4 where the variable N in the main program has a use different from that of the variable N used in the subprogram MAX which was called. This should be contrasted with remote blocks in which all variable names are global. That is, all variables used in a remote block are known by the main program as well as by all other remote blocks in that program.

Statement numbers are likewise local to subprograms. They can be identical with those in other subprograms or the main program, and no problems arise. Note that, with remote blocks, statement numbers are global.

Note that a subprogram always has an END statement as its final statement. In order to have a complete job, all the subprograms required by the main program must be placed either before or after the main program, in any order. Then the $JOB and $ENTRY control cards are placed respectively before and after this combined deck, and any data cards follow the $ENTRY control card. A typical job deck is illustrated in Figure 13.4. Each of the subprograms, as well as the main program, is referred to as a program segment. Note that each job has one and only one main program, but can have as many subprograms as required.

```
$JOB
      ————————————
      ————————————

      ————————————
END
SUBROUTINE MAX(N,X,J,SMALL)
      ————————————

      ————————————
END
$ENTRY
      ————————————

      ————————————      Data Cards

      ————————————
```

Figure 13.4

It is possible to place subprograms in a library stored
on the random-access storage devices of the computer. If this
is the case, they need not be placed with the job deck as in
Figure 13.4. The WATFIV-S compiler will locate them automatically. Whether or not programs are housed in the library is a
matter of personal preference, and this will vary from installation to installation. The programmer should consult his
installation's operating manual for details. Note however,
that such facilities are not available with remote blocks.

Example 13.5 illustrates some additional features of
subroutine subprograms. It is a main program which uses MAX
as a subprogram. Its function is to read in a vector of N
real constants, and print them out in descending order.

The effect is to call the MAX subprogram, and print out
the largest element. This element is then replaced by the
last element in the array. This means that only N-1 elements
remain to be considered, and they occupy the first N-1 positions of the array. This fact allows us to call the subprogram MAX again, this time specifying N-1 elements, rather than
N. The largest element among the N-1 is determined and
printed. Then, it is replaced by the second-last element in
the array. This process continues in the DO-loop until all
elements have been printed in descending order.

```
C EXAMPLE 13.5
      REAL A(100), LARGE
      READ, N, (A(I), I=1,N)
      DO 6 I=1,N
         CALL MAX(N-I+1, A, J, LARGE)
         PRINT, LARGE
         A(J) = A(N-I+1)
6        CONTINUE
      STOP
      END
```

Note that the arguments in the list for the CALL need not be simple variables. They can be any expressions which, when evaluated, yield a result of the proper type. The type is determined according to the type of the corresponding dummy variable in the parameter list of the SUBROUTINE statement. Thus, N-I+1 is an acceptable expression in the CALL argument list, since it yields an integer value corresponding in type to the integer N in the SUBROUTINE parameter list. On the other hand, the second argument in the CALL must be an array name, as the corresponding entry in the SUBROUTINE parameter list is X, an array name. It would be invalid to use an expression for this argument, since an expression cannot yield an array name as its value.

This example also illustrates the fact that statement numbers are local to subprograms. The statement number 6 is used in both the main program and the subprogram.

It should be noted that the action of the main program causes the original contents of the vector A to be destroyed. This happens because of the statement

$$A(J) = A(N-I+1)$$

If this is undesirable, the vector should be copied before the main part of the execution begins.

Since programs which sequence or sort data are generally useful, it seems appropriate to modify the example to be a subprogram. This is illustrated in Example 13.6.

The subroutine SORT accepts as input a vector A with N components. The effect of the computation is to shuffle the elements of A into ascending sequence.

```
C EXAMPLE 13.6
      SUBROUTINE SORT (N, A)
      REAL A(100), LARGE
      DO 6 I=1,N
         CALL MAX(N-I+1, A, J, LARGE)
         A(J) = A(N-I+1)
         A(N-I+1) = LARGE
6     CONTINUE
      RETURN
      END
```

The example illustrates that a subprogram can call a second subprogram. The second subprogram can call a third subprogram, etc., with one restriction. A subprogram may never call _itself_, either directly or indirectly. In other words, the same subprogram may not be called again until its RETURN is executed. This is identical to the rule used for remote blocks.

13.2 SUBROUTINE SUBPROGRAM SUMMARY

It is appropriate at this point to summarize and expand upon the major ideas which have been introduced concerning subroutine subprograms.

    (a)   Each subroutine subprogram has a SUBROUTINE statement as its first statement and an END statement as its last statement.

    (b)   The general form of the SUBROUTINE statement is as follows

SUBROUTINE NAME(param1, param2, ..., paramn)

The name can be any FORTRAN symbolic name. The parameter list may contain any non-subscripted variable name or array name. These parameters are referred to as dummy variables. No expressions are allowed in the parameter list. In the next chapter, we will see that subprogram names and *'s are also valid entries in the parameter list. We will also see that no parameter list is necessary.

(c) The subroutine subprogram is referenced by the CALL statement, which has the following general form.

CALL NAME (arg1, arg2, ..., argn)

When executed, it has the effect of transferring control to the first executable statement in the subroutine subprogram called NAME. The list of arguments must agree in number with the list of parameters in the SUBROUTINE statement. Wherever the corresponding parameter is a simple variable, the argument can be an expression of the same type. If the parameter is an array name, the calling argument must also be an array name.

(d) Whenever the subprogram uses one of its dummy variables, it is in actual fact using the value of the corresponding variable or expression in the calling argument list. When one of the dummy variables in the parameter list is assigned a value in that subprogram, the effect is to assign the value to the corresponding argument in the CALL list. Thus the argument and parameter lists provide a two-way means of communication between the calling program segment and the called subprogram.

(e) When a RETURN statement is executed, control is transferred back to the calling program segment. Transfer of control is to the first executable statement following the CALL.

(f) A subroutine subprogram can call other subprograms, provided it does not call itself either directly or indirectly.

(g) All variable names or statement numbers used in a subroutine subprogram are local to that subprogram.

(h) Subroutine subprograms can be in a library, or can be inserted in a job deck as program segments.

13.3   FUNCTION SUBPROGRAMS

Function subprograms are very similar to subroutine subprograms. Example 13.7 is used to point out the differences. This subprogram is designed to accept a real vector X and its dimension N as input, and to compute the sum of the components of the vector.

```
C EXAMPLE 13.7
      FUNCTION SUM (N, X)
      REAL X(100)
      SUM = 0.
      DO 6 I=1,N
          SUM = SUM + X(I)
6     CONTINUE
      RETURN
      END
```

At first glance, the only difference appears to be the use of the word FUNCTION rather than SUBROUTINE. However, one major difference is that the name, SUM, of the subprogram appears as a variable in the subprogram, and is assigned a value. This is always the case with function subprograms, and is never the case with subroutine subprograms.

The other major difference between the two types is the way in which they are called. Whereas subroutine subprograms are always called using the CALL statement, function subprograms never are. Example 13.8 is a main program which uses the subprogram SUM.

```
C EXAMPLE 13.8
      REAL A(100), B(100)
      READ, N, (A(I), I=1,N), M, (B(I), I=1,M)
      AVG = (SUM(N,A) + SUM(M,B)) / (M + N)
      PRINT, AVG
      STOP
      END
```

This program reads two vectors with real components, and computes their composite average, AVG. Note that the function subprogram is called in the same manner as SIN or COS, using its name followed by the argument list contained in parentheses. Thus, function subprograms are useful when a single value is to be returned, since the call is included as part of an expression rather than as a separate statement.

Since the name of the function subprogram is treated like a variable, it must be declared according to type in both the calling program and the subprogram. In Examples 13.7 and 13.8 this was unnecessary, since SUM begins with the letter S and is therefore real by default, in the absence of other declarations.

Suppose, however, that the subprogram SUM were designed to compute the integer-valued sum of an array of integers. It would be written as in Example 13.9.

```
C EXAMPLE 13.9
      INTEGER FUNCTION SUM (N, X)
      INTEGER X(100)
      SUM = 0
      DO 6 I=1,N
          SUM = SUM + X(I)
    6     CONTINUE
      RETURN
      END
```

Note that the subprogram name, SUM, is declared to be of integer type by placing the word INTEGER at the beginning of the FUNCTION statement. In fact, this is the only way the type of a function subprogram name can be declared explicitly in the subprogram. The following two statements, although they would seem to have an equivalent effect, are, in fact, illegal.

FUNCTION SUM(N,X)

INTEGER SUM, X(100)

Furthermore, in the calling program, SUM must be declared as an integer by using the INTEGER declaration statement.

Function subprograms may be integer type or real type, but may <u>not</u> be of character type. Thus it is not possible for a function name to be a character variable.

13.4   FUNCTION SUBPROGRAM SUMMARY

The rules for subroutine subprograms in Section 13.2 generally apply to function subprograms, when the obvious changes of wording are taken into account. Only the exceptions and additional rules will be summarized here.

(a) A function name has a type which is declared explicitly as in

REAL FUNCTION MAX (P,Q)

or by default. It may not be of type character.

(b) A function subprogram must have at least one parameter in the parameter list. Asterisks (*) may not appear as parameters.

(c) The function subprogram is called by using the name of the subprogram followed by an argument list in parentheses. The name and argument list always appear as a component in any legal expression. When the name is encountered, control is transferred to the first executable statement in the function subprogram. When the function subprogram reaches a RETURN statement, control is returned to the point in the expression which contains the name and argument list. The name assumes the value assigned to it in the subprogram, and computation of the expression is resumed.

(d) Function subprograms normally return one value to the calling program. However, they may return several by assigning values to the dummy variables, just as is the case for subroutine subprograms.

(e) The name of the function subprogram is defined in any calling program. Hence, it is not local to the subprogram, as is the case for other variables used in the subprogram.

13.5 STATEMENT FUNCTIONS

The FORTRAN statement function is a highly specialized feature which permits the programmer to define a function by using a single statement. Its use is illustrated in Example 13.10.

```
C EXAMPLE 13.10
      AREA(A,B,C) = SQRT(S*(S-A)*(S-B)*(S-C))
      SUM = 0.
      DO 8 I=1,10
         READ, X, Y, Z
         S = (X+Y+Z) / 2.
         SUM = SUM + AREA(X,Y,Z)
8     CONTINUE
      PRINT, SUM
      STOP
      END
```

The first statement is known as a statement function definition which, in this case, defines the function AREA with three dummy variables A, B, and C as parameters. This function evaluates the area of a triangle with sides of lengths a, b, and c, by using the formula

$$area = \sqrt{s(s-a)(s-b)(s-c)}$$

$$where \quad s = \frac{a+b+c}{2} \quad .$$

The first executable statement in the example is SUM=0.. The effect of the program is to read the lengths of the sides of ten triangles into the computer and calculate the total of the areas of these triangles. In the statement SUM=SUM+AREA(X,Y,Z), the function, AREA, is referenced. Note that the arguments agree in order, number, and type with the dummy variables in the function definition statement. Also note that the expression

$$SQRT(S*(S-A)*(S-B)*(S-C))$$

contains dummy variables A, B, and C, as well as a variable S which is assigned in the course of computation. It also contains a reference to a built-in function.

13.6 FORTRAN STATEMENT FUNCTION SUMMARY

The following points summarize the rules for the use of the FORTRAN statement function.

(a) In general, the statement function definition has the form

NAME(list of dummy variables)=expression

The name can be any valid FORTRAN symbolic name. The name must be declared according to type in a statement prior to that of the statement function definition; otherwise, the default declaration is used. It cannot be of type character.

(b)   The list of dummy variables can contain any FORTRAN symbolic name. These variables are local to the <u>single</u> statement in which they appear.

(c)   The expression can be of any type (except character) but should not contain subscripted variables. If other statement functions are referenced in the expression, they must be defined by using earlier statement function definitions. The expression can use variables defined anywhere in the program segment, as well as the dummy variables.

(d)   The argument list in a reference to the function must have arguments which agree in number, order, and type with the dummy variables. These arguments may be expressions.

(e)   Statement function definitions should be placed in the program prior to the first executable statement.

(f)   Statement functions are defined only in the program segment in which they appear. They cannot, under any circumstances, be referenced from other segments.

13.7   ADVANTAGES OF SUBPROGRAMS

As has been pointed out, subprograms make it possible to store debugged routines in a library so that they are available to all users. They have other obvious advantages worth mentioning. They permit the programmer to write his total program in segments which are easier to debug and document. This expedites the programming and testing, and makes the final product easier for another programmer to understand. In this respect, they serve a purpose similar to that of remote blocks. Since variables and statement numbers are local to each program segment, they can be repeated at will from segment to segment. This saves a good deal of book-keeping, and reduces errors. The same feature allows several programmers to handle different segments of a large project with a minimum of consultation with each other. Consequently they are much more powerful than remote blocks.

13.8   EXERCISES

13.1   (a)   Convert the subprogram of Example 13.2 to a function subprogram.

(b)   Convert the main program of Example 13.3 to use the function subprogram of (a).

13.2   Write a subprogram to do each of the following:

(a)   Compute the average of the elements of a one-dimensional array.

(b)   Find the maximum value of the elements of a one-dimensional array.

13.3   Write a main program which reads in a two-dimensional array containing marks for several students in each of various courses. Use the subprograms of Example 13.2 to assist in the production of a class list, printed in descending order of student averages.

13.4   Write a subroutine subprogram which accepts any positive integer as input, and determines whether or not it is prime. A variable should be set to one if the integer is prime, and to zero otherwise.

13.5   Suppose we have a one-dimensional array, X, of ten elements.

   (a)   Write a subroutine SUMS, with parameters X, S, S2, which computes the sum, S, and the sum of squares, S2, of the ten elements of the array X.

   (b)   Write a main program which reads the elements of a 10 by 10 array A. Then, the program should use SUMS on each row of A to form two new vectors of 10 elements each. Use SUMS on these vectors to produce an over-all sum and sum of squares of elements in A.

13.6   (a)   Write a function subprogram which evaluates a polynomial, given the coefficients in array form and a value for the independent variable.

   (b)   Modify the function subprogram in part (a) so that it evaluates the derivative as well as the function. In the process, change it to a subroutine subprogram.

13.7   Write a subprogram to compute the median of a set of n integers, regardless of the sequence in which they appear.

13.8   Write subprograms which accomplish the matrix operations outlined in Exercise 9.11. Include careful documentation with your subprograms, so that other programmers could use them.

13.9   Write subprograms which accomplish the vector operations outlined in Exercise 9.10. Include careful documentation with your subprograms, so that other programmers could use them.

13.10 Write a subprogram which computes the greatest common divisor of two positive integers.

13.11 Write a subprogram which computes all of the prime factors of a given positive integer. These factors are to be returned to the main program, stored in an array.

13.12 The FORTRAN language does not have built-in functions for secant and cosecant. Write statement-function definitions for each of these. In a main program, use the statement functions to tabulate the two functions over a convenient range.

13.13 (a) Write a subprogram which will convert any non-negative integer, less than 500, to the corresponding binary integer. The binary integer should be stored using an integer variable.

   (b) Write a subprogram which will convert any non-negative binary integer, of 10 or fewer digits, into the equivalent decimal integer. The binary integer should be input to the subprogram as an integer constant consisting only of ones and zeros.

Chapter 14

SUBPROGRAMS - ADDITIONAL FEATURES

In Chapter 13 we discussed the basic ideas involving the use of subroutine and function subprograms. There are many other features of these subprograms; as well, there are other facilities in the FORTRAN language which tend to make the use of subprograms easier and more flexible. The purpose of this chapter is to describe some of these additional features.

14.1   COMMON BLOCKS

It has been noted that variables used in a main program or in a subprogram are local to that program segment. COMMON statements provide a means of declaring selected variables to be in a common area in the memory of the computer, and thus accessible to all program segments. This common area is referred to as a common block, because all variables in the area are adjacent to one another in memory. Consider Example 14.1, which is a reprogramming of Example 13.3 and its associated subprogram, Example 13.2.

The statement

COMMON K, A, M, ANS

declares that the variables K, A, M, and ANS, referenced in the main program, are to be located in the common block. Since A is a subscripted variable of 100 elements, the block requires 103 storage locations. The subroutine contains a similar statement,

COMMON N, X, J, LARGE

which declares that the variables N, X, J, and LARGE used within it are in the common block. Since there is only one common block, the effect is to have K and N use the same storage location in computer memory. Similarly, the arrays A and X occupy the same memory locations, as do the variables M and J and the variables ANS and LARGE.

```
C EXAMPLE 14.1
      REAL A(100)
      COMMON K, A, M, ANS
      READ, K, (A(I), I=1,K)
      CALL MAX
      PRINT, M, ANS
      STOP
      END

      SUBROUTINE MAX
      REAL X(100),LARGE
      COMMON N, X, J, LARGE
      LARGE = X(1)
      J = 1
      DO 1 I=2,N
         IF (X(I) .GT. LARGE) THEN
            LARGE = X(I)
            J = I
         ENDIF
1     CONTINUE
      RETURN
      END
```

The statement

SUBROUTINE MAX

has no list of dummy variables, and, similarly, the CALL statement has no argument list. The CALL merely transfers control to the first executable statement in MAX which is

LARGE = X(1)

When the subprogram is dealing with variables N, X, J, and LARGE, it is, in fact, dealing with the corresponding variables K, A, M, and ANS in the common block. When the RETURN is executed, control is, as usual, returned to the statement following the CALL. Hence, the values of M and ANS are printed.

The use of a common area has eliminated the need for a parameter list in the the SUBROUTINE and CALL statements. There has been an _implicit_ transfer of variables between the subprogram and its calling program. The reader should observe that the function achieved by the combination of the COMMON statement with the subprogram is similar to the effect of using a remote block. With a remote block, all variables are global and no parameters are used when it is invoked.

It is not necessary to eliminate all the variables in the SUBROUTINE and CALL lists. Some of the variables could be placed in COMMON; the remaining ones could be passed explicitly, using arguments in the CALL. The use of common blocks is a matter of personal preference, and provides an extra degree of freedom to the programmer. However, there is one important rule; variables cannot appear both in the parameter list and in the common list.

It should be noted that variables in the two COMMON statements are in exact one-to-one correspondence according to type and number. For the moment, this should be accepted as the rule. However, it may be legally violated, as will be discussed in Chapter 24.

As an extra convenience to the programmer, the dimensions of subscripted variables can be declared in the COMMON statement. For example, if the COMMON statement in the main program had been written as

COMMON K, A(100), M, ANS

the need for the statement

$$REAL\ A(100)$$

would have been eliminated. In fact, the presence of both statements would create a redundant condition which would be signalled as an error.

If more than one COMMON statement appears in a single program or subprogram, the effect is cumulative; the variables in the first COMMON statement are the first variables in the common block, and are followed by those in the second, etc. This means that the statements

```
COMMON A, B, C
COMMON D
```

are equivalent to the single statement

```
COMMON A, B, C, D
```

Example 14.1 has illustrated the use of COMMON statements associated with the main program and a single subprogram. If several subprograms were used, the COMMON statement could be used in all of them, or in any subset of them. In fact, the COMMON statement can be used in some of the subprograms, and not appear in the main program at all.

14.2   LABELLED COMMON

As an added convenience to the programmer, the common area can be extended to include as many labelled or named common blocks as desired. The statement

```
COMMON /AREA1/ A, B, C
```

would set up a separate common area called AREA1 containing the variables A, B, and C. COMMON statements in various program segments would use the identical name AREA1 to place their variables in the same labelled common area. These names can be any valid FORTRAN symbolic name.

The unlabelled common area used in the last section is known as <u>blank</u> <u>common</u>. Labelled common areas and associated COMMON statements are used according to the same rules as are their blank common counterparts. One set of program segments can have as many common areas as is convenient to the programmer.

A single COMMON statement can define variables as members of both blank common and labelled common areas.

The statement

COMMON A, B /AREA1/C, D /AREA2/E, F

defines A and B as members of blank common, C and D as belonging to the common block named AREA1, and E and F as belonging to AREA2. An equivalent form of the same statement is

COMMON /AREA1/C/ /A, B /AREA1/D /AREA2/E, F

Note that blank common is defined using two consecutive slashes. A further rule is that a comma never immediately precedes or follows a slash. This example illustrates the general flexibility in setting up common areas using the COMMON statement.

The reader may wonder why named common is available. One use of named common is to provide "private" common areas between program segments. Suppose we wanted several subprograms in the library to form an integrated set. They undoubtedly would share common areas for data. On the other hand, the user might not need to know about these common areas. However, he might wish to use common areas for his own purposes. In this case, the subprograms would use specific labelled common blocks, and the other common blocks would be left to the user. All he must know is the names of the labelled common blocks so that he does not use them again.

14.3 EXECUTION-TIME DIMENSIONING OF ARRAYS

It has been pointed out that an array whose name appears in a subprogram parameter list should have the same dimension specifications in both the calling program and the called subprogram. This means that both the calling program and the subprogram must be modified if a different array size is to be used. This is frequently a nuisance, especially since the subprogram is probably in a library, and thus not readily available to the programmer for him to make changes. Furthermore, changes of this type to the library could be disastrous, since many people might be using the library simultaneously.

To overcome this difficulty, a way has been provided to permit the calling program to include the dimension information as part of its input to the subprogram; thus, the dimension in the subprogram is assigned at execution time, rather than at compile time. Example 14.2 incorporates this feature into the subroutine MAX of Example 13.2.

```
C EXAMPLE 14.2
      SUBROUTINE MAX (M, N, X, J, LARGE)
      REAL X(M), LARGE
      LARGE = X(1)
      J = 1
      IF (N .EQ. 1) THEN
          QUIT
      ELSE
          DO 6 I=2,N
              IF (X(I) .GT. LARGE) THEN
                  LARGE = X(I)
                  J = I
              ENDIF
6         CONTINUE
      ENDIF
      RETURN
      END
```

The changes are:

(a) The declaration statement has become

```
      REAL X(M), LARGE
```

with the variable M replacing the constant 100.

(b)   The parameter list has one more parameter, namely, M, an integer variable.

(c)   If only one value is supplied, i.e. N is 1, the subprogram returns X(1) for LARGE.

Declaration statements of this type can occur only in subprograms, and never in the main program.

Example 14.3 shows the modification necessary to solve the same problem as Example 13.3.

```
C EXAMPLE 14.3
      REAL X(100), LARGE
      READ, N, (X(I), I=1,N)
      CALL MAX(100, N, X, J, LARGE)
      PRINT, J, LARGE
      STOP
      END
```

Note that, since the array X is of size 100 in the calling program, the corresponding parameter in the CALL statement is set at 100 to ensure that the subprogram receives the proper dimension information. The dimension in the called program must be identical with the dimension in the calling program.

The following additional points should be kept in mind when using execution-time dimensioning of arrays.

(a)   Dimensions can be assigned at execution time in both function and subroutine subprograms.

(b)   Only arrays which appear as elements in the parameter list of the FUNCTION or SUBROUTINE statement can have variable dimensions. Thus, they cannot be contained in any common blocks.

(c)   The integer variables which indicate the dimensions of the array are usually members of the parameter list, and have their values assigned when the subprogram is called. Alternatively, they can be in a common block.

- 186 -

(d)   The integer variables which indicate the dimensions of the array should not be reassigned new values in the course of execution of the subprogram.

14.4   EXTERNAL STATEMENTS

Example 14.4 is a function subprogram for approximating the integral

$$\int_a^b f(x) \ dx$$

using the trapezoidal rule. The formula employed is

$$\int_a^b f(x) \, dx \doteq \frac{h}{2}\left[f(a) + 2f(a+h) + 2f(a+2h) + \ldots + 2f(a+(n-1)h + f(b)\right]$$

where h = (b-a)/n, and n is the number of trapezoids.

```
      C EXAMPLE 14.4
            FUNCTION TRAP (A, B, N, FX)
            H = (B-A) / N
            SUM = 0.
            K = N - 1
            DO 6 I=1,K
               SUM = SUM + FX(A+I*H)
      6     CONTINUE
            TRAP = (FX(A) + FX(B) + 2.*SUM) * (H/2.)
            RETURN
            END
```

The subprogram TRAP calls another function subprogram FX which defines the function which is the integrand of the integral. The name of this function, FX, appears as one of the entries in the parameter list, and therefore must be supplied by the calling program, just as any other parameter would have to be supplied. We illustrate this in Example 14.5, which is designed to approximate

$$\int_{0}^{.4} \sin x^2 \, dx + \int_{.1}^{.3} \cos x^2 \, dx$$

using TRAP with 5 trapezoids.

```
C EXAMPLE 14.5
      EXTERNAL FX1, FX2
      APPROX = TRAP(0., .4, 5, FX1) + TRAP(.1, .3, 5, FX2)
      PRINT, APPROX
      STOP
      END

      FUNCTION FX1 (X)
      FX1 = SIN(X**2)
      RETURN
      END

      FUNCTION FX2 (X)
      FX2 = COS(X**2)
      RETURN
      END
```

The example consists of the main program and two function subprograms to define the integrands. The function subprogram names FX1 and FX2 appear in the calling argument lists when TRAP is used in the main program. However, an additional statement

EXTERNAL FX1, FX2

becomes necessary in the calling program. This is a special declaration which must be used in every calling program which passes the name of a subprogram or built-in function to another subprogram. Basically it tells the compiler that wherever it sees the names in the program segment, it should treat them as subprogram names and not merely as variable names. This is the only circumstance when the EXTERNAL statement is used.

14.5 MULTIPLE ENTRIES

Sometimes two subprograms are similar in that the statements in one are identical with a subset of the statements in the other. In situations like this, it is desirable to combine the two in some way, in order to save memory space and some programming time. One way is to use only the larger subprogram, and have **multiple** entry **points** to it. Then, if the whole program is needed, the normal entry point is used; if only the subset is needed, an alternate entry point is used. This use of multiple entries will be illustrated in Example 14.6 below.

```
C EXAMPLE 14.6
      SUBROUTINE CLINP (X, N)
      REAL X(20,20)
      DO 6 I=1,20
         DO 60 J=1,20
            X(I,J) = 0.
60       CONTINUE
6     CONTINUE
      ENTRY INP(X, N)
      DO 7 K=1,N
         READ, I, J, X(I,J)
7     CONTINUE
      RETURN
      END
```

If the subprogram is called using the statement

              CALL CLINP (A, K)

control transfers as usual to the first executable statement following the SUBROUTINE statement, in this case, the first DO. The effect is to set all elements of array A equal to zero, and to read N new elements into the array. (The ENTRY statement is non-executable, and so can be ignored.) If, however, the subprogram is called using the statement

              CALL INP(A, K)

control transfers to the first executable statement following the ENTRY statement, since the ENTRY statement defines the entry point INP. The effect is to read N new elements into the array A without initializing it to zero, as happens in a call to CLINP.

As many entry points as desired can be set up using ENTRY statements. Each one must have a distinct name in order to reference it. The entries in the list of dummy parameters of the ENTRY statement must correspond to the entries in the calling list according to order, type, and number, as is the case for SUBROUTINE and FUNCTION statements. However, the lists in the ENTRY statements do not have to correspond to each other, or to the lists in the SUBROUTINE or FUNCTION statements. All that is required is that the variables to be manipulated in the part of the subprogram that is used be assigned values prior to their use. This could be done in many ways, including the use of COMMON statements.

When ENTRY statements are used within function subprograms, the entry point name is treated like a variable, and so must be declared according to type if necessary. The FUNCTION name and ENTRY names can be of differing types. However, neither can be of type character.

The following additional points about ENTRY statements should be kept in mind.

(a) The ENTRY statement can be used only in subroutine and function subprograms. It can never appear in the main program.

(b) The ENTRY statement cannot appear within the range of a DO nor should it be within a block controlled by an IF, LOOP, WHILE, AT END, or REMOTE BLOCK.

(c) If statement function definitions are used in a subprogram which has ENTRY statements, these definitions should be placed, as usual, prior to the first executable statement in the total subprogram.

14.6   MULTIPLE RETURNS FROM SUBROUTINE SUBPROGRAMS

When a RETURN statement in a subroutine subprogram is executed, control is returned to the statement immediately following the CALL statement in the calling program. However, it is possible to return control to other statements in the calling program by using the multiple return feature, as illustrated in Example 14.7.

```
C EXAMPLE 14.7
      SUBROUTINE TEST (ARG, A, *, B, *)
      INTEGER A(100), B(100), ARG
      DO 8 I=1,100
         IF (ARG .EQ. A(I)) RETURN 1
         IF (ARG .EQ. B(I)) RETURN 2
    8    CONTINUE
      RETURN
      END
```

The subroutine TEST accepts an integer ARG and two integer vectors A and B as input. Its function is to scan the elements in A and B in a search for ARG. If ARG is found in A, the subprogram uses the statement RETURN 1 to exit; if ARG is found in B, the subroutine uses the statement RETURN 2 to exit. If ARG is not found, the normal RETURN statement is executed. The asterisks in the list of dummy variables provide the means of communication of statement numbers from the CALL statement to the subroutine subprogram. For example

          CALL TEST(STUDNO, CLASS1, &10, CLASS2, &20)

will test to see whether a certain student having student number STUDNO is in class 1, class 2, or neither. If he is in class 1, control is returned to statement 10 in the calling program. If he is in class 2, control is returned to statement 20 in the calling program. If he is in neither class, control is returned to the statement following the CALL. Note that the <u>alternate returns</u> to statement numbers 10 and 20 are indicated by inserting &10 and &20 in the appropriate places in the calling argument list. The appropriate places are those corresponding to the *'s in the associated parameter list of the subroutine subprogram. The first * is associated with RETURN 1, the second * with RETURN 2.

The subprogram can be set up to have as many alternate returns as are required. Normally, these returns are numbered consecutively, beginning with RETURN 1, RETURN 2, etc. Whenever the subprogram executes the statement RETURN n, it uses the nth return. This return is defined using the nth asterisk (*) in the parameter list of the SUBROUTINE statement. This asterisk will correspond to an entry in the argument list of the CALL statement. This entry is always of the form &s, where s is a statement number in the calling program.

The n in RETURN n can be an integer variable, provided its value is appropriate, i.e., a positive integer having the required magnitude.

The multiple return feature is used _only_ in subroutine subprograms. It makes no sense to use it in function subprograms, nor can the main program use the statement RETURN n.

14.7   EXERCISES

14.1   Modify any of the programs for the examples or exercises in Chapter 13 so that one or more of the parameters of the subprogram list are in COMMON.

14.2   Write a real-valued function subprogram named J35 which computes

$$\sqrt{1 - (f(x))^2}$$

The parameter list should include the variable X and the function name FX. Test J35 by tabulating it for f(x) = sin x and x = 0, .1, .2, .3, ..., 1.0. Compare the results with the corresponding values of cos x.

14.3   Convert the subprogram in Exercise 13.4 to have two
       returns, one if the integer is prime, the other if
       it is not. In this case, it is not necessary to use
       the variable which indicates whether or not the
       integer is prime.

       A main program reads data cards containing
       integer values. Use the subprogram to test the
       integer values to determine whether or not they are
       prime. Print a list of the input integers with the
       words PRIME or NOT PRIME adjacent to them.

14.4   Consider the following two subprograms.

       1)   The subprogram A is to accept an array X as
            input and compute the median value, Y, of the
            elements of X.

       2)   The subprogram B is to accept an array X as
            input and compute the median value, Y, of the
            squares of the elements of X.

       In each case, the original contents of the array X
       are to be left unchanged. Thus, a work area could
       be provided in which to store, in ascending
       sequence, the elements of X or their squares, prior
       to calculating the median value, Y.

       The two subprograms can be organized to use the
       same work-area, and thus save space. Accomplish
       this in the following two ways.

       (a) Write the two subprograms so that they share
            the same labelled common block for work space.

       (b) Combine the two subprograms into one with two
            entry points. By employing the same variable
            names, the same work space can be used for each
            problem. As well, with careful planning, parts
            of one program can be overlapped with parts of
            the other, to save program space.

Chapter 15

LOGICAL OPERATIONS

In many of the examples of previous chapters we have used
IF statements with logical expressions embedded in them. To
this point, we have treated such expressions rather casually.
All we have noted is that they yield a result which is either
true or false. The purpose of this chapter is to introduce
logical computations more formally.

15.1   LOGICAL CONSTANTS

There are only two logical constants and they are represented in FORTRAN as .TRUE. and .FALSE..

15.2   LOGICAL VARIABLES

Variables capable of being assigned values which are
logical constants are said to be logical variables. A logical
variable can be any valid FORTRAN symbolic name which is
declared in a LOGICAL declaration statement. For example, the
statement

LOGICAL A, B, SAM, T(10), D

declares each of A, B, SAM, and D to be logical variables and
T to be a logical one-dimensional array.

15.3   LOGICAL OPERATORS

Since logical variables and constants are not arithmetic quantities, they cannot be manipulated using the arithmetic operators +, -, *, /, and **. Three special <u>logical</u> <u>operators</u> are available; they are .AND., .OR., and .NOT..

Suppose X and Y are logical variables. The following statements define .AND., .OR., and .NOT..

(a)   The expression

X .AND. Y

has the value .TRUE. if and only if both X and Y have the value .TRUE.. Otherwise, it has the value .FALSE..

(b)   The expression

X .OR. Y

has the value .TRUE. if either or both of X and Y have the value .TRUE.. Thus the expression has the value .FALSE. if and only if both X and Y are .FALSE..

(c)   The expression

.NOT.X

has the value .TRUE. if X is .FALSE. and .FALSE. if X is .TRUE..

These definitions can be summarized in tabular form as follows.

X	Y	X.AND.Y	X.OR.Y	.NOT.X
.TRUE.	.TRUE.	.TRUE.	.TRUE.	.FALSE.
.TRUE.	.FALSE.	.FALSE.	.TRUE.	.FALSE.
.FALSE.	.TRUE.	.FALSE.	.TRUE.	.TRUE.
.FALSE.	.FALSE.	.FALSE.	.FALSE.	.TRUE.

15.4   RELATIONAL OPERATORS

There are six relational operators available in FORTRAN. Most of these have been encountered in examples used in previous chapters.

Operator	Meaning
.EQ.	equal to
.NE.	not equal to
.LT.	less than
.LE.	less than or equal to
.GT.	greater than
.GE.	greater than or equal to

These operators are binary operators which have two arithmetic expressions as operands; the result of the binary operation is always a logical value. Consider the following examples.

	FORTRAN	Algebra
(a)	I .GT. 4	$i > 4$
(b)	(I+2*J) .LT. K	$i + 2j < k$
(c)	(A+2*X) .EQ. 6.4.	$a + 2x = 6.4$
(d)	(X+COS(X)). NE. T(I)	$x + \cos x \neq t_i$
(e)	(I+4) .GE. ((X+J)/3)	$i + 4 \geq (x+j)/3$

Examples (a) and (b) have integer-valued expressions as operands. Examples (c) and (d) have real-valued expressions as operands, and (d) illustrates that functions and subscripted variables can be used in the expression. Finally, Example (e) illustrates that mixed-mode arithmetic can be used; in this case, one of the operands is an integer expression and the other is a real expression.

Each of the examples is an assertion which is either true or false. We can paraphrase the expression I.GT.4 as follows:

The current value of I is greater than four; this assertion is either true or false. Thus the expression I.GT.4, when computed, yields the result .TRUE. or .FALSE., depending on the current value of I. Similar explanations can be given for the other examples.

15.5   LOGICAL-VALUED EXPRESSIONS

Any expression which, when evaluated, produces a logical result is said to be a logical-valued expression, or, more briefly, a logical expression. Assuming that A, B, and X are variables of integer or real type, and that U, V, and W are of logical type, the following are examples of logical expressions.

(a)   .TRUE.

(b)   A .GT. B

(c)   A .GT. 6.4

(d)   .NOT.(A .GT. 6.4)

(e)   ((X+3.2) .LT.(SIN(A**2+1.))) .AND. (B .EQ. 3.)

(f)   U

(g)   .NOT.U .OR. V .AND. W

(h)   V .OR. .TRUE.

(i)   X .LE. .5

When arithmetic operators were introduced, the notion of operator priority was discussed. In a similar way, priorities for logical and relational operators have to be established. The complete operator list of FORTRAN, in order of decreasing priority is as follows.

function evaluations

**

* and /

+ and - (including unary + and -)

.EQ., .NE., .LT., .LE., .GT., and .GE.

.NOT.

.AND.

.OR.

Thus the logical expression (e) could be written as follows

X+3.2 .LT. SIN(A**2+1.) .AND. B .EQ. 3.

and would have exactly the same meaning, because of the rules of priority. This illustrates the fact that parentheses, while sometimes redundant, are nevertheless useful to help clarify the meaning of an expression. The expression (g) might be more clearly understood if written in the equivalent form

(.NOT.U) .OR. (V.AND.W)

15.6   LOGICAL ASSIGNMENT STATEMENTS

The general form of a logical assignment statement is

logical variable = logical expression

Examples are:

X = .TRUE.
Y = A .GT. B .OR. Y
Z = U .AND. V .OR. W

where X, Y, Z, U, V, and W are logical variables, and A and B are of real or integer type.

The computer first evaluates the logical expression, then assigns the result to the logical variable to the left of the equals sign.

Extended assignment statements can be used to assign more than one logical variable in a single FORTRAN statement. For example, the statement

$$U = V = W = .TRUE.$$

would assign the constant .TRUE. to each of the logical variables U, V, and W.

15.7   LOGICAL IF STATEMENT

In a previous chapter we defined and illustrated the use of the logical IF statement. It remains to be said that the logical expression used in the logical IF statement can be more flexible than has been illustrated in any examples to this point. The logical IF might look like any of the following:

(a)   IF (A .EQ. X+3.) QUIT

(b)   IF (A .LT. 1.0 .AND. B**2 .GT. 25.) PRINT, A

(c)   IF (X*SIN(Y) .GT. 0.) A(I) = B(I)

(d)   IF (.NOT.(A .EQ. B)) CALL SUBR(X, Y)

15.8   EXAMPLES USING LOGICAL OPERATIONS

Suppose TABLE is an array containing integer variables. Example 15.1 illustrates a subprogram for determining if a specific integer ARG is a member of the array. The logical variable RESULT will be .TRUE. if ARG is in the table; otherwise, RESULT will be returned as .FALSE..

```
C EXAMPLE 15.1
      SUBROUTINE LOOK (ARG, TABLE, SIZE, RESULT)
      INTEGER ARG, SIZE, TABLE(SIZE)
      LOGICAL RESULT
      RESULT = .FALSE.
      I = 1
      WHILE (.NOT.RESULT .AND. I .LE. SIZE)
          IF (ARG .EQ. TABLE(I)) RESULT = .TRUE.
          I = I + 1
      ENDWHILE
      RETURN
      END
```

Example 15.2 is identical with Example 15.1, except that a function subprogram is used instead of a subroutine subprogram.

Note that the variable LOOK, which is also the name of the function subprogram, is declared as logical in the first statement of the subprogram. This variable must also be declared as logical in the calling program.

```
C EXAMPLE 15.2
      LOGICAL FUNCTION LOOK (ARG, TABLE, SIZE)
      INTEGER ARG, SIZE, TABLE(SIZE)
      LOOK = .FALSE.
      I = 1
      WHILE (.NOT.LOOK .AND. I .LE. SIZE)
          IF (ARG .EQ. TABLE(I)) LOOK = .TRUE.
          I = I + 1
      ENDWHILE
      RETURN
      END
```

Logical variables can be useful in time-tabling and scheduling problems. Suppose that an institution operates on a schedule of 50 one-hour periods per week, and that 100 courses numbered 1 to 100 are taught. The time-table might be represented as in Figure 15.1.

The symbol T, representing true, indicates the periods at which a particular course meets. For example, course 3 meets

in periods 2 and 50, but not in periods 1, 3, 4, and 49. This
information could be stored as a two-dimensional table with
logical entries, set up with the declaration statement

LOGICAL TTABLE(100,50)

The time-table would probably be read into the computer from
data cards.

Period Course	1	2	3	4	.	.	49	50
1	T	F	F	T			F	F
2	F	F	F	F			T	F
3	F	T	F	F			F	T
4	F	F	F	F			F	F
.								
.								
99	T	F	F	F			F	F
100	F	F	T	F			T	F

Figure 15.1

Assuming the time-table is stored in memory, Example 15.3
shows how a subprogram could be written to detect whether or
not a conflict would arise as a result of the selection of a
particular set of courses. The set of N selected courses is
assumed to be stored in the vector called COURSE. The subroutine CNFLCT returns RESULT as .TRUE. if there is a conflict or
.FALSE. if not.

The inner WHILE loop employs the variable USED to indicate the availability of time period J. The first course
which requires time period J causes USED to assume the value
.TRUE. as a result of the statement

USED = USED .OR. TTABLE(COURSE(I),J)

- 201 -

```
C EXAMPLE 15.3
      SUBROUTINE CNFLCT (TTABLE, COURSE, N, RESULT)
      LOGICAL TTABLE(100,50), RESULT, USED
      INTEGER COURSE(10), N
      RESULT = .FALSE.
      IF (N .NE. 1) THEN
          J = 1
          WHILE (RESULT .AND. J .LE.  50)
              I = 1
              USED = .FALSE.
              WHILE (RESULT .AND. I .LE. N)
                  IF (USED .AND. TTABLE(COURSE(I),J)) THEN
                      RESULT = .TRUE.
                  ELSE
                      USED = USED .OR. TTABLE(COURSE(I),J)
                  ENDIF
                  I = I + 1
              ENDWHILE
              J = J + 1
          ENDWHILE
      ENDIF
      RETURN
      END
```

If a subsequent course also requires time period J, the IF statement causes RESULT to assume the value .TRUE., indicating a conflict. As a result, control transfers out of both the inner and outer WHILE loops since both test if RESULT is true. If, after checking all time periods using the outer WHILE-loop, no conflict is found, the subprogram returns RESULT as .FALSE.

This example also illustrates the use of a subscripted variable used as subscript, namely, TTABLE(COURSE(I),J).

15.9   FORMAT-FREE I/O OF LOGICAL VALUES

Whenever a logical variable appears in the list of a format-free PRINT statement, its value is printed as T or F depending on whether it has the value .TRUE. or .FALSE. Thus, the sequence of statements

```
            LOGICAL U, V, W
            X = 3.25
            I = 4
            U = V = .TRUE.
            W = .FALSE.
            PRINT, U, X, V, W, I
```
would cause the following line to be printed.

```
      T     3.2500000     T   F   4
```

Entire arrays of logical values can be printed, just as is the case for real or integer arrays. Consider the following examples with reference to the time-table described above.

(a)   PRINT, TTABLE

(b)   PRINT, ((TTABLE(I,J) ,I=1,100) ,J=1,50)

(c)   PRINT, ((TTABLE(I,J) ,J=1,50) ,I=1,100)

The first statement causes the entire time-table to be printed in storage order, which is column by column. The second statement uses a pair of nested implied DO's, and accomplishes exactly the same result as the first. The third statement causes the time-table to be printed row by row.

It is legal to use logical expressions in format-free PRINT or PUNCH statements. Thus the sequence of statements

```
            U = .TRUE.
            I = 3
            J = 4
            PRINT, I, J, I.GT.J, .NOT.U, .FALSE.
```
would cause the following line to be printed.

```
      3    4    F    F    F
```

Example 15.4 illustrates the use of format-free output of logical variables and also shows how logical operations can be useful in problems involving sets. Suppose three sets A, B, and C are defined as follows:

A: All points inside or on the circle

$$x^2 + y^2 = 25$$

B: All points inside the ellipse

$$\frac{x^2}{36} + \frac{y^2}{16} = 1$$

C: All points (x,y) which satisfy the condition $y > 1-x$

The program in Example 15.4 causes a data card containing the
co-ordinates of a point (x,y) to be read; it then determines
whether or not (x,y) is a member of each of the following
sets:

U: $A \cap B \cap C$

V: $\overline{A} \cap B \cap A \cap C$

W: $\overline{A} \cap (B \cup C)$

```
C EXAMPLE 15.4
      LOGICAL EA, EB, EC, EU, EV, EW
      READ, X, Y
      EA = (X**2 + Y**2) .LE. 25.
      EB = (X**2/36. + Y**2/16.) .LT. 1.
      EC = Y .GT. (1.-X)
      EU = EA .AND. EB .AND. EC
      EV = .NOT.EA .AND. EB.OR.EA .AND. EC
      EW = .NOT.EA .AND. (EB .OR. EC)
      PRINT, X, Y, EU, EV, EW
      STOP
      END
```

Logical constants can be read using the format-free input
statement READ. They can be punched as T or F, or as .TRUE.
or .FALSE., or as any combination of these representations.
Each constant must be separated from the next by a comma or by
at least one blank column. Thus an input data card might be
punched as follows.

T F .TRUE. .TRUE. ,T .FALSE.,F T

The rules for READ are otherwise identical with those outlined in the chapter entitled "Simple Input and Output".

15.10   FORMAT FOR I/O OF LOGICAL VALUES

The format code used for logical variables is Lw, where w denotes the width of the field. On output, the letter T or F is printed, depending upon whether the value is .TRUE. or .FALSE.. The T or F is right-justified in the field. For example, the statements

```
          LOGICAL U, V
          U = .TRUE.
          V = .FALSE.
          I = 3
          J = 760
          PRINT 5, I, U, J, V
    5     FORMAT('0', I5, L7, I4, L4)
```

would cause the following line to be printed.

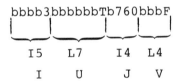

On input, a field of width w which consists of the next w columns of the card is scanned from left to right until T or F is encountered, and, correspondingly, .TRUE. or .FALSE. is assigned to the variable. For example, the time-table in Example 15.2 could be punched into 100 cards, one for each course. Column 1 to 3 would contain the course number and columns 4 to 53 would contain T's or F's depending upon the time-table for the particular course. These cards could be read as follows:

```
          DO 5 K=1,100
              READ6, I, (TTABLE(I,J), J=1,50)
    5     CONTINUE
    6     FORMAT(I3, 50L1)
```

If the input field is blank, the value .FALSE. is assigned to the corresponding variable.

15.11   EXERCISES

15.1   Suppose a data deck contains forty cards, each of which contains a student number and the student's marks in three examinations. These numbers are recorded as integers. Write a program which does the following:

(a)   reads the cards, and stores the student number and marks in four separate vectors.

(b)   scans the mark vectors, and sets up three logical vectors of forty elements each. These vectors reflect whether or not the student passed or failed the particular subject by using .TRUE. if the mark is greater than or equal to 50 and .FALSE. otherwise.

(c)   prints these logical vectors.

15.2   This is a continuation of Exercise 15.1. Use the three logical vectors as data to determine the total number of students who

(a)   passed each course, (that is, add up the number of "trues" in each vector).

(b)   passed all three courses

(c)   passed at least two courses

(d)   passed at least one course

(e)   passed courses one and two, failed three

(f)   passed course one or course two, failed course three

(g)   did not pass any courses

(h)   did not pass course one.

15.3   Write a logical-valued function subprogram called
ODD which accepts an integer value as input, and
determines whether or not it is odd. If it is odd,
the function returns a value of .TRUE.; otherwise,
the function returns a value of .FALSE.. The
subprogram should work for negative, zero, or positive integers.

15.4   The values for the elements of a two-dimensional
array of integers are read into the computer from
data cards. Use the function subprogram ODD,
written in Exercise 15.3, to help solve the
following problem.

(a)   The program is to compute the total number of
odd integers in the array.

(b)   Write a second program which determines the
number of pairs of odd integers in each column
of the array. A pair of odd integers is
defined as two consecutive elements, both of
which have odd values. Thus, if the column had
ten elements, all of which are odd, it would
have nine pairs.

15.5   With reference to Example 15.4, write a program
which reads several data cards, each containing a
pair of co-ordinates defining a point (x,y). Determine how many of the points are in each of the
following sets.

(a) $A \cup B \cup C$

(b) $\bar{A} \cup \bar{B} \cup C$

(c) $\overline{A \cup B \cap C}$

15.6 Test the subroutine CNFLCT used in Example 15.3 by punching some data for a time-table, storing it, and reading in other data for students' course selections. To reduce the volume of data, it is probably best to reduce the number of courses and periods to 20 and 15 respectively.

15.7 Suppose each course were offered in two sections, with each section at two different time periods. Thus, if a conflict existed for one time period, it might not for the other. Re-program the subroutine CNFLCT to reflect this extension of the problem. Note that this is not just a trivial modification of CNFLCT, but requires a complete re-thinking of the various aspects of the problem. For example, how will the time-table be stored? Also, when no conflict is found, how are the appropriate sections indicated?

    The problem can be further extended by allowing a variable number of sections for each course, some of which may be at the same time period.

15.8 Use format statements whenever input-output is required in the above problems if you have not already done so. For example, the time-table data could be punched in consecutive columns of the card, thus saving space on the card.

15.9 Given a square array of points, connection between points is defined by horizontal and vertical lines.

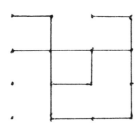

One way of representing a connection between two points is to define two arrays to represent horizontal and vertical connections of points. For example, the element HOR(I,J) of a logical array has a value .TRUE. if, in row I, the J'th point starting from the left is connected to the (J+1)'st point. Thus, in the following diagram

```
    HOR(1,1)      HOR(1,2)      HOR(1,3)

 .━━━━━━━━━━━━.              .━━━━━━━━━━━.

    HOR(2,1)      HOR(2,2)      HOR(2,3)

              .━━━━━━━━━━━━━.
```

HOR(1,1), HOR(1,3), and HOR(2,2) would have value .TRUE., and HOR(1,2), HOR(2,1), and HOR(2,3) would have value .FALSE.. A similar technique could be used to define vertical connections using a logical array, VER, say.

Write a program which reads in a set of connections between n^2 points, which represents internally the required figure (assume $2 \leq n \leq 5$), and which determines the number of squares formed by the connections. (E.g., for the given figure there are two squares of size 1, and 1 square of size 2). Your program should print the number of squares of each size.

Chapter 16

DOUBLE PRECISION

It is often desirable to do computations using real arithmetic, but with more significant digits than the seven allowed using single-precision constants. When this need arises, it is convenient to employ the double-precision features of the FORTRAN language. It should be noted that these features should not be used indiscriminately, since more memory space is required in the computer, and the computations usually proceed more slowly.

16.1   DOUBLE-PRECISION CONSTANTS

Double-precision constants are similar to real constants except that each of them occupies double the physical space in the computer's memory. As a consequence, over 16 significant digits are recorded. The range of magnitude remains between 10^{-78} and 10^{75}, approximately. Note that, while the term "double precision" implies a doubling of the precision, in actual practice, more than a doubling is achieved. This is because of the nature of the hardware in the IBM 360 computer. Since the precision is not really doubled, this feature is frequently referred to as extended precision rather than double precision.

Now that we have introduced double precision, it will be convenient to refer to the other real constants and variables as having single precision.

Examples of double-precision constants are as follows:

(a)　12.3456789

(b)　12.3456789D-11

(c)　1.25D2

(d)　0.D0

(e)　12345678.12345678D6

Note that the constant (a) has more than seven digits, and so is automatically taken to be in double precision. In Example (b), the letter D is used to denote exponentiation (recall that E was used in single-precision constants). Example (c) shows that the constant can have fewer than eight digits and still be a double-precision constant, because of the presence of the D. Example (d) shows how zero can be written as a double-precision constant.

The following are examples of invalid double-precision constants.

(a)　1.2D+362　　Magnitude out of range.

(b)　3,865D3　　Comma not allowed.

(c)　3　　　　　No decimal - this is an integer constant.

16.2　DOUBLE-PRECISION VARIABLES

Variables capable of being assigned values which are double-precision constants are said to be double-precision variables. A double-precision variable can be any valid FORTRAN symbolic name which is declared in a DOUBLE PRECISION declaration statement. For example, the statement

DOUBLE PRECISION A, B, C(18)

declares A and B to be double-precision real variables, and C to be an array with the 18 double-precision elements, C(1), C(2), C(3), ..., C(18).

- 211 -

16.3   DOUBLE-PRECISION EXPRESSIONS

Any expression which, when evaluated, produces a double-precision result is said to be a <u>double-precision</u> <u>expression</u>. If variables have been declared using the statements

        DOUBLE PRECISION A, B, C
        REAL X, Y, Z
        INTEGER I, J, K, L, M, N

the following are examples of double-precision expressions.

  (a)   1.3D20

  (b)   A

  (c)   (.1D0 * A + B) / (C**A - 8.2D0)

  (d)   (A + X + I + L) / (A*X - I**L)

  (e)   A + .1D0

  (f)   A + .1

Examples (a) and (b) illustrate the simplest of double-precision expressions.

Example (c) illustrates the fact that the arithmetic operators can be used in a double-precision expression, with the usual rules of priority applying.

Examples (d), (e), and (f) show that it is completely acceptable to mix modes between real, integer, and double-precision operands. In general, the resulting expression is a double-precision expression. Evaluation proceeds from left to right, taking into account priority of operators and parenthesized expressions. Whenever a binary operator has only one of its operands in double precision, the other is converted to double precision. This conversion is done by

  (a)   filling out single-precision constants with zeros,

  (b)   converting integers exactly.

Thus the expressions A+.1D0 and A+.1 do not produce the same result. In the first case, .1D0 is a double-precision constant, accurate to 16 figures; in the second case, .1 is converted to a double-precision value but the converted value is accurate only to seven figures. This illustrates that care must be taken when using mixed-mode expressions.

To complete this section, it is in order to mention that logical expressions of the type A.GT.X or A.LE.I are allowed. In other words, the expressions used as the two operands can be of different types, including double-precision.

16.4   DOUBLE-PRECISION ASSIGNMENT STATEMENTS

The general form of a double-precision assignment statement is

double-precision variable = any arithmetic expression

Assuming A, B, and C to be of double-precision, examples are:

   (a)   A = 1.2D10

   (b)   B(10) = A**2 + 3

   (c)   B(J) = B(J-1)

   (d)   A = D

   (e)   A = .1

The computer first evaluates the arithmetic expression, then assigns the result to the double-precision variable to the left of the equals sign. If the arithmetic expression is not of double precision, the result is converted to double-precision using the same rule stated for evaluation of mixed-mode arithmetic expressions. Thus, in Example (e) the variable A would not be assigned the double-precision version of .1; it would be assigned the single-precision version filled out with zeros.

16.5   DOUBLE-PRECISION BUILT-IN FUNCTIONS

Many double-precision built-in functions are available. For example, DSQRT(d) will evaluate the double-precision square root of a double-precision expression d. Similarly, we can evaluate the double-precision sine, cosine, arctan, exponential, logarithm, and absolute value, using DSIN(d), DCOS(d), DATAN(d), DEXP(d), DLOG(d) and DABS(d). A complete list of available built-in functions can be consulted in Appendix A.

Since the WATFIV-S compiler knows about the double-precision built-in functions, it can provide a type for them automatically. Thus, as a convenience to the programmer, there is no need to declare their names to be of type double precision in a program segment which might use them.

The functions DBLE(r) and SNGL(d) deserve special comment. DBLE(r) takes the calculated value of a real expression r and converts it to a double-precision result. This is done by filling out the single-precision constant with zeros. SNGL(d) converts the value of the double-precision expression d to single precision by truncating the extra digits; rounding does not take place. Note also that SNGL is a single-precision real function.

16.6   EXAMPLE

Extended precision is useful, and often necessary, in many types of computations. Most examples require a specialized understanding of the numerical properties of the particular problem being considered, and so are not of general interest. In order to give an illustration of the mechanics of using double precision, the following problem is considered.

Each term of the Fibonacci sequence

$$1, 1, 2, 3, 5, 8, 13, 21, 34, \ldots$$

is formed by taking the sum of the previous two terms. Thus, if the sequence is written as

$$f_1, f_2, f_3, f_4, \ldots, f_n, \ldots$$

it can be defined using the rule

$$f_1 = f_2 = 1 \qquad f_{n+2} = f_{n+1} + f_n$$

Mathematicians have discovered that the ratio of consecutive terms approaches the constant value $(1 + \sqrt{5})/2$, as n approaches infinity. In mathematical notation

$$\lim_{n \to \infty} \frac{f_n}{f_{n-1}} = \frac{1 + \sqrt{5}}{2}$$

Consider the problem of calculating $(1+\sqrt{5})/2$ as accurately as possible using double precision, and of determining how large n must be in order to have the ratio f_n/f_{n-1} at least as accurate. A program to do this could be written as in Example 16.1.

```
C EXAMPLE 16.1 - FIBONACCI PROBLEM
      DOUBLE PRECISION CONST, RATIO, DABS
      DOUBLE PRECISION FNM2, FNM1, FN
      CONST = (1.D0 + DSQRT(5.D0)) / 2.D0
      PRINT, CONST
      N = 3
      FNM2 = 1.D0
      FNM1 = 1.D0
      LOOP
          FN = FNM1 + FNM2
          RATIO = FN / FNM1
          IF (DABS(CONST-RATIO) .LT. 1.D-15) QUIT
          FNM2 = FNM1
          FNM1 = FN
          N = N + 1
      ENDLOOP
      PRINT, N, RATIO
      STOP
      END
```

The output for Example 16.1 is illustrated below, and shows that one must go as far as the 38'th term of the sequence in order to produce the constant $(1 + \sqrt{5})/2$ to 16 digits by taking the ratio of consecutive terms.

        0.1618033988749894D 01
    38   0.1618033988749894D 01

16.7   FORMAT-FREE I/O OF DOUBLE-PRECISION VALUES

Whenever a double-precision variable appears in the list of a format-free PRINT statement, its value is printed with 16 digits of precision using the D exponent. As is the case for single-precision variables, entire arrays can be printed by using the array name in the PRINT list. Also, double-precision expressions can appear in the PRINT list, and their computed values are printed.

It is possible to assign values to double-precision variables by using the READ statement. In this case, the double-precision constants are punched on data cards, and are separated by a comma or at least by one blank column. They can be punched in D exponent form, or as real constants without exponents. For example, .1 can appear on the data card; when assigned to a double-precision variable by using a READ statement, it will be converted with 16 digits of precision, just as if it had been punched as .1D0.

16.8   FORMAT FOR I/O OF DOUBLE-PRECISION VALUES

Double-precision values can be printed using either D format or F format; E format cannot be used.

D format works exactly like E format, except that more significant digits can be printed, and the symbol D is used to denote exponentiation, as seen in the output from

Example 16.1. The format code Dw.d specifies that the variable whose value is to be printed is of double precision, and is to be printed right-justified in the next w print positions, with a precision of d significant digits. In general, the output will be according to the following pattern.

$$\underline{+}0.\underbrace{xxxxxxxxxx}D\underline{+}xx$$

d digits

Thus it follows that, unless $w \geq d+7$, a format error will occur.

When double-precision values are printed using F format, the rules are identical with those for real variables.

For input, double-precision values are read using the F and D format codes. The rules are essentially the same as those for reading single-precision values using the F and E format codes, as outlined in Chapter 10.

16.9   EXERCISES

16.1   (a)   Write a program to compute n! (n factorial) for n = 0, 1, 2, ..., 18. Note that double-precision real arithmetic is the easiest way to achieve accurate results.

   (b)   Modify the program so that it becomes a subprogram, FACT, which stores the nineteen values in an array.

   (c)   Write a subprogram, COMB, designed to compute the number of combinations of n things taken r at a time using the formula

$$(n \text{ choose } r) = \binom{n}{r} = \frac{n!}{r!(n-r)!}.$$

- 217 -

This subprogram should use the array formed by the previously written subprogram.

(d)   Write a main program which reads data cards containing values for n and r, and uses COMB and FACT to compute (n choose r). Note that FACT should be executed only once, i.e., it is an initializing subroutine.

16.2   In the computation of compound interest, it is important to have tables of the function

$$(1+i)^n$$

where i is an interest rate, and n is an integer indicating a number of time periods. These tables are often required to eight or more decimal places. Write a program to compute this function for i = .0025 and n = 1, 2, 3, ..., 50. Each answer should be rounded to eight decimal places. Printing should be controlled, by using format, to produce only eight decimal places.

16.3   The mathematical functions sine, cosine, and exponential can be evaluated using the following series.

$$\sin x = \frac{x}{1!} - \frac{x^3}{3!} + \frac{x^5}{5!} - \frac{x^7}{7!} + \ldots$$

$$\cos x = 1 - \frac{x^2}{2!} + \frac{x^4}{4!} - \frac{x^6}{6!} + \ldots$$

$$\exp x = 1 + \frac{x}{1!} + \frac{x^2}{2!} + \frac{x^3}{3!} + \ldots$$

Write a program which evaluates each of these functions, using both the extended-precision built-in
functions and the above series. Determine, for x =
.1, the number of terms of the series which are
required, in each case, to produce the same precision as the built-in function.

16.4 In Exercise 5.11, we wrote a program to do extended-
precision multiplication with integers. Suppose we
now consider extended-precision division. The dividend has 16 significant digits, and is stored as two
integer constants, the first set of eight digits as
one integer, and the second set of eight digits as
the other.

(a) Write a program which divides an extended-precision integer by another integer of up to
eight digits of precision. The result is to be
a quotient of no more than eight digits. The
program should be designed to reject divisions
by zero or divisions which would result in a
quotient of more than eight digits.

(b) Make the necessary modifications to your
program for part (a) so that it computes the
eight-digit remainder as well.

(c) Try the program on the computer for various
values of the dividend and divisor. Check to
see that it handles all possible combinations
of signs.

Chapter 17

COMPLEX OPERATIONS

FORTRAN permits arithmetic computations with complex numbers. This is accomplished by defining complex constants, complex variables, and complex functions, and using them in the appropriate FORTRAN statements. It is also possible to do complex arithmetic in extended precision.

17.1   COMPLEX CONSTANTS

In mathematical textbooks, complex numbers are usually written in the form a+ib, where a and b are real numbers and $i^2=-1$. At times they are written in vector form as (a,b), with the first component "a" representing the real part and the second component "b" representing the imaginary part. This latter technique is used in FORTRAN. Thus typical complex constants would be

$$(1.24,-6.8)$$
$$(0.,0.)$$
$$(.2456E-8,-7.3)$$

Note that both components are real constants, they are separated by a comma, and the pair is enclosed in parentheses. Illegal forms follow.

(1,2)   Integer constants must not be used.
(2.68,X)   A variable must not be used.

17.2   COMPLEX VARIABLES

Variables capable of being assigned values which are complex constants are said to be complex variables. A complex variable can be any valid FORTRAN symbolic name which is declared in a COMPLEX declaration statement. For example, the statement

COMPLEX A, B(25), K

declares A and K to be complex variables, and B to be an array of 25 complex elements.

17.3   COMPLEX-VALUED EXPRESSIONS

Any expression which, when evaluated, produces a complex result is said to be a complex-valued expression, or, more briefly, a complex expression. If A and B are complex variables, the following are legal complex expressions.

(a)   A + B

(b)   A - B

(c)   A*B

(d)   A/B

(e)   (A+B)**2 - A/(2.0,3.0)*B

(f)   2*A + 3.6*B + 5

(g)   CSQRT(A*B)

Examples (a), (b), (c), and (d) illustrate how complex numbers can be added, subtracted, multiplied, or divided. Of course, the rules of complex arithmetic are used, and the result is a complex constant.

Example (e) illustrates the use of all possible arithmetic operators in a single expression. The established rules of priority apply to complex operations. It is important to note that exponentiation of complex expressions is permitted, but the exponent <u>must</u> be an integer expression. Furthermore, complex expressions can never be used as exponents of any type of expression.

Example (f) illustrates that mixed-mode arithmetic is permitted. As the expression is evaluated, the constants 2, 3.6, and 5 are converted to the complex constants (2.0,0.), (3.6,0.0), and (5.0,0.0), and the final result is complex.

Example (g) includes a complex built-in function which will be explained later.

17.4   COMPLEX ASSIGNMENT STATEMENTS

A complex variable can be assigned a value using a complex assignment statement of the form

    complex variable = expression

If the expression is complex, the complex variable assumes this value. If the expression is not complex, its value is converted to a complex value before assignment takes place; the value of the expression is assigned to the real part and zero is assigned to the imaginary part. Of course, the expression cannot be logical-valued, nor can it be a char-acter value.

Assuming A, B, and C to be complex, the following are valid assignment statements.

                    A = (2.0,-4.8)
                    B = (A+3)*B
                    C(I,3) = (A+B)**2
                    B = 6
                    A = 0

17.5   COMPLEX BUILT-IN FUNCTIONS

Many of the commonly used mathematical routines are available as built-in functions. For example, CSQRT(c) will compute the square root of the value of a complex expression c. Of course, the result is, in general, another complex number. Some other available functions are CSIN(c), CCOS(c), CEXP(c), and CLOG(c), to calculate the sine, cosine, exponential, and logarithm respectively. As a convenience to the programmer, WATFIV-S automatically assumes these built-in functions to be of type complex. A complete list is given in Appendix A.

It is worth underlining the usefulness of the function CMPLX(r_1,r_2). It has already been pointed out that it is illegal to write a complex constant as

$$(X,3.4)$$

where X is a real variable or real expression. This is accomplished by using the built-in function CMPLX as follows:

$$CMPLX(X,3.4)$$

The function CMPLX is used extensively in the examples which follow.

It is also worth noting that, while most functions used with complex numbers yield complex values as their result, some of them produce real values. For example, CABS(c) produces $\sqrt{a^2 + b^2}$, where a+ib is the complex constant produced when c is evaluated. In a similar fashion, REAL(c) produces the real number a (the real part of c); and AIMAG(c) produces the real number b (the imaginary part of c).

17.6   EXAMPLES

Example 17.1 tabulates the function

$$w = 1+z+z^2$$

for $z = x+iy$

$$x = 0, .1, .2, \ldots, 1.0,$$

and $y = 0, .2, .4, \ldots, 3.0$

This example uses mainly real arithmetic, but changes to complex arithmetic in the statement Z=CMPLX(X,Y) just in time evaluate the complex arithmetic and print the results.   The loops are controlled using the real and imaginary parts of the complex independent variable.

```
C EXAMPLE 17.1
      COMPLEX W, Z
      Y = 0.
      LOOP
          X = 0.
          LOOP
              Z = CMPLX(X,Y)
              W = 1. + Z + Z**2
              PRINT, Z, W
              X = X + .1
              IF (X .GT. 1.) QUIT
          ENDLOOP
          Y = Y + .2
          IF (Y .GT. 3.) QUIT
      ENDLOOP
      STOP
      END
```

The same problem can be solved using the built-in functions REAL and AIMAG as illustrated in Example 17.2.

Note that REAL and AIMAG are not declared as complex functions because they produce real results.   Also REAL and AIMAG do not have to be declared as REAL, because any variable or function name beginning with letters other than I to N inclusive is automatically real, unless declared otherwise.

```
C EXAMPLE 17.2
      COMPLEX Z, W
      Z = 0.
      LOOP
          LOOP
              W = 1. + Z + Z**2
              PRINT, Z, W
              Z = CMPLX(REAL(Z)+.1, AIMAG(Z))
              IF (REAL(Z) .GT. 1.) QUIT
          ENDLOOP
          Z = CMPLX(0., AIMAG(Z)+.2)
          IF (AIMAG(Z) .GT. 3.) QUIT
      ENDLOOP
      STOP
      END
```

Example 17.3 illustrates how the function

$$\overline{w} = \cos(1 + \sqrt{z} + z^2)$$

could be tabulated in the circular region

$$|z| < 1$$

```
C EXAMPLE 17.3
      COMPLEX Z , W
      Z = (-.9,-.9)
      LOOP
          LOOP
              IF (CABS(Z) .LT. 1.) THEN
                  W = CONJG(CCOS(1. + CSQRT(Z) + Z**2))
                  PRINT, Z, W
              ENDIF
              Z = CMPLX(REAL(Z) + .1, AIMAG(Z))
              IF (REAL(Z) .GT. .9) QUIT
          ENDLOOP
          Z = CMPLX(-.9, AIMAG(Z) + .1)
          IF (AIMAG(Z) .GT. .9) QUIT
      ENDLOOP
      STOP
      END
```

To illustrate the use of a complex FUNCTION subprogram, we will write a routine called MAX which is designed to find the complex number of largest magnitude in an array of complex numbers.

```
C EXAMPLE 17.4
      COMPLEX FUNCTION MAX (N, A)
      COMPLEX A(N)
      MAX = A(1)
      IF (N .NE. 1) THEN
          DO 7 I=1,N
              IF (CABS(A(I)) .GT. CABS(MAX)) MAX=A(I)
7         CONTINUE
      ENDIF
      RETURN
      END
```

Note that the function name MAX is declared complex in the statement

COMPLEX FUNCTION MAX(N,A)

Furthermore, MAX must be declared as complex in the calling program segment.

17.7   <u>EXTENDED</u> <u>PRECISION</u> <u>WITH</u> <u>COMPLEX</u> <u>NUMBERS</u>

Any complex constant can have extended precision, provided <u>both</u> of its real components have double precision. Examples are

(1.0D0,-8.D11)

(.123456789,0.D0)

Extended-precision complex variables can be declared in a COMPLEX*16 declaration statement. For example

COMPLEX*16 A, B, C(8), D

declares A, B, and D as extended-precision complex variables and declares C to be an array with 8 extended-precision complex elements.

Double-precision complex expressions are those which give a computed result which is of double precision complex. All the rules for single-precision complex expressions apply in a similar fashion to double-precision complex expressions.

Furthermore, it is permissible to mix modes between single-precision complex, extended-precision complex, real, double-precision, and integer expressions. In all cases, the output of an expression is re-typed to suit the type of arithmetic which is to be done, and, wherever possible, precision is not reduced. Remember that it is never possible to use a complex number, either with single or extended precision, as an exponent. Also, exponents of complex expressions can only be integer expressions.

As an illustration of one of the rules for mixed-mode arithmetic, consider the expression:

$$1.2D6 + (1.0,6.3)$$

The result would be an extended-precision complex constant. This is because the constant 1.2D6 is first converted to the extended-precision complex constant (1.2D6,0.D0); then the constant (1.0,6.3) is converted to extended precision by filling out the real and imaginary components with zeros. Finally, the two extended-precision complex constants are added together.

A set of extended-precision complex built-in functions is available. For example, CDSQRT(epc) computes the square root of the computed result of the extended-precision complex expression epc. The result is an extended-precision complex number. The complete list of built-in functions is in Appendix A. Since they are built-in functions, WATFIV-S provides their proper type automatically.

17.8   FORMAT-FREE I/O OF COMPLEX VALUES

Whenever a complex variable appears in the list of a format-free PRINT statement, its value is printed as two real constants side by side. If the variable is of single precision, the two constants are printed with seven digits of precision and use the E exponent; if the variable is of extended precision, the two constants each have 16 digits of precision and use the D exponent. An entire array of complex constants can be printed by placing its name in the PRINT list. Complex expressions can appear in the PRINT list, and their computed values are printed.

When format-free input is used with complex variables, the complex values must be punched on the data cards in the same manner they would appear in a FORTRAN program. Thus, they must be pairs of real constants, separated by a comma, and enclosed in parentheses. If more than one complex constant is punched on a single data card, a comma or at least one blank column must separate each from its successor.

17.9   FORMAT FOR I/O OF COMPLEX VALUES

There is no special format code for handling complex values. Since every complex number is really a pair of real numbers, we use either a pair of E or a pair of D format codes, depending upon whether single or extended precision is needed. For either precision, a pair of F codes can be used instead of the E or D codes, or a combination of F and E or F and D is acceptable.

For example, consider the statements:

```
          X = (1.0,-8.6)
          PRINT 5, X
     5    FORMAT('0', E20.8, E20.8)
```

The printer would double space, and the two components 1.0 and -8.6 would be printed, using the E20.8 code. Alternatively, the FORMAT statement could have been any of the following:

```
     5    FORMAT('0', F20.4, E18.6)
     5    FORMAT('0', 2F20.6)
     5    FORMAT('0', E14.5, F18.6)
```

For input, complex numbers are punched as two real constants, both having either single or double precision. They are read in using any combination of E and F for single precision, and any combination of D and F for double precision.

17.10   EXERCISES

17.1   Write a program which reads in two complex numbers A and B, using format-free input. Perform the following computations.

(a)   C = A + B

(b)   C = A - B

(c)   C = A*B

(d)   C = A/B

Verify that the results are consistent with the rules of complex arithmetic.

17.2   Write programs which tabulate the following functions. Here, $i^2 = -1$.

(a) $f(x) = (1+i)x^2 + (7+3i)x + 5 - 6i$ for $x = 0, -1, -2, \ldots, -8$.

(b) $f(z) = z^3 + 3z + y$ where $z = x + iy$
       for $x = 0, 1, 2, \ldots, 7$,
       and $y = -3, -1, 1, \ldots, 9$,
       for each value of x.

(c) $f(z) = e^z + \sqrt{\sin z}$
       where $z = x + iy$
       for $x = 0, .8, 1.6, \ldots, 4.0$,
       and $y = 0, .5, 1.0, \ldots, 3.0$,
       for each value of x.

(d) $f(x) = (x^2+3x+6) + i(2x^2+7)$

for x = 0, 1, 2, ..., 10.

17.3 It is well known that sin x and exp x can be represented by the following series:

$$\sin x = x - \frac{x^3}{3!} + \frac{x^5}{5!} - \frac{x^7}{7!}$$

$$\exp x = 1 + \frac{x}{1!} + \frac{x^2}{2!} + \frac{x^3}{3!}$$

The series can also be used if x is a complex number.

(a) Write a program that evaluates sin x and exp x, where x = a+ib for a = 1, 2, 3, ..., 5, and b = -2, -1, 0, 1, ..., 4, for each value of a. Use both the series (ten terms) and the built-in functions CSIN and CEXP. Compare your results.

(b) How many terms of the series are required to compute the real and imaginary parts of sin x and exp x to five decimal places for x = 1+i?

17.4 The quadratic equation

$$ax^2 + bx + c = 0,$$

where a, b, and c, are real values, has complex roots when $b^2 < 4ac$. Write a program which uses complex arithmetic to compute the roots of any quadratic equation (note that a is not equal 0) regardless of whether the roots are complex or not. Test your program using the following values of a, b, and c:

a	b	c
5	5	4
2	4	2
1	0	16
3	0	37
1	2	0
3	0	0

17.5 Calculate the modulus and complex conjugate of the function

$$f(z) = z^2 + \sin z + e^z$$

for $x = y$, where $z = x+iy$. Use the values 0, 1, 2, ..., 10, for x.

17.6 Write a program to do the following:

(a) Generate a 3 by 3 matrix A, with complex entries, such that

$$A_{jk} = j + ik \qquad i^2 = -1$$

(b) Print out the matrix.

(c) The complex conjugate, $\overline{A}$, of A has elements

$$\overline{A}_{jk} = j - ik$$

Calculate the complex conjugate $\overline{A}$, and print it out.

(d) Multiply the 2 matrices A and $\overline{A}$, using complex arithmetic, and print out the product.

17.7 Develop a logical-valued statement function, called TEST, designed to take, as inputs, two complex numbers X and Y. This statement function is to have the value .TRUE. if $|X^2 + Y^2| < \sqrt{2}$, .FALSE. otherwise. Using one program, test your statement function on the following two cases:

(a) X = 1 + i

Y = 2 - i

(b) $X = \dfrac{1}{2} + \dfrac{1}{5}i$

$Y = \dfrac{3}{10} - \dfrac{1}{4}i$

Your program should print (using FORMAT statements) the values for X and Y, as well as the word .TRUE. or the word .FALSE., depending upon the value yielded by TEST.

17.8 Write a subroutine subprogram, called TEST, designed to accept as input a square matrix A with complex numbers for elements. Determine if the matrix A satisfies both of the following properties:

(a) $A_{kk} = k + ik$ $k = 1, 2, \ldots, N$ $(i^2 = -1)$

(b) $A_{kj} = 0$ $k \neq j$ $k, j = 1, 2, \ldots, N$

$(N \leq 25)$

The output from the subroutine should be a logical-valued variable having the value .TRUE. if the input matrix satisfies both of the conditions above, .FALSE. otherwise.

Chapter 18

HARDWARE-DEPENDENT FEATURES

It has often been said that languages such as FORTRAN are
machine-independent, that is, programs written in FORTRAN are
capable of being processed on any computer for which a
compiler exists. Although this would be ideal, in actual fact
there are many variations of FORTRAN. These differ slightly
because any particular computer for which a compiler has been
created will have its own special features. Consequently,
programs written in FORTRAN may require some modification if
they are to yield the same results when run on different
computers.

This chapter is meant to outline features of the IBM
computer which, to some extent, affect the results obtainable
by FORTRAN programs written to be processed using WATFIV-S.
It will also put the reader in a better position to understand
those features of FORTRAN, peculiar to the IBM computer,
described in succeeding chapters.

The WATFIV-S compiler was originally written for use with
the IBM 360 series of computers, and the information that
follows in this chapter mentions the IBM computer as if it
were the only one available for WATFIV-S users. That is not,
in fact, the case since over the years other computers have
been introduced that are basically the same as the 360 line;
it is now possible to run WATFIV-S on various computers. Some
newer computers are the 370, 3000, 4300 series from IBM, and

compatible machines produced by other manufacturers such as the Amdahl Corporation and the Magnuson Systems Corporation.

18.1   MEMORY AND ADDRESSING

The memory of the IBM computer is composed of eight-bit modules called bytes. The size of the memory on a particular machine depends on the computer model used and on the economic resources of the installation. Memory sizes vary from several thousand to several million bytes. However, a programmer may not have all the memory of a particular machine at his disposal, since he may have to share it with other programs which are in the computer at the same time. Machines which use WATFIV-S have at least 128K bytes, where K equals 1024.

Each byte is assigned a reference number called its address. Addresses always start at zero, and increase by unity to the number of bytes in the memory. Machine-language instructions gain access to a particular byte in memory by specifying the address of that byte.

Certain machine-language instructions operate on adjacent groups of bytes which are referred to as half words, full words, and double words. These consist of two, four, and eight bytes respectively. Often a full word, or four bytes, is called a word, for brevity. The address of a group of bytes is the address of its farthest left or lowest-numbered byte. An address which is a multiple of 2, 4, or 8 is called a half-word, full-word, or double-word boundary respectively. Note that all double-word boundaries are also full-word boundaries and half-word boundaries, but not vice-versa.

The original IBM 360 line of computers was designed so that when a half word in memory was referenced, the half word had to be stored aligned on a half-word boundary. Similarly, full-word and double-word operands had to be properly aligned in memory on their corresponding boundaries. Invalidly aligned operands, when referenced at execution time, would cause the program to terminate with an error condition. Newer models of computers, e.g., IBM 370, 3000, 4300 series and compatible machines of other manufacturers, now have hardware that automatically corrects for invalidly aligned operands, so that boundary alignment is not the problem it was on the 360 series machines. However, even the newer computers suffer some degradation in performance when the hardware references invalidly aligned operands.

The FORTRAN programmer usually need not concern himself with proper boundary alignment because the compiler takes care of storage allocation for variables and automatically provides the alignment. The exception is that the programmer can construct a common block which can force invalid boundary alignment for some variables in the block. The compiler diagnoses this, however, and provides a warning message. Furthermore, if the block is not reconstructed to provide the proper alignment, the compiler, at execution time (if the program executes on a 360-type machine), will move invalidly aligned operands, when referenced, to valid boundaries before performing any operations on them. If the program executes on a 370 or newer type machine, the hardware automatically compensates for the invalid alignment. In either case execution of the program can be slowed, and invalid alignment should be avoided when possible.

18.2   INTEGER VARIABLES

A FORTRAN integer variable occupies a full word of memory. Positive values are stored in true binary form, and negative values in twos-complement form. The farthest-left bit in the word is taken as the sign, with zero representing plus, one representing minus. This storage scheme restricts integer values to the range from -2^{31} to $2^{31}-1$, i.e., -2147483648 to 2147483647.

In a previous chapter, we warned the reader that it was the programmer's responsibility to ensure that results of computations with integers do not fall outside this range, since the compiler gives no indication of such occurrences. If, for example, two integers such as 2147483645 and 129 are added, the result cannot be stored in a full word; the result overflows a word, or a fixed-point overflow is said to occur. The computer ignores the over-flowed part of the result, and proceeds with the part that will fit into a word. This can lead to unexpected results. The term fixed-point constant is also used as a synonym for integer constant.

The computer has machine-language instructions for doing integer arithmetic with half-word operands. The farthest-left bit of the half word is used as the sign; positive values are in true binary and negative values in twos-complement notation. Thus, the range of values is from -2^{15} to $2^{15}-1$, i.e., -32768 to 32767. Half-word integers allow a saving in space at the expense of a decrease in precision of values that may be used. Also, fixed-point overflow can occur with improper use of half-word integers.

18.3 REAL VARIABLES

A FORTRAN real variable occupies a full word of memory, and is stored according to the notation for single-precision normalized floating-point numbers in the computer. This means that a word contains both a fraction and an exponent which specify the value of the number. A different notational system - hexadecimal - is used for arithmetic, and a few words might be said about this notation.

The base used in hexadecimal arithmetic is 16, and hence
16 symbols are required to express numbers to this base. For
convenience, the characters 0, 1, 2, 3, 4, 5, 6, 7, 8, 9, A,
B, C, D, E, and F, are used as hexadecimal digits. A number
expressed in hexadecimal notation can be expressed in binary
notation by expanding each hexadecimal digit to an equivalent
four-bit binary number (see Figure 18.1). Thus, the decimal
number 156 has hexadecimal representation 9C or binary representation 10011100, since 1001 and 1100 are binary representations of hexadecimal digits 9 and C respectively. Similarly,
any binary integer can be expressed in hexadecimal form by
grouping the bits into groups of four from the right, and
replacing each group by the equivalent hexadecimal digit.

0	1	2	3	4	5	6	7
0000	0001	0010	0011	0100	0101	0110	0111

8	9	A	B	C	D	E	F
1000	1001	1010	1011	1100	1101	1110	1111

Figure 18.1

Hexadecimal Digits and Binary Equivalents

Figure 18.2 (b) shows the internal format of a floating-
point number in the IBM computer, corresponding to a number
written symbolically as .f x 16^e. Here f represents a hexadecimal fraction different from zero, and e represents the exponent of the base 16. For example, .A4 x 16^1 is equivalent to
the decimal number .1025 x 10^2. The fraction f is stored as

six hexadecimal digits, $h_1h_2h_3h_4h_5h_6$, in the three farthest-right bytes of the word; the sign of f is the first bit of the farthest-left byte, and is zero for positive and one for negative. Normalized numbers always have h_1 greater than zero. To allow for positive and negative exponents, <u>excess-64</u> notation is used, that is, the <u>characteristic</u> is obtained by adding 64 (=40, hexadecimal) to the exponent e, and this is stored in the seven farthest-right bits of the first byte.

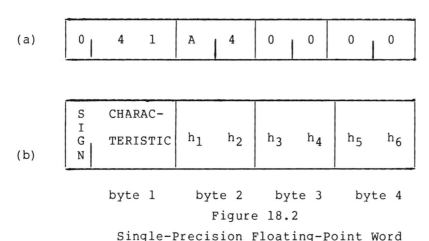

(a)

| 0 | 4 | 1 | A | 4 | 0 | 0 | 0 | 0 |

(b)

| S I G N | CHARAC- TERISTIC | h_1 | h_2 | h_3 | h_4 | h_5 | h_6 |

byte 1　　　　byte 2　　byte 3　　byte 4

Figure 18.2

Single-Precision Floating-Point Word

A seven-bit characteristic allows for a range of from 0 to 127, with a corresponding range of exponent from -64 to 63. Thus, the largest real number which can be represented in this format is .FFFFFF x 16^{63}, or approximately .7237005 x 10^{76} in decimal notation. The smallest in magnitude (except for zero, represented as a full word of zero-bits) is .1 x 16^{-64}, or approximately .5397605 x 10^{-78} in decimal notation.

An attempt to compute a non-zero value with magnitude greater than .7237005 x 10^{76} or less than .5397605 x 10^{-78} results in an <u>exponent</u> <u>overflow</u> or <u>exponent</u> <u>underflow</u> respectively, since the resulting exponent cannot be stored in the seven bits allotted to it. This situation is usually considered a program error, and the program is terminated, since further calculations involving the invalid result are usually meaningless.

The hexadecimal integer FFFFFF is equivalent to $2^{24}-1$ or 16,777,215 (decimal). For this reason, WATFIV-S prints out at most seven significant decimal digits for a real value, although computations proceed with slightly more accuracy, using the equivalent of about 7.2 decimal digits.

18.4   DOUBLE-PRECISION VARIABLES

A FORTRAN double-precision variable occupies a double word of memory, and is stored in double-precision floating-point notation. This differs from the single-precision form only in that the extra four bytes are used to supply eight additional hexadecimal digits of precision to the floating-point fraction. Figure 18.3 shows the internal format of such numbers.

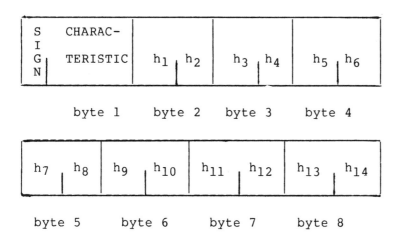

Figure 18.3

Double Precision Floating-Point Format

Since the exponent is identical with that used by single-precision numbers, the range of magnitudes is essen-

- 239 -

tially the same. However, the hexadecimal integer FFFFFFFFFFFFFF is equivalent to 72,057,594,037,927,935 (decimal — $2^{56}-1$). For this reason, WATFIV-S prints double precision values to a maximum of sixteen significant decimal digits; in fact, computations proceed with the equivalent of about 16.7 decimal digits.

The details on internal formats of numbers covered above allow us to discuss the differences in the numbers 1.3, 1.3D0, and the value of the built-in function DBLE(1.3). The single-precision constant 1.3 has internal format equivalent to .14CCCD x 16^1; the double-precision constant has internal format equivalent to .14CCCCCCCCCCCC x 16^1; the value of DBLE(1.3) has internal format equivalent to .14CCCD00000000 x 16^1. The differences just illustrated are important considerations for programs which use mixed-mode calculations.

18.5   COMPLEX VARIABLES

A FORTRAN complex variable occupies two adjacent full words of memory, one for the real part and one for the imaginary part. Both parts are stored as single-precision floating-point numbers with the real part in the farther-left or lower-addressed word.

Extended-precision complex variables are similar, except the real and imaginary parts occupy adjacent double words.

The address of a complex number is the address of its real part.

18.6   LOGICAL VARIABLES

A FORTRAN logical variable occupies a full word of memory, but in actual fact only the farthest-left byte is used to store the logical value. WATFIV-S uses a string of eight one-bits to represent .TRUE., and a string of eight zero-bits to represent .FALSE.. The three low-order bytes are ignored in logical calculations.

If a program makes extensive use of logical variables, especially of large logical arrays, considerable memory is wasted. Thus it would be better if the programmer had a means of restricting the size of logical variables to, say, one byte. This is, in fact, possible, and will be illustrated in the next chapter.

18.7   EXERCISES

The following exercises are meant to give the reader an opportunity to familiarize himself with the ways in which values are stored in the memory of the computer. No programs are necessary to complete these exercises; however, the reader may choose to develop programs to accomplish some of the conversions.

18.1 (A) Convert the following hexadecimal numbers to binary numbers using Figure 18.1.

(a)   00FA1234   (d)   00000000

(b)   12345678   (e)   11111111

(c)   FEDCBA98   (f)   ABCDEFFF

(B) Convert the following sixteen-bit binary values to their corresponding hexadecimal representations.

(a) 1010101010101010   (c)   1111111111111111
(b) 0111111010110001   (d)   0000000000000000

18.2 (A) Convert the following decimal numbers to their corresponding (a) binary representations, (b) hexadecimal representations.

- 241 -

(a) 46   (d) 127

(b) 32   (e) 32767

(c) 7632   (f) 1234567

(B) Convert the binary values in Exercise 18.1 (B)
to their corresponding decimal representations.

18.3 The internal format of a single-precision floating-point constant is illustrated in Figure 18.2.
Convert the following hexadecimal representations of floating-point numbers to their corresponding
decimal representations. Recall that this calculation involves two steps; the first is to calculate
the exponent, and the second is to convert the fraction to its decimal representation.

(a) 41100000   (d) C2560000

(b) 41200000   (e) 437F0000

(c) 41480000   (f) A4630500

18.4 Convert the following decimal values to their corresponding hexadecimal representations using normalized floating-point notation.

(a) 1.3   (d) 1.11

(b) 10.5   (e) -6.125

(c) 1.5   (f) 256.354

18.5 Perform the following operations which involve hexadecimal values. Check your answers by performing
the operations in decimal arithmetic.

(a) 00FF + 0013   (c) 0080 / 0010

(b) FFFF - 1234   (d) 00E1 / 000F

Chapter 19

DECLARATION STATEMENTS

Although the type-declaration statements INTEGER, REAL, COMPLEX, LOGICAL, and CHARACTER, have been introduced in previous chapters, they have some features not yet discussed. Some of these features are connected with the hardware-dependent concepts described in the previous chapter. The new features will be discussed in this chapter.

In addition, a new declaration statement - IMPLICIT - is introduced and explained.

19.1   INTEGER DECLARATIONS

The integer declaration statement

INTEGER I, X(3), MABLE, SOON

declares the symbolic names I, X, MABLE, and SOON, to be integer variables. In addition, the variable X represents an array of 3 integer values.

If the statement were written as

INTEGER I/2/, X(3), MABLE/-8/, SOON

the variables would not only be declared as integer type, but I and MABLE would have assigned to them the initial values 2 and -8 respectively. This means that the programmer could assume that the variables I, MABLE, would have the values 2, -8, at the time his program begins execution. These assignments are made at compile time, and the process is often referred to as <u>initialization</u>. The statement also shows that all variables declared need not be initialized.

Example 19.1 shows a program which computes the sum of squares of the first fifty integers. The integer variable TOTAL is initialized to zero, at compile time, to act as an accumulator.

```
      C EXAMPLE 19.1 - USING INITIALIZATION
            INTEGER TOTAL/0/
            DO 43 INT=1,50
               TOTAL = TOTAL + INT*INT
      43    CONTINUE
            PRINT, TOTAL
            STOP
            END
```

Although initialization is a very useful feature of the declaration statement, its action must be understood for effective use. Example 19.2 will illustrate how this feature can be misused. It is an attempt at the following problem: Read in a data card containing the number of students, say n, in a class. Then read in n cards, each containing a mark, and calculate the average. Repeat this process for a number of classes, and terminate when a value of zero is read for n.

```
      C EXAMPLE 19.2 - CLASS AVERAGES
            INTEGER SUM/0/, STUDNT
            LOOP
               READ, N
               IF (N .EQ. 0) QUIT
               DO 24 STUDNT=1,N
                  READ, MARK
                  SUM = SUM + MARK
      24       CONTINUE
               PRINT, SUM / N
            ENDLOOP
            STOP
            END
```

The program produces incorrect results for all classes but the first, since the value of SUM is not reset to zero for each class. Thus the statement SUM=0 should be included as the first statement in the loop. The point illustrated is that the initialization in the declaration statement is performed only once, at compile time.

The initialization feature finds its greatest use in initializing variables which remain constant throughout the execution of a program, for example,

INTEGER YEAR/365/, WEEK/7/, DAY/24/

Entire arrays may be initialized in declaration statements, as the following example statement shows.

INTEGER I/2/, X(3)/3*5/, MABLE

This statement declares X to be an integer vector of dimension 3; also, its three elements are all to be initialized to the value 5. The constant 3 in the construction /3*5/ is called a replication factor, since it specifies how many times the constant following the asterisk is to be repeated in the initializing process. An alternative form of the statement, which does not use the replication factor, is

INTEGER I/2/, X(3)/5, 5, 5/, MABLE

The initializing of arrays is done in storage order, using the specified constants from left to right. The rule is that there must be exactly as many constants as there are array elements to be initialized, with any replication factors being taken into account. Thus, to initialize a table T as shown in Figure 19.1 the, following statement could be used:

INTEGER T(3,4)/50, 3, 2*0, 4, 1, 16, 0, 4, 2, 98, 220/

50	0	16	2
3	4	0	98
0	1	4	220

Figure 19.1

Initial Values for a 3x4 Table T

The dimensions of arrays can be declared separately in a DIMENSION statement, and the initial values can be specified in the type-declaration statement, e.g.,

```
DIMENSION T(3,4), X(3)
INTEGER T/50, 3, 2*0, 4, 1, 16, 0, 4, 2, 98, 220/, X/3*5/
```

There are two more rules which can conveniently be stated at this time, and they apply also to the initialization which will be described in the next three sections of this chapter.

(a) The constant used for initialization must be of the same type as the variable to be initialized. Thus the statement

INTEGER Z/2.38/

is illegal, since 2.38 is not an integer constant.

(b) Subprogram parameters and function names may not be initialized.

The previous chapter mentioned that the IBM computer could operate with integers stored in half-word form. The FORTRAN programmer is able to use this facility by declaring particular variables as half-word integer variables. Thus the statement

INTEGER*2 JACK, BALL, Z

has the effect of specifying that variables JACK, BALL, and Z

are of integer type, but occupy only two bytes of memory
rather than the four bytes used for ordinary integer variables. The use of half-word integer variables can produce a
saving of space, if this is critical, at the expense of a
decrease in the range of values which can be stored. The
range of half-word integer values is from -32768 to 32767.

Arrays of half-word integers can be declared, and half-
word integer variables can be initialized. For example, the
statement

        INTEGER*2 XRAY/28/, VEL(10)/5*3, 5*0/, BOB

declares the variables XRAY, VEL, BOB, to be half-word integers; the '*2' specifies that all variables named are of
length two bytes. VEL is declared as an array of 10 half-word
elements. Furthermore, XRAY is initialized to the value 28;
the first five elements of VEL are each initialized to 3, the
last five to 0.

Half-word integers may be mixed freely in programs with
full-word integers; the former may be used in all places in
which the latter may be used. Exceptions will be noted in the
text.

Example 19.3 shows a simple program that mixes the use of
integer variables of length two bytes and of length four
bytes.

```
         C EXAMPLE 19.3 - MIXED LENGTH INTEGERS
               INTEGER*2 HALF
               INTEGER FULL
               LOOP
                    READ, HALF, FULL
                    IF (HALF*3 .EQ. FULL) QUIT
                    HALF = HALF + 5
                    PRINT, HALF, FULL
               ENDLOOP
               STOP
               END
```

The assignment statement

$$HALF = HALF + 5$$

uses mixed-length arithmetic, since the integer constant 5 is treated as a full-word operand by the compiler. The compiler treats all integer constants in this way. The effect is that the addition of the two integer values is done to full four-byte precision; then the low-order two bytes of the resulting value are assigned to the variable HALF. It is the programmer's responsibility to make sure that no information is lost in such operations.

The two declaration statements of Example 19.3 could be replaced by the single statement

INTEGER HALF*2, FULL*4

since the INTEGER statement allows mixed declarations of this kind. The '*4' appended to FULL specifies that FULL is to be treated as an ordinary integer variable occupying a word, or four bytes, of memory. The values 2 and 4 are called the length specifications of the corresponding variables HALF and FULL. In fact, the INTEGER statement has an implied default standard length specification of four bytes, and thus the following two statements are equivalent:

INTEGER A, B(5, 3), C/-2/
INTEGER*4 A,B(5,3),C/-2/

The last statement emphasizes the fact that when a length specification is appended to the type identifier, INTEGER, that specification applies to all names which do not have an appended explicit length. Furthermore, if no length specification is appended to the word INTEGER, the standard length of 4 is assumed. Thus, the following statements all result in the same declarations:

```
INTEGER A*2, B, C*4, D*2
INTEGER*2 A, B*4, C*4, D
INTEGER A*2, B*4, C, D*2
INTEGER A*2, B, C, D*2
INTEGER*4 A*2, B, C*4, D*2
```

The length specification 2 is called the _optional length_ for integers.

The following statements show that initialization may be done and array dimensions may be declared when length specifications are included in the declaration statement.

(a)   INTEGER*2 A/-5/, C*4(5)/1,2,3,4,5/, D(3,3)/9*0/, B*2
(b)   INTEGER*4 X*2/7/, Z, Y*2(3)/1, 2*-7/, W*2, U*4, T(2,5)

The statements have the effect of declaring names A, D, B, X, Y, W, to be half-word integer variables, and names C, Z, U, T, to be full-word integers.   Furthermore, C and Y are vectors of 5 and 3 elements respectively; and D and T are matrices of dimensions 3 by 3 and 2 by 5 respectively. Initialization is supplied for variables A, X, and for the elements of C, Y, D.   Note that the '*2' appended to the name B in (a), and the '*4' appended to the word INTEGER and to the name U in (b), are redundant.

Half-word integer values can be obtained from real values by using the built-in function HFIX, as shown by Example 19.4.

```
      C EXAMPLE 19.4 - USE OF HFIX
            INTEGER*2 JACK
            READ, X
            JACK = HFIX(X+2.5)
            PRINT, X, JACK
```

19.2   REAL DECLARATIONS

Earlier chapters have introduced the REAL and DOUBLE PRECISION declaration statements and the use of variables of these types.   In particular, the previous chapter explained the internal machine forms of real and double-precision values.   There is little difference between them; real values occupy four bytes of memory, and double-precision values occupy eight.   For this reason, it is convenient to consider double-precision values as merely a variation of real values. In fact, it is possible to do away with the DOUBLE PRECISION statement entirely if we agree to consider two kinds of real variables - those with a standard length of four bytes, and those with an optional length of eight bytes.

Thus the declaration statement

REAL*8 B, A

can be used instead of

DOUBLE PRECISION B, A

In addition, the REAL statement has the same flexibility as the INTEGER statement discussed in the previous section; that is, real variables of either length can be declared in the same statement, and initialization can be specified.

A few examples should suffice, since the rules for REAL are similar to those for INTEGER.

(a)   REAL*8 A, B*4, C(25), D*4(6,3), E*4/2.718282/

(b)   REAL*4 ROOT2/1.414214/, PI*8/3.141592653589793/

(c)   REAL*8 ROOT2*4/1.414214/, PI/3.141592653589793/

(d)   REAL ROOT2/1.414214/, PI*8/3.141592653589793/

(e)   REAL*8 X(5)/5*3.8D0/, Y, Z*4(2, 3)/3*.5, 3*1./

Note that (b), (c), and (d) achieve the same result.

19.3   COMPLEX DECLARATIONS

There are two kinds of complex values in FORTRAN - those with the standard length of eight bytes and those with the optional length of sixteen bytes.   Examples of both kinds have been given in an earlier chapter, and the method of declaring each was described.   The previous chapter showed that a complex value of length eight is really stored as two adjacent real values of length four, and an extended-precision complex value is composed of two adjacent real values of length eight.

Since the COMPLEX declaration statement has the same properties as the REAL and INTEGER statements, sample statements only will be given.

(a)   COMPLEX*8 CDSORT*16, C, Z*16/(1.5D0,-1.5D0)/, P*8

(b)   COMPLEX CDSORT*16, C, Z*16/(1.5D0,-1.5D0)/, P

(c)   COMPLEX*16 CDS, Q5*8(3,.3)/9*(0.,1.)/, CDC*16

(d)   COMPLEX*16 D*8(3)/(-1.,1.), 2*(1.,-1.)/, EGGMOR

Statements (a) and (b) are equivalent.

19.4   LOGICAL DECLARATIONS

The last section of the previous chapter mentioned that a variable declared in a LOGICAL statement occupies four bytes of memory although, in fact, only one byte of the four is used for storing the logical value.   Logical variables can be restricted to occupy one byte of storage, with a resulting saving of space, if they are declared to have the optional length of one; the standard length occupied by a logical variable is four bytes.

Thus the following statements are valid, and the rules are similar to those used in the preceding sections.

(a) LOGICAL*1 GIPWAD/.TRUE./, UVZ(2)/.TRUE., .FALSE./

(b) LOGICAL*1 A*4(5)/4*.TRUE., .FALSE./, FALSE/.FALSE./

(c) LOGICAL YES/.TRUE./, NO*1/.FALSE./, TV*1(5,5) /25*T/

(d) LOGICAL*4 YES/T/, NO*1/F/, TV*1(5,5) /25*.TRUE./

Statements (c) and (d) are equivalent, since the standard length used for logical values is four bytes. These statements show also that T and F may be used as abbreviations for .TRUE. and .FALSE. when initializing variables.

When logical values of different lengths are combined using the logical operators .AND. and .OR., the result is of length four. Moreover, the logical constants .TRUE., and .FALSE. are considered to be of length four.

19.5   CHARACTER DECLARATIONS

Character variables are different from the other types of variables in that they do not have specifically fixed lengths. The length of a character variable is the number of bytes that is reserved for the variable. The default or standard length is one, and the maximum length is 255. Recall that each byte is capable of storing one character. Occasionally we use the terms 'byte' and 'character' interchangeably.

The following examples demonstrate how character strings can be initialized.

(a)   CHARACTER*4 A/'LIFE'/,B*9/'ALBATROSS'/

(b)   CHARACTER*8 C/8HABCDEFGH/

(c)   CHARACTER Z(5)/'A','B','C','D','E'/

(d)   CHARACTER H*11/'HORSE'/,W*8/'ABCDEFGHIJK'/

(e)   CHARACTER TAB*5(3,2)/3*'XXXXX',3*'YYYYY'/

Example (a) assigns the character strings LIFE and ALBATROSS to the character variables A and B, respectively.

Example (b) illustrates the use of the H-type Hollerith string.

Example (c) declares Z to be a character array with five elements, each occupying one byte. The five elements contain the letters A, B, C, D, and E.

In Example (d), we have the situation where there are only five characters in the string, whereas the variable H is capable of storing eleven characters; in this case, blanks are inserted on the right. In the case of W in Example (d), the letters IJK are truncated, since the character string has eleven characters, and the variable can store only eight.

Example (e) uses a replication factor, and sets the first column of TAB to XXXXX's and the second column to YYYYY's.

19.6　TYPE DECLARATION FOR FUNCTION SUBPROGRAMS

Previous chapters have introduced the statements

```
FUNCTION
REAL FUNCTION
INTEGER FUNCTION
LOGICAL FUNCTION
DOUBLE PRECISION FUNCTION
COMPLEX FUNCTION
```

Each of these statements always appears as the first statement of a function subprogram, and serves the purpose of identifying the name of the function and providing information about its type. (Recall that it is not permissible to have a character function.) The function's parameters are also identified by including them in a parenthesized list following the function name. Sample statements follow:

(a)　FUNCTION SUM (X, N)

(b)　REAL FUNCTION MAX (L, V, S)

(c)   FUNCTION MOD3 (T)

(d)   LOGICAL FUNCTION TEST (A, B)

In (b) and (d), the types of MAX and TEST are explicitly declared to be real and logical respectively; in (a) and (c) the types of SUM and MOD3 are taken by default as real and integer respectively. The length of each name is the standard for its type.

It remains only to point out that function subprogram names, like variable names, can be of the optional length for a particular type. To achieve this, the appropriate length specification is appended to the function name, as the following examples show.

(a)   REAL FUNCTION TVAL*8 (P, Q)

(b)   INTEGER FUNCTION ARGFU*2 (N, A, L, S)

(c)   COMPLEX FUNCTION HONK*16 (Z)

(d)   LOGICAL FUNCTION YESRNO*1 (IN, OUT)

Statement (a) could be used to head a function subprogram named TVAL; the function value, TVAL, is of real type, and has the appropriate optional length, 8 bytes. Similar descriptions could be given for (b), (c) and (d).

Note that (a) is equivalent to

DOUBLE PRECISION FUNCTION TVAL (P, Q)

It is important to note the position of the length specification in these statements - it follows the function name. The statement

REAL*8 FUNCTION TVAL (P, Q)

is not a valid function declaration.

If desired, the standard length specification of a type may be given; for example,

REAL FUNCTION VEPROD*4 (T, A)

COMPLEX FUNCTION OMEGA*8 (V, T)

The programmer must declare the type and length, if different from those assigned by default, of the function name in any program segment in which the function is called. The following Example, 19.5, illustrates this for the logical function TEST. The function has one parameter, a positive integer N, and the result of the function is .TRUE. if N is a prime number, and is .FALSE. otherwise. The main program, using TEST, determines and prints all twin primes less than 100.

```
C EXAMPLE 19.5 - FINDING TWIN PRIMES
      LOGICAL*1 TEST
      DO 1 I=3,100,2
          IF (TEST(I) .AND. TEST(I+2)) PRINT, I, I+2
1     CONTINUE
      STOP
      END

      LOGICAL FUNCTION TEST*1 (N)
      IF (N .EQ. 2) THEN
          TEST = .TRUE.
      ELSEIF (N .EQ. N/2*2) THEN
          TEST = .FALSE.
      ELSE
          I = 3
          WHILE (I*I .LE. N)
              TEST = N .NE. N/I*I
              IF (.NOT.TEST) QUIT
              I = I + 2
          ENDWHILE
      ENDIF
      RETURN
      END
```

19.7   THE IMPLICIT STATEMENT

The first version of FORTRAN developed in the mid-1950's allowed only two types of variables - integer and real.   At that time, the rule was established that variables beginning with the letters I, J, K, L, M, or N, were to be integer, all others real; there were no statements for type declaration.

Later versions of FORTRAN allowed variables of complex or logical type, as well as the declaration statements, mentioned in the previous sections, for typing names explicitly.   The original "first-letter rule" was maintained, however, for "default" typing of integer and real variables.

Some additional freedom was added with the design of FORTRAN for the IBM computer by including a very general type-declaration statement, IMPLICIT.   This statement essentially allows the programmer to specify his own "first-letter rule", and to extend it to include all types.   Moreover, the rule may be changed in each program segment.   Several examples are given to illustrate these ideas.

The statement

IMPLICIT REAL*8(D,T-Z), INTEGER*2(M,N), LOGICAL(O-S)

specifies that variable names whose first letters are D, T, U, V, W, X, Y, or Z, will be real of length 8, by default, that is, in the absence of any explicit declaration statements. Similarly, variable names beginning with letters M or N will be, by default, integer of length 2, and those beginning with the letters O to S will be logical of standard length 4, by default.   The conventional FORTRAN first-letter rule will apply for all other letters; that is, variables beginning with I, J, K, or L, are integer of standard length 4, and variables beginning with A, B, C, E, F, G, H, or $, are real of standard length 4.

As shown, standard or optional lengths can be given for a letter or range of letters, and the standard length is assumed if not specified. A range of letters is indicated by separating the first and last letters of the range by a minus sign.

The statement

```
IMPLICIT REAL(A-H, O-Z, $), INTEGER(I-N)
```

is equivalent to the conventional first-letter rule.

The IMPLICIT statement could be used to set up a "first-letter rule" for character variables of a specified length. For example, the statement

```
IMPLICIT CHARACTER*9(A), CHARACTER(B-E)
```

specifies that variables beginning with the letter A are of type character and of length 9. Variables starting with letters B through E are character variables of length 1.

Explicit declarations still override implicit typing. For example,

```
IMPLICIT INTEGER*4(A-N)
REAL*8 ABLE, JACK*4
```

explicitly declare ABLE and JACK to be of type real with lengths 8 and 4 bytes respectively; if not explicitly so declared, they would both be integer of length 4.

The statement

```
IMPLICIT REAL*4(A-Z, $)
```

might be used in a program segment which is to do computations in real arithmetic only. This could give the programmer some additional freedom in naming variables. The program could easily be converted to double-precision arithmetic by replacing the above statement by

```
IMPLICIT REAL*8(A-Z, $)
```

However, care needs to be taken if the program uses constants or makes references to built-in functions. For example, if a program referenced the built-in function SQRT, WATFIV-S would automatically assume it to be of type real, length 4, whereas the programmer would really want to use DSQRT. As a potential solution to this problem, we might make use of a statement function defined as

$$SQRT(X) = DSQRT(X)$$

There are only a few rules that apply to the IMPLICIT statement.

(a) At most <u>one</u> IMPLICIT statement is allowed per program segment; that is, each subprogram may have one or none. The regular first-letter rule applies in any program segment which does not have an IMPLICIT statement.

(b) The IMPLICIT statement, if used, must be the first in the main program and the second in any subprogram. Thus, it immediately follows the SUBROUTINE or FUNCTION statement. In a subprogram, it types a function name and any arguments, if these are not explicitly typed. Thus, for

```
FUNCTION THETA (COV, STAR)
IMPLICIT COMPLEX*16(C), COMPLEX(Q-U)
REAL STAR
```

the function THETA is of type complex and standard length 8, COV is of type complex and length 16. STAR is explicitly declared to be of type real and of standard length 4.

(c) The IMPLICIT statement, like all declaration statements, is not executable, and serves only as a guide at compile time.

19.8   <u>EXERCISES</u>

19.1 (A) Consider the following sequence of statements.
```
REAL*8 D, E
INTEGER*2 IH
R = 3.0*(1./3.)
D = 3.0*(1./3.)
E = 3.D0*(1.D0/3.D0)
I = 45678+92
IH = 45678+92
PRINT, R, D, E, I, IH
```
Predict the values which would be printed.
Verify your prediction by including the
sequence of statements in a program for the
computer.

(B) Given the following declaration statements,
```
REAL A, B*8
INTEGER I, J*2
COMPLEX C, D*16
```
state the type of each of the following expressions.

(a) A+B/I   (d) A*I*J

(b) C+I+J*A   (e) C**I+C**J

(c) D-J

19.2 (a) Using the feature of initialization in declaration statements, set up the starting, ending,
and increment values, and tabulate the function

f(x) = sin x + cos x

for x = 0, $\dfrac{\pi}{8}$, $\dfrac{\pi}{4}$, ..., π

where π = 3.14159

(b) Do Exercise 5.6 using initialization to set up the constant values required for the various calculations.

(c) Repeat part (b) using half-word integers to store the required values.

19.3 Exercises 4.3, 4.5, 4.8, 8.1(c), and 8.1(d) involve calculations with single-precision real variables, constants, and built-in functions. Make use of the IMPLICIT statement to assist in the conversion of these programs to extended-precision real arithmetic.

19.4 Exercise 17.3 involves computations with single-precision complex quantities. Modify the program to perform the computations in extended precision.

19.5 (a) Repeat Exercise 13.6 using extended-precision arithmetic.

(b) Write a main program that reads the degree and the coefficients of the polynomial

$$f(x) = x^6 + x^3 + x + 1.$$

The program is to evaluate the polynomial and its derivative for

$$x = 10, 11, 12, \ldots, 25$$

using the subprograms written for part (a).

19.6 In Exercise 9.14, we determined prime numbers. Re-write the program using half-word integers to store the values. Use it to determine all primes less than 400.

19.7 Improve the efficiency of the main program in Example 19.5 by decreasing the number of calls to the function TEST.

Chapter 20

INPUT/OUTPUT WITH SEQUENTIAL FILES

The purpose of this chapter is to describe in more detail some of the features of FORTRAN input/output that are implemented in the WATFIV-S compiler. In particular, the FORTRAN statements oriented to the use of magnetic tapes for input/output of sequential files are described and illustrated. In a subsequent chapter, input/output with direct access files is discussed.

A brief review of input/output features covered in previous chapters is included in this chapter.

20.1   FORMAT-FREE I/O

Early in Chapter 1 of this text, the reader encountered example programs which required the reading of data values or the printing of results. At that time he was introduced to the so-called format-free input/output statements of WATFIV-S, some examples of which follow.

```
READ, X, A, I
READ, (B(K), K=N,M,L) ,T
PRINT, J, P**2, (B(I), I=1,J)
```

These are the simplest forms of I/O statements available using WATFIV-S, and are particularly convenient for the beginning programmer, since he need not bother himself with the more difficult FORMAT statement. These statements allow him

the ability to input to the computer memory data values
punched on cards, and to output values to a printer for examination.

The general form of these statements is

READ, list

PRINT, list

The "list" is the means by which the values to be transmitted
to or from memory are specified to the I/O system. The list
is composed of list elements, separated by commas; list
elements may be variable names, array names with or without
subscripts, or implied DO's containing any of the previous or
other implied DO's.

With WATFIV-S, list elements in output statements may
also be any FORTRAN expressions.[1]

Occasionally the programmer has need to obtain output,
which is not printed, but instead is punched on cards,
possibly to be used as input for another program.

The format-free statement

PUNCH, list

is available for this purpose. Since values are transmitted
to be punched on 80-column cards any list items which will not
fit on the first card are punched on successive cards. Thus,
a single PUNCH statement may produce more than one card as
output, in the same way that a PRINT statement may produce
more than one line on the printer, if many values are produced
as output.

---

[1] An exception is that the expression may not start with a
left parenthesis, since this signals an implied DO. Thus
PRINT, (X+Y)/2. would be flagged with an error message.
However, PRINT, +(X+Y)/2. is valid.

20.2   FORMATTED I/O

The introduction of FORMAT greatly increased the flexibility of FORTRAN I/O since, with it, the programmer could compose print lines himself, and could also control the editing of lines and the layout of values on data cards.

The forms of the statements using FORMAT are:

```
          READ fmt, list
          PRINT fmt, list
          PUNCH fmt, list
```

where "fmt" stands for the statement number of a FORMAT statement which appears elsewhere in the program. Here "list" need not contain any elements; if it does not, the commas are omitted. Examples are:

```
          READ 12, X, A
          PRINT 784, (I, SQRT(FLOAT(I)), I=1,25)
          PUNCH 13, ((B(I,J), I=1,N), J=1,M)
          PRINT 26
          READ 43
```


20.3   GENERAL READ AND WRITE STATEMENTS

The three statements given in the previous section provide the FORTRAN user with access to a card reader, card punch, and printer, for I/O. To avoid the proliferation of statement types that could occur in permitting access to other kinds of I/O devices such as magnetic tapes, discs, or video screens, it was decided, in the course of FORTRAN's development, that uniform input/output statements should be designed to accommodate all devices. This decision resulted in the design of two general statements - one for input and one for output. Their forms are

```
                READ(unit,fmt,END=n,ERR=m) list
                WRITE(unit,fmt) list
```

Here "unit" is called the unit number[2] and n and m are statement numbers of executable statements. Rather than explain
the full significance of these statements, we will give examples in subsequent sections of this chapter to illustrate the
various forms they may take.

A few words should be said about the unit number. The
unit number is used by the programmer to specify which I/O
device he wants to associate with the I/O operation. It is
usually[3] the case that unit number 5 specifies the standard
card reader, and unit numbers 6 and 7 specify the standard
printer and standard punch respectively. Under such circumstances, the statements

```
                READ 2, X, A
                READ(5,2) X, A
```

are exactly equivalent, as are

```
                PRINT 25, Y
                WRITE(6,25) Y
```

and

```
                PUNCH 16, Z**2+3.
                WRITE(7,16) Z**2+3.
```

WATFIV-S's format-free versions of READ, PRINT, and PUNCH also
use the standard units.

The unit number in the general I/O statements may, in

---

[2] Sometimes called the data set reference number.

[3] Some installations prefer other numbers for standard reader,
   printer, punch units. You should check before running a
   program.

fact, be an integer variable name of length 4; for example,

READ(I,25) X, Y

Example 20.1 shows part of a program which gives symbolic names to the standard units; this makes it very easy to change the program if it is to be used at an installation with different standard unit numbers.

```
C EXAMPLE 20.1 - VARIABLE UNITS
      INTEGER READER/5/, PRNTER/6/, PUNCH/7/
      READ(READER,25) X, Y
      .
      .
      WRITE(PRNTER,78) A, B
      .
      .
      WRITE(PUNCH,204)(Z(I), I=1,5)
      .
      .
      END
```

20.4 MAGNETIC TAPE CHARACTERISTICS

The previous section showed that the value of an integer variable could be used to specify a unit number. Are there units other than 5, 6, and 7, and devices other than card readers, printers, and punches, available to the FORTRAN programmer?

The answer to this question depends on the computer installation whose services the programmer uses. Usually it is safe to say that other unit numbers may be used to perform I/O on magnetic tape drives or discs. Tapes are extremely useful for manipulating large volumes of data, because of their speed and data storage capacities. Magnetic tapes provide an extension of the memory capacity of the computer, and may be used by the FORTRAN programmer to store intermediate results of calculations for later use, or as data input or output media. Their use permits the convenient interchange of data between different programs or even different computers.

Since methods of doing I/O on magnetic tapes are somewhat different from methods used with the other devices mentioned so far, a brief description of magnetic tape characteristics is now given.

A computer tape drive is much like a conventional tape recorder, in that a long thin ribbon of oxide-coated plastic material, wound on a reel mountable on the drive, may have information recorded on it in the form of magnetic impressions. The recording takes place by moving the tape past a stationary read/write head on the tape drive while data is transmitted to the head from the computer memory. (This movement is accomplished by winding up the tape on one reel, while allowing it to play off another reel.) Information that has previously been recorded may be read back into the computer memory by repositioning the tape so that the data to be read again moves past the read/write head, this time with the tape drive instructed to read instead of to write. Material previously recorded may at any time be destroyed by over-writing with new data, i.e., a tape can be used many times.

Reading or writing of the tape takes place in one direction only, and, at the completion of an I/O operation, the tape comes to a stop. It is not possible to read a tape "backwards" in FORTRAN, although some modern tape drives allow this possibility. Hence, instructions must be given to position the tape to the proper place with respect to the read/write head before attempting to read or overwrite previously written information. There are special FORTRAN statements to control the backward movement of the tape, as will be seen shortly.

Near the beginning and end of the tape, there are special markers to indicate the limits between which recording can be done. The tape drive can sense these marks, and the one at the beginning is used to indicate where the first recorded information starts; the one at the end serves to prevent the accidental writing of information beyond the end of the tape.

This description, although it ignores all the details of the actual recording and the physical characteristics of any tape drives, should be sufficient to understand the examples which follow.

20.5 SEQUENTIAL FILES

Example 20.2 is a simple program which illustrates the use of a tape unit. It merely reads in the elements of vector A, punched on cards, and copies them onto the tape on the drive associated with unit number 3.

```
C EXAMPLE 20.2 - WRITING ON TAPE
      DIMENSION A(25)
      REWIND 3
      READ(5,27) A
27    FORMAT(8F10.2)
      WRITE(3) A
      STOP
      END
```

The statement REWIND 3 is a new statement. Its effect is to position the tape to the starting marker so that the first recording on the tape will be in a known fixed position. Failure to do this almost always leads to trouble. If the tape is already in this _rewound_ position, the statement has no effect. The programmer should not assume that for his job the tape is in the rewound position since the computer operator who mounts the tape on the drive may not have put it in the rewound position. It is wise to rewind a tape before doing any I/O with it.

Notice that the statement WRITE(3) A contains no reference to a format; the elements of the vector A are transmitted
directly to tape unit 3 in the form in which they are stored
within the computer. This method of output is termed writing
without format control, and is the most efficient way of
recording data on a tape in terms of both time and space.

The amount of data transmitted by a WRITE statement is
called a logical record or record for brevity. The size of a
record, when writing without format control, is determined by
the number and lengths of all list elements transmitted. For
Example 20.2, the record consists of 25 computer words or 100
bytes.

Example 20.3 shows that it is possible to have records of
varying sizes written on a tape; the number of elements of the
vector X written each time is not necessarily the same.

```
      C EXAMPLE 20.3 - VARYING RECORD LENGTHS
            DIMENSION X(100), Y(100)
            REWIND 2
            LOOP
                READ(5,63,END=4) N
      63        FORMAT(I3)
                READ 43, (X(I), I=1,N)
      43        FORMAT(8F10.3)
                WRITE(2) N, (X(I), I=1,N)
            ENDLOOP
      4     BACKSPACE 2
            READ (2) M, (Y(I), I=1,M)
            STOP
            END
```

The program loops reading various vectors from the card
reader, and, for each vector, writes the number of elements
and the vector on tape 2. When the data cards are exhausted,
control transfers to statement numbered 4, namely, BACKSPACE
2. The BACKSPACE statement works something like REWIND, in
that tape 2 is moved backwards, but only past the last logical
record written. Thus, the READ statement following statement
4 effectively reads a copy of N and the N elements of the last

vector recorded on tape 2 into variable M and the first M elements of vector Y respectively.

We can always get to the first record on a tape by doing a REWIND; we can always back up one record by doing a BACKSPACE. A BACKSPACE has no effect if the tape is already rewound.

Example 20.3 potentially writes numerous records on tape. The total collection of records recorded on a particular tape is called a <u>file</u>.[4] Specifically, a file on tape is called a <u>sequential</u> <u>file</u> since there is an implied ordering to the records. Thus, if the tape is rewound, to read the twelfth record, for example, records one to eleven must be skipped over. This is in contrast to the random order in which records may be retrieved from or written on a direct-access device such as a disc or drum.

It is the usual convention to follow the last record of a sequential file by a special character called an <u>end-of-file-mark</u> which the tape drive can sense. This is to guard against any attempt to read more information than has been recorded in the file. The statement ENDFILE 2 will write an end-of-file mark at the current position of the tape on unit 2.

The reader has probably guessed that the <u>END</u> <u>return</u> of the READ statement may be used to gain control when the end-of-file mark is sensed while reading a sequential file. Control transfers to the statement identified by the statement number following the END=. A similar affect was achieved in previous examples using the AT END, QUIT statement following the READ.

Example 20.4 is another illustration of sensing the end-of-file mark. The program reads various vectors from a tape on unit 3, and writes them alternately on units 1 and 2; it

---

[4] Sometimes called a data set.

repeats this procedure until the end-of-file mark is sensed on tape 3. Then tape 3 is rewound, and the records of tape 1 are copied onto 3, followed by the records of tape 2. An end-of-file mark is written on 3 so that the data on it can be used again.

```
      C EXAMPLE 20.4 - END RETURN FOR TAPE
            DIMENSION X(100)
            REWIND 2
            REWIND 1
            REWIND 3
            J = 2
            LOOP
                READ(3,ERR=19,END=25) N, (X(I), I=1,N)
                J = J - J/2*2 + 1
                WRITE(J) N, (X(I), I=1,N)
            ENDLOOP
      25    ENDFILE 2
            ENDFILE 1
            DO 99 J=1,3
                REWIND J
      99    CONTINUE
            LOOP
                READ(1,END=435,ERR=19) N, (X(I), I=1,N)
                WRITE(3) N, (X(I), I=1,N)
            ENDLOOP
      435   CONTINUE
            LOOP
                READ(2,ERR=19,END=8) N, (X(I), I=1,N)
                WRITE(3) N, (X(I), I=1,N)
            ENDLOOP
      19    WRITE(6,61)
      61    FORMAT(' ERROR WHILE READING TAPE')
      8     ENDFILE 3
            STOP
            END
```

The READ statements show examples of the ERR return used to gain control if an I/O device-error occurs while in the process of reading a record. This problem can arise occasionally with tapes, for example if dust or smoke particles adhere to the recording surface. If the ERR return were not present and an I/O error occurred, the program would be terminated by the compiler. Note that the positions of the END and ERR returns are interchangeable if both are present.

The reader might question why the two almost equivalent features AT END and END= exist. The END= method of determining end-of-file is allowed by most FORTRAN compilers and is the more traditional and historical approach. The AT END method is available in WATFIV-S and is more suitable for writing structured programs. Finally, note that there is no alternative for the ERR= feature.

The general forms of the tape control statements are

REWIND i

BACKSPACE i

ENDFILE i

where i is an integer constant or variable name representing the unit number.

It is entirely possible to read less information than has been written in a record, as the following example will show.

```
C EXAMPLE 20.5 - READING LESS THAN RECORD SIZE
      DIMENSION A(100), I(25), C(10,10)
      COMPLEX*8 D(40)
      READ(5,3)A
3     FORMAT(8F10.2)
      REWIND 1
      WRITE(1) A
      REWIND 1
4     READ(1) X, I
      BACKSPACE 1
5     READ(1) D
      BACKSPACE 1
6     READ(1) C
      STOP
      END
```

The one hundred elements of vector A are read from cards and written on tape unit 1. This single record of size 400 bytes is then read by three different READ statements.

The READ statement numbered 4 places the first 4 bytes of the record into variable X and the next 100 bytes into the 25 elements of integer vector I. The remaining 296 bytes of the record are ignored. The READ statement 5 places the first 320 bytes of the record into the 40 elements of the complex vector D. Thus alternate elements of A become real and imaginary parts of elements of D. Again, the last 80 bytes of the record are ignored. The READ statement 6 places the entire record, by columns, into the 100 elements of matrix C. (Note that the statement numbers on the READ statements are there only for the authors' convenience.)

This example emphasizes that the data are recorded on tape in the exact form in which they are stored. When data are retrieved from a record, as many bytes as required to fill a list item are moved directly from the record to the memory locations occupied by the list item. Thus it is the programmer's responsibility to ensure that data of type appropriate for his requirements are read into the variable; otherwise, erroneous results may be obtained. The programmer should be aware of the contents, sizes, and relative positions of the records he has placed on a file.

It is, in fact, possible to have a READ statement with no list, and this is handy for skipping records in a forward direction. For example, the statements

```
          DO 28 I=1,10
          READ(4)
28        CONTINUE
```

will skip over 10 records since each execution of the READ causes the tape drive to read a record; however, the information in it is ignored.

It is not possible to read more information than has been written in a record.

To review the ideas given above, consider Figure 20.1. A program has written m logical records, followed by an end-of-file mark, on unit 2, has rewound the tape, and has since read three records. The arrow indicates the current position of the tape with respect to the read/write head. (Direction of tape movement for reading or writing is assumed to be from right to left.)

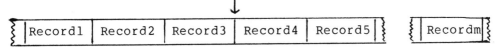

Figure 20.1

The tape is now in a position so that record 4 may be read, or a new record may be written over old record 4. If it were desired to read record 2 back into memory, the tape would first have to be repositioned by backspacing twice. If the programmer wishes to skip record 4 and read record 5, he could execute a READ with no list.

Note that if a file currently contains m records, numbered from 1 to m, and the programmer writes a new record j with j<m, he _must_ assume that the file now has only j records and that records j+1, j+2, ..., m, are no longer accessible. For Figure 20.1, if the programmer wrote a new record 4, he has, for all purposes, made records 5, 6, 7, ..., m, along with old record 4, unavailable.

20.6   DISC FILE CHARACTERISTICS

Sequential files can also be written onto and read from disc units. All of the same rules apply, just as if a magnetic tape were being used. The unit number is associated with a file on a disc, rather than with a specific tape unit. In this case, the REWIND statement merely positions the disc read mechanism at the beginning of the file, rather than "rewinding" it.

20.7 SEQUENTIAL FILES WITH FORMAT CONTROL

It is also possible to read and write sequential files with format control by including a reference to a FORMAT statement in the I/O statement. Thus

$$\text{WRITE}(2,78) \ X, \ Y, \ Z$$
$$78 \qquad \text{FORMAT}(F10.2, \ 2E16.7)$$

would write the values of X, Y, and Z, onto the file associated with unit 2 according to the formats specified. The same record could be read by a statement such as

$$\text{READ}(2,78,\text{END}=12,\text{ERR}=45) \ A, \ B, \ C$$

The records written with format control resemble the printer lines that would be created if the unit number had been that of the standard printer, except that the first character of each line is not treated as a carriage control, but is actually written on the file. This is important to consider if the file is ever to be subsequently produced on a printer.

Sequential files written with format control are not normally used for storing intermediate results of a program since considerable computer time is involved in converting values from internal form to that specified by FORMAT.

For records written without format control, the record size was specified by the total size of all the I/O list elements. When writing with format control, records are written onto the file under the control of the FORMAT statement in the same way that format codes control the generation of printer lines.

To avoid confusion with the logical records of the previous section, records written with format control are often referred to as FORTRAN records. Thus, the following statement would write three separate FORTRAN records on unit 4, since there is no field count for the E format code.

```
            WRITE(4,23) X, Y, Z
    23      FORMAT(E20.6)
```

These records could be read by one, two, or three separate READ statements: thus

```
            READ(4,23) A, B, C
```

        or

```
            READ(4,23) A, B
            READ(4,23) C
```

        or

```
            READ(4,23) A
            READ(4,23) B
            READ(4,23) C
```

Two FORTRAN records would be written if the FORMAT statement
were changed to

```
    23      FORMAT(2E20.6)
```

Note that printer lines and data cards are examples of
FORTRAN records. Records written with and without FORMAT
control may be written on the same file, but this is risky
because of the different nature of logical and FORTRAN records
and the different ways in which the information is recorded.
Records written without FORMAT control should not be read with
FORMAT control, and vice versa. In addition, BACKSPACE works
differently since it backspaces one FORTRAN record.

20.8   CONCLUDING REMARKS

As the reader should be aware, much care and organization
is needed when working with sequential files on tape or disc
in order to use them properly and effectively. More could be
said about techniques (e.g., buffering, blocking) which tend
to increase the efficiency of programs which use sequential

- 275 -

files. The previous sections have merely covered the details of the FORTRAN statements available to the programmer; he should now be able to try his hand at programs using these ideas.

Many details are left unmentioned since they are beyond the scope of this book. For example, the total number of units available to the programmer is an installation decision. What happens if the statement sequence WRITE, ENDFILE, WRITE, is executed? How is the actual connection made between the logical idea of a file and a particular physical I/O device? Suffice it to say that the answers to these questions lie in mechanisms external to the FORTRAN program, and usually need not be known by the beginning programmer.

Anyone planning to make considerable use of tapes and discs is well advised to consult the manuals relating to the operating system in use at his computer installation. For example, the answer to the questions posed above may be found in the IBM manual "FORTRAN IV Programmer's Guide".

20.9   EXERCISES

Prepare a data deck which contains 50 cards, one for each of 50 students. Each card contains a student's name and number, together with his marks in each of 6 particular courses. If no mark is available for a particular course, the corresponding field contains zeros. The deck is in student-number sequence.

20.1   Write a program which reads this data deck, writes it onto a tape, rewinds the tape, and prints it for verification purposes. Thus, this tape, which we will call the Student Master File, has a record for each student, and is in student-number sequence.

20.2   Write a program which reads the Student Master File

created in Exercise 20.1, and computes the number of students who have passed each course. Assume a pass mark to be 50 or more.

20.3 Write a program which reads the Student Master File and computes the average for each student. A new Student Master File should be written to record the average for each student, along with the rest of the data.

20.4 Assume that additional marks become available to update a student's record (recall that some of the marks were missing). Devise a program which reads data cards, in student-number sequence, and uses the new information to update the Student Master File. Note that a new file must be written.

20.5 Suppose a new student joins the class. Write a program which will insert the new student's record into the Student Master File. Note that his student number could be such that his record is not necessarily at the end of the Student Master File. (Recall that the master file is recorded in student-number sequence.)

20.6 Suppose a similar Student Master File is available for another class, the members of which take the same six subjects. Suppose further that it is our wish to merge the two files to create one new Student Master File which contains the records of all the students in sequence, by student number. Write a program to accomplish this.

Chapter 21

ADVANCED FORMAT

Various format codes have been introduced throughout this book as they were required. This chapter introduces some specialized format codes and some techniques that simplify the writing of FORMAT statements. The final section discusses a means of constructing or modifying format codes at execution time.

Although most of the examples in this chapter are illustrated by referring to punched cards for input and printed lines for output, the concepts apply to FORTRAN records read or written using any I/O device.

21.1   G FORMAT

The G format code is a generalized code which can be used to transmit (input or output) integer, real, complex, or logical values. Example 21.1 demonstrates the use of the G code for both input and output.

```
       C EXAMPLE 21.1 - DEMONSTRATE G FORMAT
              LOGICAL L
              COMPLEX C
              REAL*8 BIG
              READ 10, A, L, C, BIG
       10     FORMAT(4G8.4, G15.8)
              I = 321
              PRINT 96, A, L, C, I, BIG
       96     FORMAT(' ', 3G9.2, G9.3, G4, G12.5)
              STOP
              END
```

If the following data card were supplied,

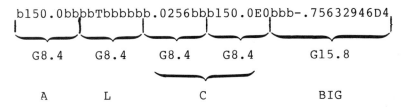

the line printed would be

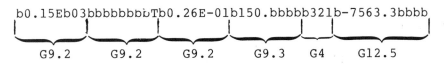

Note that the same result could have been obtained if the FORMAT statements used were

```
10     FORMAT(F8.4, L8, F8.4, E8.4,, D15.8)
96     FORMAT(' ', E9.2, L9, E9.2, F5.0, 4X, I4, F8.1, 4X)
```

The example illustrates that the G format code can be used in place of the F, E, D, I, or L, codes. The .d portion of Gw.d may be omitted for integer and logical values, and is ignored if present.

For input, the rules for the G code are the same as those for the individual codes F, E, D, I, and L; the type of the variable and the form of the number punched on the card determine which set of rules apply.

For output, integer and logical values are printed according to the rules for I and L codes, respectively. For real values, the d of Gw.d specifies the number of $\underline{significant}$ digits to be printed, and is also used to determine whether the value is to be printed with or without an exponent. If the magnitude of a value x is in the range $.1 \le x < 10^d$, d significant digits are printed with a decimal point in the proper place; in such cases, the exponent is zero, and it is replaced by four blanks. If x is not in the range just specified, the rules for Ew.d or Dw.d are used, depending on the length (4 or 8 bytes) of the value. For complex values, this rule applies to the real and imaginary parts individually. It is wise to have $w \geq d + 7$ in order to have space in the field in case the exponent has to be printed.

21.2   Z FORMAT

The format code Zw is used to transmit data in hexadecimal form, as Example 21.2 shows.

```
      C EXAMPLE 21.2 - Z FORMAT
            INTEGER*2 J
            J = 28
            X = 28.
            WRITE(6,43) J, J, X, X
   43       FORMAT(' ', I3, 4X, Z4, F6.1, Z10)
```

The output of this example is the line

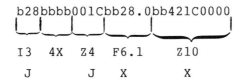

The field 001C is the hexadecimal coding of the sixteen-bit binary integer number contained in the half-word of memory that the variable J occupies. Similarly, 421C0000 is the hexadecimal representation of the contents of the word that the real variable X occupies. Since a word, or four bytes, is the equivalent of eight hexadecimal digits, the last field printed has been padded on the left with two blanks to make up the requested printer field of width 10.

Thus the Z format code allows the programmer to examine the actual bit configuration that the computer uses to store a value. On input, it may be used to set up special bit patterns in memory.

The rules for the Zw code are:

(a) For output, if the number of hexadecimal digits
     -2, 4, 8, 16, 32, for a value of length 1, 2, 4,
     8, 16, bytes respectively - is less than the field
     width w, the field is padded on the left with
     blanks. If the number of hexadecimal digits is
     greater than w, only the w farthest-right digits
     are printed.

(b) For input, leading, embedded, and trailing blanks
     in the input field of width w are treated as zeros.
     If w exceeds the number n of hexadecimal digits
     corresponding to the number of bytes occupied by
     the variable, the farthest-right digits of the
     input field are used; if w is less than n, the
     input field is padded on the left with the hexade-
     cimal digit 0. Only the hexadecimal digits
          0, 1, 2, 3, 4, 5, 6, 7, 8, 9,
          A, B, C, D, E, F, or blanks
     may appear in the input field.

21.3   T FORMAT

The T format code simplifies the construction of FORMAT
statements in which the positioning of fields in the print
line is important. The code Tw used on output does not itself
print anything, but specifies that the next field to be
printed is to start in position w of the FORTRAN record. In
this respect, its action is similar to that of a "tab-stop" on
a typewriter.

Example 21.3 illustrates how the T format code may be
used.

```
C EXAMPLE 21.3 - T FORMAT
      X = J = 10
      PRINT 16, J, X
16    FORMAT(' ', T14, 'J=', I2, T38, 'X=', F4.1)
```

The line printed is

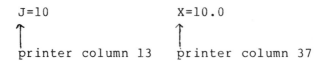

          J=10   X=10.0

          ↑   ↑

          printer column 13   printer column 37

The code T14 specifies that the next field is to start in position 14 of the record. For printer output, this corresponds to column 13, since the first character in the record is used as the printer control character.

Since the T format code specifies where in the record the next field is to start, the codes in a FORMAT statement do not necessarily have to be given in a left-to-right order. Thus, the same printer line would have resulted from the use of the statement

    FORMAT(T16, I2, T38, 'X=', T1, ' ', T40, F4.1, T14,'J=')

Although it is not normal to "tab" backwards, as in the above example, this is sometimes done to achieve special effects. Example 21.4 shows how a high-order zero can be inserted in a field.

```
C EXAMPLE 21.4 - USE OF T FORMAT
      X = 50.01
      L = K = 50
      M = J = 1
      WRITE(6,7) K, J, L, M, X
7     FORMAT(' $  .00', T3, I2,   T6, I2, 4X, '$', I2, '.',
      *          I2, 4X, '$', F5.2)
```

The values of L, M, and X are printed for comparison; the resulting line is

          $50.01 $50. 1 $50.01

This effect is achieved in the following way. In composing the record, WATFIV-S first moves the Hollerith string specified by ' $ .00' to the first seven positions of a temporary area in memory, called a buffer. The field for K is tabbed to position 3, and the characters 50 overwrite, in the buffer, the two blanks which were in positions three and four. The field for J is tabbed to position 6, but only the non-blank characters are moved into the buffer. Thus the first zero following the decimal point remains in the buffer, but the second zero is overwritten with the value, 1, of J. The other Hollerith strings and the fields for L, M and X are also moved into the buffer. When the end of the FORMAT statement is reached, the record is transmitted from the buffer to the printer for printing.

Note that care must be taken, when T format is used as above, to ensure that only the desired fields are overwritten.

On input, the code Tw indicates that the next field starts in position w of the input record, e.g., column w of a data card. Example 21.5 shows how columns 61 to 80 of a data card may be read "twice" as alphabetic data into different variables with different format codes.

```
      C EXAMPLE 21.5 - T FORMAT ON INPUT
            CHARACTER COL1(20), COL4(5)
            READ(5,2) COL1, COL4
      2     FORMAT(T61, 20A1, T61, 5A4)
```

21.4   THE SLASH (/) FORMAT CODE

The / format code is used to indicate the end of one FORTRAN record and the start of a new one. This means, for example, that more than one printer line can be described by a single FORMAT statement.

Example 21.6 shows how the / code may be used to produce multi-record formats.

- 283 -

```
C EXAMPLE 21.6 - USE OF '/'
      A = 16.
      B = 25.
      I = 35
      J = 17
      PRINT 9, A, I, J, B
9     FORMAT(' ', 'NOTE' / ' ', F7.0, I3/'0', I2, F6.1)
```

The output is

```
              NOTE
              bbbb16.b35

              17bb25.0
```

The / following the string NOTE indicates that the end of
the first record (print line) has been reached, and that a new
record is to be started for any values that remain to be
printed. Thus, the values of A and I are printed on the
second line, according to the codes F7.0 and I3 respectively.
The / which follows I3 again indicates that a new record is to
be started for any values remaining to be printed, namely, J
and B. Note that a printer control character is given at the
start of each record.

Consecutive slashes may be used, with the result that
blank records are inserted in the output. If the FORMAT
statement of Example 21.6 were changed to

```
    FORMAT(' ', 'NOTE' /// ' ', F7.0, I3 / '0', I2, F6.1 //)
```

the output would be

```
                        NOTE
      2 blank lines -
                    -
                        bbbb16.b35
      1 blank line  -
                        17   25.0
      2 blank lines -
                    -
```

The rule is that n consecutive slashes at the beginning
or end of a FORMAT statement cause n blank records to be

produced; n consecutive slashes within the statement cause n-1 blank records to be produced.

The / code can be used on input to skip to new records, to read some values, or to skip whole records entirely. Example 21.7 reads A and B from the first card, C from the second card, D from the <u>fourth</u> card; furthermore, cards five and six are skipped entirely.

```
      C EXAMPLE 21.7 - '/' ON INPUT
        READ(5,2) A, B, C, D
    2   FORMAT(2E15.7 / F4.2 // E9.1 //)
```

If the read statement were

```
        READ(1,2) A, B, C, D
```

values of A and B would be obtained from the first record of the sequential file on unit 1, C from the second record, D from the fourth record. Records three, five, and six would be skipped entirely; a subsequent read on unit 1 would input the seventh record on the file.

Finally, it should be noted that / acts like a comma as a valid separator between format codes; hence a comma is not required where a / already exists as a separator. But feel free to use a comma if you think it will improve readability, e.g.,

```
        FORMAT(F20.8, /, 3A4)
```

instead of

```
        FORMAT(F20.8/3A4)
```

21.5 GROUP COUNTS

In the same way that field count allows a single format code to be repeated a number of times, a <u>group</u> <u>count</u> allows a collection of codes to be repeated. Example 21.8 illustrates the use of a group count.

```
      C EXAMPLE 21.8 - GROUP COUNT
          REAL X(3)/-1., 0., +1./
          PRINT 10, (L, X(L), L=1,3)
   10     FORMAT(' ', 3(I3, F4.0))
```

The output is the line

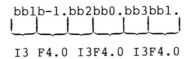

```
      I3 F4.0 I3F4.0 I3F4.0
```

The format codes to be repeated - I3, F4.0 - are enclosed
in parentheses following the group count 3.   Note that the
same result could have been achieved with the FORMAT statement

```
   10     FORMAT(' ', I3, F4.0, I3, F4.0, I3, F4.0)
```

If a group count is not specified, it is assumed to be 1.
Thus the following statements are equivalent.

```
          FORMAT((2I5, 1X, 3F4.2))
          FORMAT(1(2I5, 1X, 3F4.2))
          FORMAT(I5, I5, 1X, F4.2, F4.2, F4.2)
```

The following are sample statements which contain group
counts.

```
(a)   FORMAT('0', I5, 3(F6.1, '*', I3), F8.3/' ', 6(2I4, I7))
(b)   FORMAT(' ', 2(I6, F4.0, 3G6), 4(I2 // (F7.0, 2Z10)), I2)
(c)   FORMAT('-', 3(2G14.5, 2(I1, I3)))
```

Statements (b) and (c) show grouped format codes nested to the
maximum allowed depth of 2.

Example 21.9 shows what happens if the end of a FORMAT
statement is reached before all variables in the list have
been processed.   The example reads an integer value N from the
first data card, followed by N real numbers punched 8 per
card.   Assume N is less than or equal to 100.

```
      C EXAMPLE 21.9
          DIMENSION X(100)
          READ(5,3) N, (X(I), I=1,N)
   3      FORMAT(I3 / (8F10.4))
```

The READ statement and FORMAT statement work together as follows. The READ statement causes the first card to be read. The FORMAT statement specifies that the value of N is in columns 1 to 3 of the card. The / code indicates the end of the current record, so the next data card is obtained. Eight real values are taken from that card, and the end of the FORMAT statement is reached. If N is greater than 8, more values must be obtained, and the next card is read. Control returns within the FORMAT statement to the group count (here assumed to be 1) preceding the left parenthesis which encloses the code 8F10.4. If the end of the FORMAT statement is reached again, and all values have still not been read, the process repeats.

Note that this effect is considerably different from what would occur for the statement

3 FORMAT(I3 / 8F10.4)

In fact, the latter statement would result in an error if used with the READ statement of Example 21.9 if N were greater than 8.

The rules which apply to the use of group counts follow:

(a) Groups of format codes may be nested to a maximum depth of two. Thus, the following statement is in error.

FORMAT(3(2F4.2, 2(I2, I6, 4(I5, 2X)))))

(b) If the closing right parenthesis of the FORMAT statement is reached before all items in the I/O list have been processed, a new record is started and (a) control returns in the FORMAT statement to the group count associated with the left paren-thesis that corresponds to the second last right parenthesis, or (b) control returns to the first code of the FORMAT statement if there are no group counts.

Some pictorial examples follow.

FORMAT(...2(...)...3(...)...)

FORMAT(...(..2(..).)..2(...2(...)..))

FORMAT(...)

21.6   SCALE FACTORS

If the reader has run many programs on the computer, he
may be somewhat frustrated by the fact that discrepancies
occasionally arise when calculations are done which involve
real numbers with decimal fractions. For example

PRINT ,1./3. + 1./3. + 1./3.

produces the result 0.9999999.

These problems arise because of the inaccuracy which
results from the conversion of decimal fractions to hexadecimal floating-point numbers for the computer's internal use.

Although these discrepancies can usually be ignored, they
can be annoying when the programmer is working on a problem
that requires complete accuracy of results, for example, an
accounting problem involving money and requiring accuracy to
the nearest cent.

The programmer might consider doing all calculations
using integer arithmetic, but this might prove inconvenient
for several reasons. For example, the precision of integer
values is not as great as that of double-precision values. Or
it might prove bothersome to key-punch data as, for example,
345, when a notation such as 3.45 might be desired.

The use of scale factors in FORMAT statements can aid the
programmer in the following way. A value for a real variable
can be punched as, say, 3.45 on a data card, but can be read
in and used in the computer as the value 345., free of any

decimal fraction. Similarly, on output, the number can be scaled down to re-appear with a decimal fraction. Example 21.10 is a simple illustration of this idea.

```
C EXAMPLE 21.10 - SIMPLE P-SCALING
      READ 2, X
2     FORMAT(-2PF4.2)
      PRINT 3, X, X
3     FORMAT(' ', F6.2, 2X, -2PF4.2)
```

If the input card contains the value 3.45 punched in columns 1 to 4, the output line appears as follows:

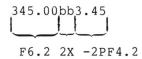

345.00bb3.45

F6.2 2X -2PF4.2

The value of X used <u>internally</u> in the computer is 345.; its value <u>externally</u> can appear as 3.45; the scaling factor -2P, applied to the F format codes, takes care of the conversion automatically.

The general form of the P code is sP, where s is an unsigned or negatively signed constant; for example,

$$-2P \ , \ 3P \ , \ 0P$$

It usually precedes a format code used for real values; for example,

$$-2PD14.2 \ , \ 0PE14.7 \ , \ 1P3F6.2$$

The number 3 appearing between the P and F in the last example is a field count for the F code.

The conversion effected by the scale factor sP is described by the rule

$$\text{external number} = 10^S \times \text{internal value}$$

The result is that X in example 21.10 is assigned the value 345. when the data field 3.45 is read with format code -2PF4.2; however, X re-appears printed as 3.45 when scaled by -2PF4.2.

Example 21.11 shows how P-scaling might be put to use in a payroll-related application. A number of data cards are read, each containing two values which represent the number of hours worked in a week by an employee and his hourly rate. The program calculates each employee's weekly gross pay, and accumulates the total gross pay for all the employees.

```
C EXAMPLE 21.11 - PAY CALCULATION
      INTEGER PAY, SUM
      PRINT 18
      SUM = 0
      LOOP
          READ(5,15) HOURS, RATE
          AT END, QUIT
          PAY = (IFIX(HOURS)*IFIX(RATE) + 50) / 100
          PRINT 16, HOURS, RATE, FLOAT(PAY)
          SUM = SUM + PAY
      ENDLOOP
      PRINT 17, FLOAT(SUM)
      STOP
18    FORMAT('1', T4, 'HOURS', T15, 'RATE', T25,
     *        'GROSS PAY')
15    FORMAT(-2PF5.2, 4X, -2PF4.2)
16    FORMAT(' ', T4, -2PF5.2, T15, -2PF4.2, T25,
     *         '$*********', T25, -2PF10.2)
17    FORMAT('0TOTAL GROSS PAY', T25, '$*********', T25,
     *         -2PF10.2)
      END
```

Some sample output follows

HOURS	RATE	GROSS PAY
40.00	3.50	$***140.00
25.00	1.99	$****49.75
41.00	3.00	$***123.00
45.50	2.55	$***116.03
TOTAL GROSS PAY		$***428.78

The data card for the first employee would be punched, starting in column 1 as

40.00bbbb3.50

The data cards for all other employees would be punched in a similar manner.

Note that the pay is calculated as an integer value rounded to the nearest cent. The built-in function IFIX is used to give the integer values corresponding to real values HOURS and RATE, and the values of PAY and SUM are changed to real values using the built-in function FLOAT. These latter values are scaled to have two decimal places for printing.

Several examples which show the effect of P-scaling on input follow:

Format Code	External Number as Input	Internal Value
-2PF5.2	26.73	2673.
2PF5.2	26.73	.2673
3PF11.2	26532000.	26532.
0PF5.1	46.5	46.5
2PE8.2	76.58E2	7658.
2PE10.2	7658.	76.58

The last two examples show that P-scaling on input applies only to F-style numbers, that is, real numbers without an E or D exponent.

P-scaling on output applies to any real value, whether written in F, E, D, or G, format. Examples of output follow:

Format Code	Internal Value	External Number as Output
2PE12.3	76532.	76.532E 03
-3PE12.6	76532.	0.000765E 08
3PF9.0	76532.	76532000.
-2PG9.2	76532.	0.00E 07

There is one other property of the P format code that remains to be explained. A scale factor, once encountered in a particular FORMAT statement, applies to all F, E, D, and G, codes which are subsequently encountered in the same statement, unless the P-scale is replaced with another scale factor. This means that the following two statements are equivalent.

```
            FORMAT(-2PF5.2, 4X, -2PF4.1)
            FORMAT(-2PF5.2, 4X, F4.1)
```

A scale factor 0P can be used to cancel the effect of any previous scale factor. For example, in the statement

```
        FORMAT(-3PF7.3, 4PE17.6, 0PF5.2, F3.0)
```

the codes F5.2 and F3.0 are not affected by any scale factor.

21.7 EXECUTION-TIME FORMAT

As has been seen, programs of a very general nature can be written using the FORTRAN language. For example, a program can be prepared that will calculate the over-all average mark for a class of virtually any size, and in which any student takes virtually any number of courses. The program could read in, as data, the number of students, a record of the number of courses that each student takes, and his mark in each course. An additional degree of flexibility could be obtained by using an integer variable as a unit number in certain READ statements of the program. In this way, the data to be processed could be stored either on cards or on tape; the value of the unit number to be used could be read in as a parameter to the program.

One degree of inflexibility does exist, however. Once the program has been compiled, any data to be used with the program must conform to the format specifications, present in the program, that will be used to read or print the data. This means that if the data are not punched in a compatible form, the FORMAT statements of the program have to be revised and the program has to be recompiled.

To avoid this undesirable possibility, a facility has been included in the FORTRAN language to allow format specifications to be read into the computer, as alphabetic data, at

execution time. This, in essence, allows a suitable FORMAT
statement to be composed after the data have been punched;
both the data and the format codes to read them can be fed
into the computer at execution time, with no modification of
the program.

Example 21.12 illustrates this idea of execution-time
format or variable format.

```
C EXAMPLE 21.12 - VARIABLE FORMAT
      DIMENSION X(100)
      CHARACTER VEC(80)
      READ(5,2) VEC
2     FORMAT(80A1)
      READ(5,VEC) N, (X(I), I=1,N)
      .
      .
```

The first READ statement reads all 80 columns into the
character array VEC, using the A format code. The second READ
statement contains the name of the character array VEC in
place of a FORMAT statement number. The result is that, at
execution time, the characters stored in the array VEC are
decoded as format specifications, and these are used to read N
and the first N elements of X. The character data read into
the array VEC must look exactly like any FORMAT statement,
except that the word FORMAT does not precede the parenthesized
list of codes. For example, the data card for VEC might be

(I3 / (E14.7, 2X, 3F10.2 / 6F8.4))

Note that the format list could be at most 80 characters long
(including the outer parentheses), since VEC has dimension 80.
This number was chosen only for illustration, and could be
changed to suit the programmer.

An execution-time format must be stored in an array, even
if the array consists of only one element, and the array name
may be used in any I/O statement in place of a FORMAT statement number. Valid statements are

```
      WRITE(I,VEC) P, W, R
      READ(3,FMT,END=12,ERR=2) (Y(I), I=1,N)
      PRINT ARRAY, A, B, C, D
```

where VEC, FMT, Y, and ARRAY are arrays.

A final example will show that execution time formats can, in fact, be constructed and modified by the program, i.e., they need not be read in.

```
C EXAMPLE 21.13 - VARIABLE FORMAT
      REAL A(10,10)
      CHARACTER DIGIT(10)/'1', '2', '3', '4', '5', '6',
     *             '7', '8', '9', '10'/
      CHARACTER*6 VF(3)/'(1H0', '  ', 'F12.6)'/
      READ, N
      .
      .
      VF(2) = DIGIT(N)
      WRITE(6,VF) ((A(I,J), J=1,N), I=1,N)
      .
      .
      END
```

Example 21.13 initializes the elements of the vector DIGIT to the character strings shown. The vector VF has its three adjacent elements initialized to the character string

$$(1H0bbbbbbbF12.6)$$

A value is read in for N, and this is subsequently used in the statement

$$VF(2) = DIGIT(N)$$

to replace the six blanks initially stored in VF(2). For example, if N equals 6, the vector VF is modified to

$$(1H0bb6bbbbbF12.6)$$

Recalling that blanks in a FORMAT statement are ignored, the reader will see that the effect of the WRITE statement is to print the elements of a 6 by 6 matrix by rows, double-spaced, with one row per printed line.

21.8   EXERCISES

21.1   Write a program which declares four variables I, A, C, and L to be of integer, real, complex, and logical type respectively. As well, the variables I, A, C, and L should be initialized to have the values 3225, 625.629, (32.4,16.E5), and .FALSE. respectively. Then print the variables, using the statement

PRINT 17, I, A, C, L

with each of the following FORMAT statements:

(a)   17 FORMAT('0', 5G16.7)

(b)   17 FORMAT('0', G4, 3G14.6, G9)

(c)   17 FORMAT('0', 5G4.0)

(d)   17 FORMAT('0', G3, 4G15.2)

(e)   17 FORMAT('0', 5(G16.5, 4X))

(f)   17 FORMAT('0', 5('VALUE IS', 5G16.3))

(g)   17 FORMAT('0', G15.6)

(h)   17 FORMAT('0', 8G15.6)

It is instructive to predict what the results will be before actually running the program on the computer.

21.2   Example 21.3 demonstrates how the T format code can be used to position fields in a print line. Write a program that calculates a table of sines, cosines, tangents, and square roots for x = 0, 1, 2, ..., 25. Use the T format code to position the headings and the columns to be printed.

21.3 The first card of a data deck contains the size n of a square matrix A (assume $n \leq 16$). The rest of the deck consists of n data cards, each card containing n integer values, punched using format I5. Write a program that reads the entire data deck, using one READ statement. Assume that the values are punched in row sequence. Print the matrix and a suitable heading, using one PRINT statement.

21.4 (a) A data deck consists of 100 real values, each having two decimal places. Write a program that reads the values, using a scaling factor to multiply each value by 100. Find the sum of the values, using integer arithmetic, and print the result, again using scaling to divide the result by 100. If the sum contains more than 7 digits, use an extended-precision variable to print the final result.

(b) Repeat part (a), but this time use T format to read each value twice, once with scaling and once without scaling. Perform all calculations using real arithmetic. Compare the two results.

21.5 (a) Punch a set of data cards according to some format of your choice. The first data card should contain the necessary list of format codes to input your data. Write a program that reads the format list into an array, and then uses the variable-format feature to read the data cards into another array.

(b) Modify the data deck so that the second data card contains a list of format codes that could be used to output the array. Write a program to read in the two format lists, and then use these to read and print your data.

21.6 Exercise 15.9 describes a figure consisting of a set of points, some of which may be connected by either vertical or horizontal lines. Write a program that reads data which describes the connections for a particular figure of your choice, and that prints the figure using *'s to denote the points and .'s to denote the connections.

21.7 Write a subprogram which accepts an integer N as input, and prints a "square" with N asterisks on each side. The figure will not be square, because the horizontal spacing on the printer is different from the vertical spacing.

21.8 Write a subprogram which accepts two integers N and M as input, and prints a "rectangle" with N asterisks as the width and M asterisks as the length.

21.9 (a) Write a subprogram which accepts the value r as input, and outlines the circle

$$x^2 + y^2 = r^2$$

on the printer, using the asterisk symbol. The circle should take up as much room as possible on the printed page. Some indication defining the scale should be printed.

(b) Part (a) should suggest a technique for "plotting" functions using the printer. Design a subprogram which has the kind of graphic output for functions of the type

$$y = f(x).$$

21.10 Your answers for Exercise 18.2, and Exercise 18.4 can be verified by reading in the constants from data cards, and printing their values, using the Z format code. Write a program to do this.

Chapter 22

CORE-TO-CORE INPUT/OUTPUT

In a previous chapter, we have discussed the general input/output statements

```
READ(unit,fmt,END=n,ERR=m) list
WRITE(unit,fmt) list
```

and their particular forms and applications in terms of I/O with card readers, printers, punches, tapes, and direct-access devices. In each of these cases, "unit" referred to a specific physical device (or part of a physical device) which was external to the main memory. For example, if "unit" were 5, a READ would cause a card or cards to be read sequentially from the card reader.

WATFIV-S allows another form of the "unit" parameter in these generalized statements. When "unit" is a variable of type character, the character string thus referenced is treated as an I/O device similar to the card reader or printer. The interesting thing is that no actual I/O device is involved; the effect is to create a memory-to-memory transfer of data, under format control. This format control gives the programmer the facility to transform data from one form to another within the computer. This feature is called core-to-core I/O,[5] and has many useful applications.

---

[5] The term "core-to-core" stems from the days when computer memory was made of small ferrite cores; memory was often referred to as core.

22.1   EXAMPLES

Let us consider a number of simple examples to illustrate the mechanics of the process.   Then we will introduce more comprehensive examples, and will conclude with a summary of the rules.

```
      C EXAMPLE 22.1
            CHARACTER*11 A/'1.234-86.45'/
            READ(A,2) X, Y
      2     FORMAT(F5.3, F6.2)
            Z = X + Y
            PRINT, Z
            STOP
            END
```

In Example 22.1, the character variable A may be considered as a card of 11 columns.   The READ statement references "unit" A; since "unit" A has been declared a character variable, the contents of variable A are "read" in the same way as we would read information from an eleven-column card.   The reading is under control of FORMAT statement 2.   Thus, the real variables X and Y are assigned the values 1.234 and -86.45, respectively.

If the FORMAT statement were incorrect in any way, an error message would result.

Let us consider a few modifications of the FORMAT statement, together with their effects.

(a)   2 FORMAT(F4.2, F7.2) The variable X is assigned the value 1.23, but an error occurs for Y, since the field 4-86.45 can not be interpreted by the format code F7.2.

(b)   2 FORMAT(F4.2, 2X, F4.1) The variables X and Y are assigned the values 1.23 and 86.4 respectively. The 2X causes the 4- to be skipped, and 5, the eleventh character, is ignored.

(c) 2 FORMAT(F5.2, F8.2) An error occurs because the FORMAT statement attempts to reference 13 characters, whereas A has a capacity of only 11 characters.

(d) 2 FORMAT(F5.3 / F6.2) Here, X is assigned the value 1.234 according to the format code F5.3. The "/" indicates that a new record is to be used for the value of Y. An error message results, indicating that we have run out of data, since the character variable A consists of only one string or record.

To allow for the possibility of reading more than one record in core-to-core I/O, the "unit" may be a character array. For example, if we define A by

```
        CHARACTER A*11(2) /'1.234', '-86.45'/
```

then the statements

```
              READ(A,2)   X, Y
        2     FORMAT(F5.3 / F6.2)
```

result in values of 1.234 and −86.45 for X and Y respectively. In effect, the elements of array A can be considered as a collection of sequential records. Example 22.2 provides another illustration of this idea.

```
        C EXAMPLE 22.2
              INTEGER X/2579/
              CHARACTER*20 B(5)/5*' '/, Y/'ZZZ'/
              WRITE(B,2) X, Y
        2     FORMAT(I10, 3X, 'ABC' / A20)
              PRINT, B
              STOP
              END
```

In Example 22.2, the WRITE statement references the character array B. The 5 elements of the array B can be considered as 5 lines on the printer, each one having 20 print positions. Thus, after the WRITE is executed, elements B(1) and B(2) would contain

bbbbbb2579bbbABCbbbb

and

ZZZbbbbbbbbbbbbbbbbbb

respectively; the values of B(3), B(4), and B(5) are not affected. No carriage-control character need be used in the FORMAT statement, since no actual printing takes place.

Consider the following FORMAT statements and their corresponding effects.

(a) 2 FORMAT('A' / 'B' / 'C' / I4 / A18) After the WRITE statement of Example 22.2 is executed, the contents of array B are as follows:

    B(1)   Abbbbbbbbbbbbbbbbbbb
    B(2)   Bbbbbbbbbbbbbbbbbbbb
    B(3)   Cbbbbbbbbbbbbbbbbbbb
    B(4)   2579bbbbbbbbbbbbbbbb
    B(5)   ZZZbbbbbbbbbbbbbbbbb

(b) 2 FORMAT(I10, A20) Here an error message results because the length of the first element of B is only 20, and the FORMAT statement is attempting to store 30 characters in it.

(c) 2 FORMAT(// I10 / A20 /) Here twenty blanks are stored in each of B(1), B(2), and B(5); B(3) and B(4) are as follows:

    B(3)   bbbbb2579bbbbbbbbbbb
    B(4)   ZZZbbbbbbbbbbbbbbbbb

(d) 2 FORMAT(//// I10 / A20) This results in an error message since we are trying to write six records, and the character array contains only five elements.

The core-to-core "unit" may also be specified as a char-
acter-array element. An example is

                    READ(B(I),2) list

This has the effect of starting the READ at the Ith element or
record of B.

22.2   RE-READS WITH CORE-TO-CORE I/O

    One of the important applications of core-to-core I/O is
the provision of a method of reading a record several times
using different FORMAT statements. For example, an input deck
can consist of cards with several different data formats in
any order. Thus, before we read a card, we have no idea which
of several FORMAT statements to use. Example 22.3 assumes
that the input cards are of three types, and each type is
identified by a code of 1, 2, or 3 in column 80. Core-to-core
I/O can be used to overcome the problem, as indicated in the
following example.

    Here the first 79 columns of the card are read into a
character variable STRING, and column 80 is read into TYPE.
Then the type of card is determined, using the case construct.
Subsequently, the first 79 columns are re-read from STRING,
using core-to-core I/O and the appropriate FORMAT statement.

```
C EXAMPLE 22.3
      CHARACTER*79 STRING
      INTEGER TYPE
      READ 2, STRING, TYPE
2     FORMAT(A79, I1)
      IF (TYPE .EQ. 1) THEN
          READ(STRING,7) LIST
7         FORMAT(...)
             .
             .
      ELSEIF (TYPE .EQ. 2) THEN
          READ(STRING,8) LIST
8         FORMAT(...)
             .
             .
      ELSEIF (TYPE .EQ. 3) THEN
          READ(STRING,9) LIST
9         FORMAT(...)
             .
             .
      ELSE
          PRINT, 'ERROR IN CARD-', STRING, TYPE
      ENDIF
      STOP
      END
```

22.3   MODIFYING EXECUTION-TIME FORMATS

Another important application of core-to-core I/O is the convenient ability which it gives to the programmer to modify execution-time formats. For example, in the statement

```
      CHARACTER*13 F(1)/'(1H0,10X,1H*)'/
         .
         .
      WRITE(6,F)
```

the format parameter in the WRITE statement is given as the character variable F. F is initialized to the character string

```
      (1H0,10X,1H*)
```

and this is a list of format codes. Thus, the WRITE statement results in an asterisk being printed in the eleventh print position. A character array, or a character array element, can be used to store the string of format codes. An array of a different type could also be used.

```
C EXAMPLE 22.4
      CHARACTER*13 F(1)
      DO 3 I=1,20
         WRITE(F,2) I
2        FORMAT('(1H0, ', I2, 'X, 1H*)')
         WRITE(6,F)
3     CONTINUE
      STOP
      END
```

In this example, we have two WRITE statements within the range of the DO-loop. The first WRITE sets up a format list in the character variable F using core-to-core I/O. It is used as an execution-time format for the second WRITE. Note that, each time through the loop, the contents of F are changed according to the current value of I. The effect is that twenty lines are printed, each containing one asterisk, where the asterisk is in print position 2 of line 1, print position 3 of line 2, etc.

22.4   CORE-TO-CORE I/O SUMMARY

Core-to-core I/O uses the two generalized statements

```
      READ(unit,fmt,end=) list
      WRITE(unit,fmt) list
```

"Unit" is either a character variable, a subscripted character variable, or a character array name. If "unit" is an array, each element of that array is considered as a sequential record whose length is indicated by the number of bytes in each element of the character array.

The "fmt" parameter is either a statement number of a FORMAT statement or the name of an execution-time format list.

The "list" is similar to the list used in other I/O operations in FORTRAN.

22.5   EXERCISES

22.1   A card contains one or more integer constants, separated from one another by semicolons. Write a generalized program which reads cards of this type and which calculates and prints the sum of the integers on each card. Test your program using the following data cards.

column 1

↓

123;-86;12678;+35
-8;+3;-0;+0;896;34286

22.2   (a)   Key-punch the program of Example 22.4 and verify that it works by testing it on the computer.

(b)   Modify the program by replacing the DO statement with the following four statements

```
            J = 5
            DO 3 K=1,11
              I = J**2
              J = J - 1
```

Run the program, and note the pattern of asterisks. What function are you plotting, and for what values of the variables?

Chapter 23

INPUT/OUTPUT WITH DIRECT-ACCESS FILES

In this chapter, we describe the rules for creating and processing direct-access files using WATFIV-S. The programmer should be aware that direct-access I/O is a very specialized method. In general, before writing programs which use this feature, he should check with his installation for any local rules concerning the use of direct-access I/O.

23.1   DIRECT-ACCESS FILES

In Chapter 20, we discussed the use of magnetic tapes for the storage and processing of data files. Vast quantities of data can be recorded rapidly and economically using tape. However, this procedure possesses a disadvantage: because of the sequential nature of tape, half of a file must be processed in order to read a record in the centre of the file. This can mean a retrieval time in the order of several minutes for that particular part of the file. This retrieval time is, of course, a function of the tape unit being used and of the actual length of the file; thus, the average retrieval time can vary from fractions of a second to minutes, depending on the circumstances.

This timing problem is the reason that magnetic tapes are seldom used to store records which have to be retrieved at random. Fortunately, many file processing applications are of a sequential nature, and magnetic tapes are ideal in such cases; however, when random retrieval of information is required, we use direct-access devices such as magnetic drums or disks.

It is beyond the scope of this book to describe the physical details of the various direct-access storage devices. However, these devices use a variety of hardware techniques to achieve a common goal; that goal is to read a record from any part of the file into computer memory within a fraction of a second. These hardware techniques include multiple read/write heads, moving read/write heads, and different physical arrangements of the storage media.

23.2   DIRECT-ACCESS FILES IN FORTRAN

The user can consider that his file consists of a number of records, each of which has an index which indicates the relative position of the record in the file. The first record has index 1, the second has index 2, etc., with the indices increasing by unity for each record up to the end of the file. Thus, the index is a way of referring directly to a record within the file. Any one of these records can be located and read into memory in less than one second. FORTRAN files which are set up in this way are known as direct-access files, and are created and processed using direct-access I/O statements.

Suppose we wish to set up a direct-access file with one record for each of the 1869 students in a school. Furthermore, assume that the students have been assigned student identification numbers from 1 to 1869. In order to begin our file of information, we punch a card containing student number and name, for each of the 1869 students. Example 23.1 illustrates a simple program for creating the file and storing this information.

The DEFINE FILE statement causes a portion of available random-access memory to be associated with to unit number 12 (also referred to as data set reference number 12, or, informally, as file 12). This file is to have 2000 records, each of 150 bytes in length. The E indicates that each record will be read or written using format control. INT is an integer variable, and is known as the associated variable; its purpose will be described later.

```
C EXAMPLE 23.1 - CREATING A DIRECT-ACCESS FILE
      INTEGER STUDNO
      CHARACTER NAME*20
      DEFINE FILE 12(2000, 150, E, INT)
      DO 22 I=1,1869
          READ 3, STUDNO, NAME
          WRITE(12'STUDNO, 4) NAME
22    CONTINUE
3     FORMAT(I4, A20)
4     FORMAT(A20)
      STOP
      END
```

The WRITE statement causes the records to be written into the file. It is an example of the general WRITE statement discussed earlier, i.e.,

WRITE(unit,fmt) list

In this case, the "unit" parameter is replaced by 12'STUDNO, which means "file 12, that specific record whose index is the current integer value of STUDNO". The "fmt" and "list" are 4 and NAME respectively.

The program reads a student number and name from each card, and stores only the name in the record indexed according to the student number. This procedure is repeated in the DO-loop for each of the 1869 cards. Note that the cards are not required to be in any particular sequence. The direct-access WRITE statement will seek out the proper record prior to transferring the name from memory to random-access storage.

Note that we reserved 2000 records, although there were only 1869 students. This is to allow for an increase in student population. Also, note that we used only 20 bytes of the 150 bytes reserved for each record. This permits us, at some future time, to store additional information about a student, such as examination marks. In the meantime, the 130 unused positions contain blanks. These blanks were automatically stored to fill out the record when the name was written into the first 20 bytes.

Example 23.2 shows how the file can be expanded to record marks for a particular examination. A card is prepared containing student number and mark for each examination, and these cards make up the data deck for the program.

```
C EXAMPLE 23.2
      INTEGER STUDNO, ASSOC
      CHARACTER NAME*20
      DEFINE FILE 12(2000, 150, E, ASSOC)
      LOOP
          READ(5,1) STUDNO, MARK
          AT END, QUIT
          READ(12'STUDNO, 2) NAME
          WRITE(12'STUDNO, 3) NAME, MARK
      ENDLOOP
      STOP
1     FORMAT(I4, I3)
2     FORMAT(A20)
3     FORMAT(A20, I3)
      END
```

The program reads a card, and subsequently reads the corresponding student record from file 12.

The FORTRAN statement

READ(12'STUDNO, 2) NAME

causes the specific record indexed by the value of STUDNO to be read from file 12, using FORMAT statement 2. The name is read and is stored in the character variable NAME. Then the record is re-written into the same physical location in file 12; this time, the name and mark are recorded.

- 309 -

Note that, once again, the cards in the input data deck can be in random sequence, and only those students who have received a mark on the examination have their records updated. Note also that, in order to add a mark to a record, we have to read it first, then write it. This is because it is not possible to write onto a part of a record. Each WRITE causes the entire record to be altered. Thus, if there is any information in a record which must be retained, the record must be read first, and then written, with all the information to be recorded placed in the output list of the WRITE statement.

A DEFINE FILE statement is included in Example 23.2; it specifies the same characteristics with which the file was originally created.

The program in Example 23.3 prepares a list giving student number, name, and examination mark for each of a selected group of students. This selected group is identified by punching the student number of each onto separate cards; these cards form the data deck for the program.

```
C EXAMPLE 23.3
         INTEGER STUDNO
         CHARACTER NAME*20
         DEFINE FILE 12(2000, 150, E, INT)
         LOOP
             READ(5,1) STUDNO
             AT END, QUIT
             READ(12'STUDNO, 2) NAME, MARK
             PRINT 3, STUDNO, NAME, MARK
         ENDLOOP
         STOP
1        FORMAT(I4)
2        FORMAT(A20, I3)
3        FORMAT('0', I8, 3X, A20, I6)
         END
```

The program reads a data card, reads the appropriate record in the direct-access file, and prints one line. This procedure is repeated for each of the data cards. If the data cards are in a random sequence by student number, the output listing will be in the same sequence.

- 310 -

The example illustrates a weakness in our planning in the previous examples. A problem arises when no mark has been previously recorded for a particular student. Execution of the statement

READ(12'STUDNO, 2) NAME, MARK

then results in assigning a value of zero to the integer variable MARK, since the record contains blanks rather than a three-digit integer. There is no indication that this is not a legitimate mark of zero. Exercise 23.5 suggests one method for overcoming this difficulty. Of course, there are other ways of applying controls in a situation like this. The matter is raised here only to bring the general problem to the attention of the reader.

23.3   DIRECT ACCESS WITH FORMAT CONTROL

The previous examples have been concerned with a direct-access file with which FORMAT statements were used to control input/output. This section is meant to consolidate some of the ideas, and to summarize the various rules.

(a)   The file is always set up using a DEFINE FILE statement of the following type:

DEFINE FILE unit(number, size, E, associated variable)

This statement must be executed prior to reading or writing into the file. It may appear more than once in a program or its associated subprograms, but second and subsequent definitions of a file are ignored.

The "unit" could be any integer from 1 to 99 inclusive, depending on the conventions used at any particular installation. The reader must be aware of these local conventions before using direct access features of FORTRAN.

The "number" is an integer constant which indicates the number of records in the file.

The "size" is an integer constant which indicates the number of bytes in each record.

The letter E indicates that I/O will be done under format control.

The "associated variable" is an integer variable. If n is the index of the record last processed by a read or write operation, the associated variable is assigned the integer value n+1. Thus, this variable has a value which is the index of the next sequential record in the file following a read or write operation. This can be useful to read a direct-access file sequentially, as in Example 23.4.

```
      C EXAMPLE 23.4
            DEFINE FILE 12(2000, 150, E, INT)
            CHARACTER NAME*20
            INT = 123
            DO 5 J=1,10
                READ(12'INT, 4) NAME
                PRINT 6, NAME
      5     CONTINUE
            STOP
      4     FORMAT(A20)
      6     FORMAT('0', A20)
            END
```

In Example 23.4, the DO-loop is executed ten times. The first READ causes record 123 to be read. Then INT is automatically set to 124, since it is the associated variable. The second READ thus causes record 124 to be retrieved. Ultimately, each of records 123 to 132 (inclusive) is read and printed.

The associated variable has all of the usual properties of an integer variable, but has some restrictions. It cannot appear as part of the "list" of a READ or a WRITE statement involving direct-access I/O on the associated file. Also, its use as a subprogram parameter is somewhat limited for this reason: Suppose the DEFINE FILE appears in the main program but I/O is done by READ's and WRITE's in a subprogram. The results of the READ's and WRITE's in the subprogram will cause the associated variable in the main program to be updated, but not any copies of it that may have been passed as subprogram arguments. Hence, if an associated variable is to be used in various subprograms, it is wisest to put it in a common block shared by the subprograms.

(b) Records are written using statements of the form

WRITE(unit'index, fmt) list

The "unit" is an integer constant or an integer variable of length four which has a value between 1 and 99, and which corresponds to the file which will be written. This file has been previously defined using a DEFINE FILE statement.

The "index" is an integer expression whose value indicates the index of the record to be written, for example,

WRITE(4'2*I+1, 6) X, Y

"Fmt" is a statement number which refers to the FORMAT statement to be used. If execution-time format is being used, "fmt" is the name of the array containing a string of characters which specifies the format.

"List" defines the data to be written, and has properties similar to those of "lists" for other output statements defined in this text. For example, a "list" will usually contain one or more FORTRAN variable names, separated by commas, as list elements. However, a list can be empty, or it can contain FORTRAN expressions as list elements. In the latter case, these expressions are evaluated, and the result is the data to be written.

Example 23.5 gives an illustration of the use of the empty list. This program causes twenty blank characters to be written in the first twenty byte-positions of each of the 2000 records in file 12. In fact, the remaining 130 byte-positions in each record are also automatically filled with blanks.

```
C EXAMPLE 23.5
        DEFINE FILE 12(2000, 150, E, INT)
        DO 22 I=1,2000
          WRITE(12'I, 4)
22      CONTINUE
4       FORMAT('                        ')
        STOP
        END
```

(c) Records are read using statements of the form

READ(unit'index, fmt, ERR=d) list

The parameters "unit", "index", "fmt", and "list", have already been defined in our discussion of WRITE. The 'ERR=d' is optional, and is used to cause a transfer of control to the statement numbered d, if an error should occur in reading.

(d) The record being written can be thought of as a line on the printer. This line has a width equal to the number of bytes in the record. If we write

- 314 -

with a FORMAT statement which uses only part of a
line, the remainder is filled with blanks. On the
other hand, if the FORMAT statement requires more
positions than the record allows, an error message
occurs. For example, it is not possible to use the
following sequence of statements for file 12, which
was defined in earlier examples.

```
          WRITE(12'125, 4) Z
4         FORMAT(140X, F18.3)
```

The FORMAT statement implies a record of 158 bytes,
and the record size for file 12 is defined as
having only 150 bytes. However, the following
sequence of statements would work:

```
          WRITE(12'125, 4) Z, T
4         FORMAT(120X, E20.3)
```

Here two records are written. First, Z is written
in record 125. Then, since the end of the FORMAT
statement is reached, a new record is begun (this
is comparable to a new print line); consequently, T
is written in record 126. Each of these records
has 120 blanks, followed by Z or T recorded in
E20.3 format, followed by 10 blanks. Note that, as
a result, the associated variable would have a
value 127.

Format for the READ statement can be considered as being analogous to that used for reading
punched cards. However, each "card" is logically
extended to have a number of columns equal to the
number of bytes in the record. The statement

```
          READ(12'235, 5) NAME
5         FORMAT(// A20)
```

would cause records 235 and 236 to be skipped.
Then the contents of the first 20 bytes of record

237 would be read into the array NAME using format 5A4. The associated variable would have the value 238 after the READ was completed.

(e) Several direct-access files can be defined in one DEFINE FILE statement. As an example, consider

DEFINE FILE 8(100,25,E,IV), 3(6908,120,E,LGV)

(f) REWIND, ENDFILE, and BACKSPACE statements which reference direct-access files are ignored.

23.4 DIRECT ACCESS WITHOUT FORMAT CONTROL

Data can be recorded more efficiently, both from the point of view of file space and machine time, if they are read and written without format control. This means that the information written is an exact image of its representation in memory. For example, consider the following sequence of statements.

```
DEFINE FILE 3(1200, 30, U, INT)
X = 3.468
WRITE(3'172) X
```

Here file 3 is defined to have 1200 records. Each of those records is 30 words (120 bytes), since the file will be written or read without format control (indicated by the letter U). The WRITE statement causes the four bytes containing the value of the real variable X to be written into the first full word (four bytes) of record 172. The remainder of the record is padded with zeros. Under no condition could the list of elements associated with the WRITE statement create a record which requires more than 30 full words. For example, the statements

```
DEFINE FILE 3(1200, 30, U, INT)
REAL X(40)/40*1.3/
WRITE(3'172) X
```

would cause an error to occur. This is because the array X requires 40 words, and the record size is only 30 words.

If the DEFINE FILE statement has the letter U as its fourth parameter, the file must always be read or written without format control. Furthermore, the third parameter (record size) must be given as the number of full words. Subsequent READ and WRITE statements associated with this file must omit the format parameter. In other respects, the READ/WRITE statements are the same as those described in the previous section.

23.5   DIRECT ACCESS WITH OR WITHOUT FORMAT CONTROL

It may be convenient to define a direct-access file so that it can be read or written with or without format control. This is done by using the letter L as the fourth parameter in the DEFINE FILE statement. The third parameter (record size) must then be indicated in bytes. The statement

```
DEFINE FILE 27(1800, 200, L, INT)
```

defines file 27 with 1800 records, each of 200 bytes, and the records can be read or written with or without format control, as required.

23.6   THE FIND STATEMENT

The direct-access READ statement must perform two functions.

    (a)   It must locate the record on the direct-access storage medium (a process which usually requires the physical movement of the storage medium or read-write heads). This could take up to one second.

    (b)   It must transfer the data from the record in the direct-access storage device to computer memory.

The FIND statement permits the programmer to perform the first of these functions in advance, thus reducing the time required to process the READ statement. For example, when the FIND statement is encountered in the sequence

```
FIND(17'127)
         .
         .

READ(17'127) X, Y, Z
         .
         .
```

it will cause the direct-access control mechanism to begin to locate record 127 in file 17. Then the processing of statements by the computer will continue while the record is being located. By the time the READ instruction is encountered, the record may be located, in which case the READ can be executed more quickly, as only a data transfer is necessary. If the record has not yet been found, processing will pause temporarily, and the READ statement will subsequently be executed.

The FIND statement is always of the form

```
FIND(unit'index)
```

where "unit" and "index" are defined as they are for the READ or WRITE statement. After the FIND statement has been executed, the associated variable has a value equal to the value of "index" in the FIND statement. Of course, the subsequent READ statement will cause the associated variable to be updated to point to the next record.

23.7   EXERCISES

23.1   Prepare a data deck for the program in Example 23.1, and use the program and data deck to create a direct-access student record file. It is unlikely that you will want to prepare 1869 data cards so be sure to change the DO statement to suit your special requirements.

Choose your student numbers so that they begin at 1 and use consecutive integers. Assign the student numbers to the student names at random.

23.2   Write programs which read the student record file and list student number and name for each record in the file

(a)   in increasing sequence by student number

(b)   in decreasing sequence by student number.

23.3   Suppose we are required to print the student record file in alphabetic order by name. Since the original student numbers were assigned at random, the solution to the problem is not trivial. There are many ways to solve the problem and the following is one solution.

(a)   Prepare a data deck which contains one card for each student in the file. Each card should contain only the student number. Sort this deck manually so that the sequence of student number will represent the students in alphabetic order by name. Write a program which reads this data deck and prints the file in alphabetic sequence.

(b) The data deck prepared for (a) is really a "list" of pointers to the records. This list could be permanently stored in a direct-access file and used whenever an alphabetic listing is required. Write a program to create this special file; subsequently, use the file to produce an alphabetic listing.

(c) Instead of creating a special file to store the list, as suggested in (b), we could place a "pointer" in each record; this indicates the next record in alphabetic sequence. Thus, if we know the position of the first record in alphabetic order, we could print the entire file in alphabetic sequence. Write a program which reads the data deck prepared for (a) and modifies the entire file to add the appropriate pointers to each record. Note that the last record (alphabetically) must have a special pointer (zero for example) to indicate the end of the "chain".

23.4 Keeping files up-to-date always presents special problems. For example, suppose we wish to add two new students to the student record file, and that we also wish to delete one particular student who has withdrawn. First we must assign student numbers to the two new students. Then we must prepare a data deck which contains three cards, one for each of the new students, and one for the student who is to be removed from the file. These data cards contain not only student number and name, but also a special code which indicates the action to be taken. For example, the new students could be indicated by code 1, and the student to be deleted could be indicated by code 2.

(a) Write a program which updates the file as created in Exercise 23.1.

(b) Write a program which updates the file or files as modified in Exercise 23.3 (b) and Exercise 23.3 (c).

23.5 In Example 23.3, we encountered a problem: it was impossible to tell whether or not a mark of zero was legitimate. One way of overcoming the problem is to read the record twice. The first time we use A format, and test for blank characters in the MARK field of the record. Subsequently, when we read the record using the second format, we are aware of the status of this field. Modify the program to use this technique, and have it print 'NO MARK' whenever there is a blank MARK field.

Chapter 24

ODDS AND ENDS

This chapter is concerned with a number of topics which
seemed to have little place in any of the preceding chapters.
Either their use was not required, or their introduction would
have added considerable detail at an inappropriate point.
Hence, it was decided to collect these ideas and present them
in this chapter.

24.1   THE DATA STATEMENT

The DATA statement is a non-executable FORTRAN statement
that is used to specify the compile-time initialization of
variables. In this respect, its effect is much like that of
declaration statements which include initialization information. The rules for the DATA statement are similar to those
of declaration statements, and a few examples should be sufficient to outline the specific differences.

The statement

    DATA PI/3.14/, I/27/, X/2.5/, J/-3/, OK/.TRUE./

assigns, at compile time, the initial values 3.14, 27, 2.5,
-3, and .TRUE. to the variables PI, I, X, J, and OK respec-

tively. The same initialization is obtained by using the statements

REAL PI/3.14/, X/2.5/

INTEGER I/27/, J/-3/

LOGICAL OK/.TRUE./

The basic difference between DATA statements and type declaration statements is that DATA statements contain no type declaration information; any variable named in the statement has a type given by default, or by a previous declaration statement.

Another difference is that the variable names to be initialized may be written in a list, followed by a list of the initializing constants. For example, each of the statements

DATA PI, I, X, J, OK/3.14, 27, 2.5, -3, .TRUE./

DATA PI, I/3.14, 27/, X/2.5/, J, OK/-3, T/

has the same effect as the above DATA statement.

Single array elements or whole arrays may be initialized, but array dimensions must be declared in previous declaration statements. Consider the statements

DIMENSION JP2(10), X(5)

REAL MORT(3,3), ZQ(6)

DATA JP2, MORT, X(3)/10*0, 6*-1., 4*5.8/, ZQ(1)/-4.3/

Each of the ten elements of the integer array JP2 is initialized to the value 0; each of the first six elements of the real array MORT is initialized to the value -1.; each of the last three elements of MORT, as well as the element X(3) of the vector X, is initialized to the value 5.8. The initialization of MORT is done in storage order, that is, by columns. Furthermore, the single element ZQ(1) of the vector ZQ is initialized to -4.3.

WATFIV-S allows implied DO's in DATA statements; they can be used to initialize parts of arrays, as the following example show.

```
DIMENSION A(3,3), X(10), Y(3)
DATA B, (X(I), I=1,7,2), Y(2), A /15*3.42E3/
```

Here, the variable B, the first, third, fifth, and seventh elements of X, the second element of Y, and all of the elements of the matrix A, are initialized to the value 3.42E3. Nested implied DO's may be used if desired. The only restriction is that the initial value, the increment, and the test value of any implied DO must be integer constants; they should not be variables, as is the case in the DO statement.

The following are several further examples of DATA statements

```
LOGICAL L1, L2, L3
REAL*8 D1, D2
COMPLEX C1, C2
DIMENSION A(10), B(2,3), N(5), M(3), L(3)
DATA L1 /.TRUE./, D1, C2, X /15.5D3, (7.2,-7.6), 25.6/
DATA A, G, B(1,2), N, M(3) /10*0., 2*.04, 5*1, -3/
DATA L2, C1, Q, L3 /'ABCD', 'DEFGHI', -14.3, F/
```

Data statements may be placed almost anywhere in a program segment. Most programmers place them near the beginning of the segment.

24.2   HEXADECIMAL CONSTANTS

A hexadecimal constant consists of the letter Z followed by a string of hexadecimal digits; an example is Z1A5B. These constants may be used as initial values in type-declaration or DATA statements to set up special bit patterns in memory.

Some examples are:

(a)   REAL X/Z00100000/, Y/Z7FFFFFFF/

(b)   DATA X, Y /Z00100000, Z7FFFFFFF/

(c)   INTEGER*2 M1 /ZF/, M2 /Z01020304/

Examples (a) and (b) achieve the same result; the variables X and Y are initialized to hexadecimal values which, incidentally, represent the smallest and largest floating-point numbers respectively. Both variables are of full-word size, and thus can contain a hexadecimal constant of eight digits.

Example (c) illustrates that the constants specified can contain fewer or more hexadecimal digits than can be stored in the corresponding variable. If fewer digits are given than can be stored, the constant is padded on the left with zeros; if more are given than can be stored, only the farthest-right are used. Both M1 and M2 are half-word integer variables; thus, each can store a four-digit hexadecimal constant. Hence, Example (c) is equivalent to the statement

INTEGER*2 M1/Z000F/, M2/Z0304/

24.3   EQUIVALENCE

Occasionally a programmer writes a very long program, and, when finished, finds that he has used, possibly by accident, two or more names for the same variable. One solution is to re-write the program to make the variable names consistent. A second alternative uses the EQUIVALENCE feature of FORTRAN. The statement

EQUIVALENCE (XP5, A, Q4)

informs the compiler that the variables named in the parenthesized list are to be assigned to the same storage locations in memory. This means that A and Q4 are synonyms for the variable XP5.

Another more common use for this feature is to provide alternative ways of referencing data in a program. For example, the statements

```
          COMPLEX Z
          DIMENSION X(2)
          EQUIVALENCE (X, Z)
```

specify that the complex variable Z and the vector X occupy the same two consecutive full words. Thus, a reference to X(1) is a reference to the real part of Z, and a reference to X(2) is a reference to the imaginary part of Z. Similarly, with the statements

```
          CHARACTER CARD*80, CHARS*1(80)
          EQUIVALENCE (CARD, CHARS)
```

references to elements of CHARS provide access to the individual bytes of variable CARD. As illustrated in an earlier chapter, it is sometimes convenient to reference the entire string, particularily for I/O, while it is sometimes necessary to reference each character of the string individually.

The statements

```
          DIMENSION V(5)
          EQUIVALENCE (Q, V(3))
```

specify Q as a synonym for V(3).

The statements

```
          DIMENSION A(10,10), B(10), C(10), D(100)
          EQUIVALENCE (A, B, D), (A(1,2), C)
```

provide various ways of referencing the elements of matrix A. Vectors B and C occupy the same storage as columns one and two, respectively, of A, since two-dimensional arrays are stored by columns. Similarly the elements of the ten columns of A, in storage order, are the one hundred elements of the vector D.

Another common use of the EQUIVALENCE statement is to achieve a saving of storage in programs which use large arrays. For example, suppose a program requires two large arrays specified by

DIMENSION X(100,100), Y(100,100)

It may not be possible to have this much storage available for the program. However, if the program is such that the matrix X is not needed in the part of the program that uses Y, and vice versa, X and Y can share storage if we make them equivalent; thus, the statement

EQUIVALENCE (X, Y)

could be used.

As the examples have illustrated, an array name can appear with or without subscripts in an EQUIVALENCE statement. If no subscripts are used, the first element of the array is implied. Thus, if A is an array of two dimensions, the statements

EQUIVALENCE (A, B)

EQUIVALENCE (A(1,1), B)

achieve the same result. An additional simplification is allowed; one subscript may be given to specify the position of an element of a multi-dimensional array when the array appears in an EQUIVALENCE statement. For example, given the statement

DIMENSION A(10,5), B(10)

the following two statements are acceptable, and produce the same result.

EQUIVALENCE (A(1,2), B)

EQUIVALENCE (A(11), B)

This is the only exception to the rule that an array must always be used with the same number of subscripts as it has dimensions.

Any number of variables may appear in the list, and any number of lists may appear in a single EQUIVALENCE statement. The following examples illustrate this, and, as well, illustrate that the same variable can be made equivalent to more than one other variable. The two statements, in fact, produce the same result.

EQUIVALENCE (A, B, C, D, E, F, G), (I, X, K, TOM), (F, T2Q)
EQUIVALENCE (A,B,C), (E,A,D), (A,T2Q,G,F), (I,X), (K,TOM,X)

Contradictory effects of the EQUIVALENCE statement are detected by the compiler and are considered as errors. An example is

DIMENSION A(10), B(10), C(10)
EQUIVALENCE (A, B(3)), (A, C(5)), (B, C)

Here A(1) and B(3) are made equivalent by the first list; this implies that A(5) and B(7) are also equivalent. The second list makes A(1) equivalent to C(5), and, by implication, makes B(7) and A(5) equivalent to C(9). The third list attempts to make B(1) equivalent to C(1), which is clearly a contradiction.

One problem can arise when variables which occupy different amounts of memory are made equivalent to one another. Consider the example

LOGICAL*1 I(4)
INTEGER A, B
EQUIVALENCE (I(2), B), (I, A)

In this case, not both of A and B can be aligned in memory on a full-word boundary. The compiler diagnoses this problem, and issues a warning message, since, if left uncorrected, time-consuming execution-time boundary alignment must take place. Ways of avoiding invalid boundary alignment are discussed in the next section.

Subprogram parameters may not appear in EQUIVALENCE statements.

Finally, it should be emphasized that the EQUIVALENCE statement is non-executable; its purpose is to supply the compiler with information to be used when it allocates storage for variables at compile time.

24.4   MORE ON COMMON BLOCKS

This section adds a few details to the information on common blocks which was given in a previous chapter. Some of the details are connected with valid and invalid uses of the EQUIVALENCE statement.

The order of appearance of the variable names in COMMON statements determines the order of the storage locations for the variables in common blocks. Thus, it is illegal to attempt to make two variables equivalent in one common block, or in two different common blocks. Hence, the following EQUIVALENCE statement is invalid.

```
COMMON /BLK1/X, Y /BLK2/A, B
EQUIVALENCE (X, B)
```

However, any variable not in a common block may be made equivalent to a variable within the block, e.g.,

```
COMMON P, Q
EQUIVALENCE (Z, P)
```

If Z were an array, this could have the implicit effect of

increasing the size of the common block. Thus, for the statements

DIMENSION Z(5)

COMMON P, Q

EQUIVALENCE (Z, P)

the size of the blank common block is 20 bytes, since the entire vector Z is brought into the block by the EQUIVALENCE statement; we say that the block has been extended to the right.

The first variable named in a COMMON statement is always the first element in the block in which it is stored. An attempt to extend any common block to the left by use of the EQUIVALENCE statement would violate this rule.

Thus, the statements

DIMENSION R(5)

COMMON S, T

EQUIVALENCE (S, R(3))

are invalid, since they attempt to have the elements R(1) and R(2) precede S in the block.

It is not necessary that the blank common block be the same size in two different segments; the compiler allocates storage by using the largest size required for the block when all segments are considered. A warning is issued, however, since the condition might indicate an error in the program. For example, consider the following two statements.

(a)   COMMON X, Y, Z

(b)   COMMON X, Z

If (a) were to be used in a main program and (b) in a subprogram, the block size allocated would be 12 bytes. But note that the variable Y in (a) and the variable Z in (b) are stored at the same location in the block.

A labelled common block should be the same size in all program segments that reference it.

To avoid problems, some programmers simply duplicate any COMMON statements, and insert the duplicates into subprograms that require them.

The lay-out of a common block can be quite different in the various segments. For example, consider the following sets of statements.

    (a)   COMMON X, Y, Z

    (b)   COMPLEX P
           COMMON P, I

    (c)   LOGICAL*1 L(12)
           COMMON L

If (a) were used in one subprogram, (b) in a second subprogram, and (c) a third subprogram, the single blank common block established would contain 12 bytes; these 12 bytes would have a different significance in each subprogram. This is not illegal, and is, in fact, occasionally desirable. It is the programmer's responsibility to be aware of the differences, and to make allowances, if necessary.

Normally, the compiler automatically provides the proper boundary alignment for variables used in a program. However, since COMMON and EQUIVALENCE statements specify the order in which variables are to be stored, their use can occasionally lead to assignment of storage such that proper alignment cannot be provided for some variables. For example, conside the following case.

        LOGICAL*1 L
        REAL*8 D
        COMMON L, D

The compiler always aligns the first element of any common

block on a <u>double-word boundary</u>. This means, for the example
under consideration, that the double-word quantity D cannot be
aligned on a double-word boundary, since the COMMON statement
specifies it must be stored adjacent to the one-byte quantity
L. Although this is not strictly an error, it should be
avoided if possible, since it can lead to a decrease in the
efficiency of the program; extra processing must be done at
execution time to compensate for the improper alignment.

One way to avoid the situation is to arrange the common
block so that the variables appear in decreasing order
according to length, i.e., all double-word variables are
placed first, all full-word variables second, all half-word
variables third, and all byte variables last. Proper align-
ments will result, since the block starts on a double-word
boundary. An alternative is to pad the block with dummy
names. For the example above, the statements

```
          LOGICAL*1 L, UNUSED(7)
          REAL*8 D
          COMMON L, UNUSED, D
```

result in proper alignment for all variables.

Similar methods can be used to correct improper alignment
caused by the use of the EQUIVALENCE statement.

24.5   <u>BLOCK</u> <u>DATA</u> <u>SUBPROGRAMS</u>

A <u>block</u> <u>data</u> <u>subprogram</u> is a special subprogram which is
specifically used to assign initial values to variables in
common blocks. The following example illustrates a number of
points.

The first statement of such subprograms is always BLOCK
DATA, and, as with every subprogram, the last statement is
always END. If an IMPLICIT statement is used, it must be the

second statement in the subprogram. A block data subprogram is never called; note that it does not have a name. Moreover, there are never any executable statements in the subprogram.

```
BLOCK DATA
IMPLICIT COMPLEX*8(C), LOGICAL(U-W)
DIMENSION P(6)
COMMON /BLK1/X(3), YZ /BLK2/U, V, W
COMMON P/BLK3/C1, C2
DATA X, V, C2 /3*0., .TRUE., (1.,2.)/
INTEGER*2 YZ/-35/, P*4
EQUIVALENCE (P, IQ)
DATA IQ/2/
END
```

There must be at least one COMMON statement, since the purpose of the subprogram is to provide initializing data for variables in common blocks. The example illustrates that initial values may be entered into more than one common block by a single block data subprogram. Note that not all variables in a block need be initialized. However, all variables in a particular block must be specified in COMMON statements; this is required so that the compiler is made aware of the complete structure of the block in order to perform the proper initialization.

Block data subprograms are not required for programs written to be compiled by WATFIV-S, since WATFIV-S allows variables in common blocks to be initialized by statements in any program segment. However, if used as described above, much of the information about the various common blocks in a program is localized in one program segment. This serves a valuable documentary purpose, and also simplifies the changing of any initial values in blocks, if changes are required.

Most FORTRAN compilers require that variables in common blocks be initialized only by means of block data subprograms. Thus, such subprograms should be used if a program is likely to be compiled by a compiler other than WATFIV-S.

24.6   SUBPROGRAM ARGUMENTS

This section contains a number of details about subprogram arguments. These details will likely be of interest only to experienced programmers, or to those who plan to make extensive use of subprogram capabilities.

*   *   *

Hollerith strings may be used as subprogram parameters, as shown by the following example.

CALL OUTMES ('THIS IS AN EXAMPLE.', 5, 18, Y)

Since WATFIV-S allows variables of type character, it is natural to pass a Hollerith string argument to a subprogram parameter that is a character variable of appropriate length. An alternate method is available and works as follows: WATFIV-S treats a Hollerith string used as a subprogram argument as if the characters forming the string, taken in groups of four, are the elements of a vector; blanks are supplied on the right of the last element if the length of the string is not a multiple of four. This argument may then be passed to any appropriately dimensioned vector.

In the above example, the Hollerith string is considered as a real vector of dimension five. The subprogram OUTMES could contain a statement supplying this dimension for a real array used as the corresponding dummy parameter. Alternatively, an execution-time dimension could be used. For example, the PRINT statement in the following sequence

```
          SUBROUTINE OUTMES (X, N, M, P)
          DIMENSION X(N)
          .
          .
          PRINT 22, X
22        FORMAT (' ', 5A4)
          .
          .
          END
```

- 334 -

would produce the printed line

THIS IS AN EXAMPLE.

* * *

A subprogram should not change the value of any parameter for which the calling argument is a constant, an expression, or a DO-parameter. Unexpected results can occur if this rule is violated. Consider a subprogram which contains the following statements:

```
SUBROUTINE SQVAR(N, X, M)
    .
    .
N = N + 1
M = N
    .
    .
X = X**2
    .
    .
END
```

A calling program segment containing the following statements violates the above rule for each argument.

```
DO 1 I=1,20
    .
    .
CALL SQVAR(2, 3.*SIN(A), I)
    .
    .
1       CONTINUE
```

An equivalent call to SQVAR, which obeys the rule, could be accomplished as follows:

```
        DO 1 I=1,20
          .
          .
            L = 2
            K = I
            Z = 3.*SIN(A)
            CALL SQVAR(L, Z, K)
          .
          .
          .
    1       CONTINUE

              *     *     *
```

The following details relate to the means by which argument values are transmitted to a subprogram when it is called.

Consider the subprogram which contains the following statements

```
        SUBROUTINE THING4 (X, N, P)
          .
          .
        X = X + 2
          .
          .
        N = P*X
          .
          .
        RETURN
          .
          .
        END
```

The variables X, N, and P are considered to be dummy variables, that is, they have no values until the subprogram is called, at which time each is assigned the value of the corresponding argument. The compiler does, however, reserve space in memory to be occupied by the values of X, N, and P; a full word is reserved for each of them.

When the subprogram is called by a statement such as

        CALL THING4(Z, K, 28.7)

part of the effect of the call is to copy the values of the arguments Z, K, and 28.7 into the storage locations reserved for X, N, and P. Thus, when the subprogram operates on X, N, and P, it is, in effect, operating on copies of the values of the calling arguments. When a RETURN is executed in the subprogram, the values in the storage locations reserved for the parameters X, N, and P are copied back into the storage locations reserved for the values of the arguments in the calling program. This copying action is performed automatically by the compiler, and the technique is referred to as call by value.

Call by value is the method most frequently used to pass arguments back and forth between calling and called segments. There is another technique, referred to as call by location, available to the programmer. To illustrate how this is used, suppose the above SUBROUTINE statement is replaced by the statement

SUBROUTINE THING4 (/X/, /N/, P)

The slashes around the parameter names X and N specify that they are to be treated by the compiler as call-by-location parameters. This means that the compiler reserves no storage - in the subprogram - for the values of X and N. Parameter P has storage reserved for it, since it is a call-by-value parameter.

When the subprogram is called by a statement such as

CALL THING4(Z, K, 28.7)

the value 28.7 is copied into the space reserved for P in the subprogram. However, the values of Z and K are not copied. Instead, the addresses of the memory locations occupied by Z and K are supplied to the subprogram. Any references that the subprogram makes to its parameters X and N are, in fact, references (by means of these addresses) to the actual values of Z and K, not to copies of Z and K, as is the case for call-by-value parameters. When a RETURN is executed, only the call-by-value parameters are copied back into the calling program; in the above case, only the value of P is copied back.

Although call by location is treated here as if it were a new concept, in actual fact, the technique has been used earlier in this book. Array names used as dummy parameters are treated automatically by the compiler as call-by-location parameters. This is done in order to avoid the wasteful duplication of memory space for arrays. As well, no time-consuming copying of the arrays needs to take place at the time of a call. Subprogram names used as dummy parameters are also treated automatically as call-by-location parameters.

One potential use of a call-by-name parameter would be to pass the associated variable of a direct-access file to subprograms that want to use the variable and that also do I/O on the file. By passing it using call-by-name, only a single image of it exists at any time, and consequently will will be updated by any READ or WRITE executed in no matter which program segment. However, as stated in the chapter on direct-access I/O, a simpler and possibly less error-prone scheme is to share the associated variable in a common block.

*　　*　　*

To this point it has been stressed that subprogram arguments must agree in type and number with their corresponding parameters; in particular, a parameter which represents an array should be passed to an array name with the same number of dimensions. WATFIV-S allows, in fact, a relaxation of this rule so that an array element may be passed to an array name. The passed array element then becomes the starting location (or base address) of the parameter array. This scheme makes it convenient for passing sub-arrays, particularly column vectors of a matrix (recall that matrix columns are in "storage order"). For example

```
        DIMENSION A(5,12)
        .
        .
        DO 1 K=1,8
        .
        .
        CALL VECTIT(A(1,K),   5)
1       CONTINUE
        .
        .
        SUBROUTINE VECTIT (X, N)
        DIMENSION X(N)
        .
        .
```

demonstrates how the first 8 columns of matrix A can be passed
in sequence to a subprogram that operates on a vector.

The only rule that must be adhered to is that the size of
the parameter array (as declared in the called subprogram)
must not exceed the size of the portion of the argument array
that follows and includes the passed array element. Basically, this rule makes it impossible for the subprogram to
index beyond the bounds of the actual array.

*   *   *

As a further extension to the mechanism of passing arrays
to subprograms, WATFIV-S will pass certain array size information to subprograms so that parameter arrays will automatically inherit dimensioning information from the passed array.
This can free the subprogram from having to be concerned about
dimensions for parameter arrays. However, the programmer must
signal his desire for this effect by declaring the last dimension of the parameter array to be 1. Thus, in

```
DIMENSION A(25), B(12)
.
.
CALL CVD(A)
CALL CVD(B)
CALL CVD(A(5))
.
.
SUBROUTINE CVD (X)
DIMENSION X(1)
.
.
C = X(I)
.
.
```

when the first call to CVD takes place, the parameter array X
will inherit the actual dimension 25.

When the second CALL statement is executed, X inherits
the dimension 12. When the third CALL statement occurs, X
inherits the dimension 8.

This technique is known as crypto-variable dimensioning,
and can be used as well with multi-dimensional arrays, e.g.,

```
                SUBROUTINE ARR (Y)
                DIMENSION  Y(7,1)
                     .
                     .
```

As usual, a subscript cannot exceed the corresponding
array dimension. In the sample statement C=X(I) above, I
could not exceed 25, 12, 8, the crypto-variable dimensions
passed for the first, second, third calls respectively.

*   *   *

A few additional rules must be added, concerning parameters in ENTRY statements. Call-by-location parameters may be
used in ENTRY statements within a subprogram. However, a
parameter must be used consistently, by location or by value,
if it appears in more than one entry point of a subprogram.
Thus the statements

```
        SUBROUTINE MAX (/N/)
        .
        .
        ENTRY MIN (N)
        .
        END
```

are in error.

A subprogram parameter must not be used in any executable statement of the subprogram prior to its appearance in a parameter list. The statements

```
        FUNCTION F (X, A, N)
        .
        .
        X = 3.*Q
        .
        .
        ENTRY G(X, Q)
        .
        .
        END
```

violate this rule, since Q is used before it appears in the parameter list of entry point G. This rule is required, since the compiler must give special treatment to names used as parameters.

24.7   ADDITIONAL RULES FOR FORMAT-FREE INPUT

The following rules are given to complete the list of features of format-free input.

(a)   Any field containing a T or an F may be used as
      input for a logical variable. The field is scanned
      from left to right, and the first T or F encoun-
      tered determines the logical value as .TRUE. or
      .FALSE., respectively.

      For example:

```
                LOGICAL L1, L2, L3
                READ, L1, L2, L3
```
with the data card
```
                CAT, ALFA, BATTLE
```
results in the assignment T, F, T, for L1, L2, L3, respectively.

(b) Data items may be separated by one comma and/or blanks.

> For example:
> ```
>                 READ, A, B
> ```

with data fields punched as 4.2bb,bbbb3.8 yields the same result as 4.2,3.8 or 4.2b3.8

(c) Hexadecimal constants may be used as input. Thus,
```
                READ, X, Y
```
with the data card
```
            Z41100000,ZC1200000.
```
assigns the indicated hexadecimal numbers to X and Y (these numbers are the floating-point representations of 1. and -2., respectively).

(d) If successive elements of the read list are to be assigned the same value, a replication factor may be used. For example,
```
                DIMENSION A(100)
                READ, A
```
could have the data card
```
                50*1.,50*-1.
```

(e) As special instances of the general READ and WRITE statements, the forms
```
            READ(unit, *, END=n, ERR=m) list
            WRITE(unit, *) list
```
are available to designate format-free I/O. Thus READ(5,*) X, Y is equivalent to READ, X, Y. These

general forms allow use of format-free I/O on other than the standard reader, printer, punch units, as well as providing the END and ERR returns for READ.

24.8   NAMELIST I/O

The NAMELIST feature of FORTRAN provides a method of doing I/O without reference to a FORMAT statement. In this case, it is similar to the format-free I/O features of WATFIV-S. Consider the following example, which illustrates basically how NAMELIST can be used to output variables.

```
      C EXAMPLE 24.1 - OUTPUT USING NAMELIST
            DIMENSION IGD(3)
            COMPLEX XRAY
            REAL*8 A1/-13.7D0/
            NAMELIST /ALPHA/XRAY, LAMBDA, IGD, A1
            LAMBDA = 5
            IGD(1) = 6
            IGD(2) = -16
            IGD(3) = 0
            XRAY = (25.38,-0.05)
            WRITE(6,ALPHA)
            STOP
            END
```

The non-executable NAMELIST statement declares the FORTRAN symbolic name ALPHA to be the name of the list of variables XRAY, LAMBDA, IGD, A1. The NAMELIST name ALPHA can then be used in a subsequent WRITE statement to print the values of all the variables which appear in the list. This is done in the WRITE statement; there, ALPHA is used where one might normally expect a format specification to appear.

If this simple program were executed, the output resulting from statement 3 would appear as follows:

    &ALPHA
    XRAY=(25.38,-0.05),LAMBDA=5,IGD=6,-16,0,A1=-13.7D0,&END

Note that the compiler supplies formatting automatically, and

explicitly identifies each variable printed. In the case of
an array, for example, IGD, the elements of the array are
printed in storage order, separated by commas. The significance of the additional fields &ALPHA and &END will become
more apparent when we discuss NAMELIST input.

Example 24.2 illustrates that more than one NAMELIST name
can be declared in a program, and that variables can appear in
more than one list.

```
C EXAMPLE 24.2 - MORE NAMELISTS
      NAMELIST /X/A, B, C/Z/P, A, Q, S
      NAMELIST /Y/C, P
      .
      .
      WRITE(6,Y)
      .
      .
      IF (A .NE. B) WRITE(6,X)
      .
      .
      WRITE(6,Z)
      STOP
      END
```

The first statement declares two NAMELIST names, X and Z,
and the second declares one NAMELIST name, Y. If the program
were to assign values of -1.25, 3.89, 6.2, 16.2, -13., 7500.
respectively, to the variables A, B, C, P, Q, S, and, if all
three WRITE statements were executed in the order shown, the
output would appear as follows:

```
&Y
C=6.2,P=16.2,&END
&X
A=-1.25,B=3.89,C=6.2,&END
&Z
P=16.2,A=-1.25,Q=13.,S=7500.,&END
```

The NAMELIST feature is often used as a simple and convenient means of producing output when debugging a program. It can also be used to input values to a program, but the rules are somewhat more detailed, as the following example will show.

```
C EXAMPLE 24.3 - NAMELIST INPUT
      COMPLEX Z
      DIMENSION X(3), B(2)
      NAMELIST /INLST/I, X, B, P, J, C, Z /VVB/A, B, X
16    READ(5,INLST)
      .
      .
      READ(5,VVB)
      .
      .
      STOP
      END
```

A data card to be read by the READ statement numbered 16 could be punched as

&INLST B(2)=-5.3,J=11,Z=(0.,-2.5),X=1.,-7.,6.,&END

↑
column 2

Column one of the card must be blank. The field &INLST, punched in columns two to seven, indicates that a NAMELIST data group follows. At least one blank column separates this field from any data items which follow. A data item, for example, B(2)=-5.3, specifically identifies the variable or array element and the value it is to receive as a result of the READ operation. Each data item is followed immediately by a comma, and the special field &END marks the end of the data group.

This particular card assigns values to the variables J and Z, to the array element B(2), and to all three elements of array X. Note that the names J, Z, B, X, appear in the list declared for NAMELIST name INLST in the program. Names not appearing in the list INLST may not appear in the data group. If an array name without subscripts appears, followed by a list of constants, the constants are assigned to the elements of the array in storage order. It is not necessary to specify values in the data group for all variables appearing in the NAMELIST list; the current value of any omitted variable (I, C, B(1), P, in Example 24.3) is left unchanged by the READ statement.

Data items may not contain embedded blanks. For example,

AbBCb=7.3b,XbY=b6b5bb,

are not valid data items, whereas

ABC=7.3,bbXY=65.,

are valid.

The usual rules of agreement between the type of variable and type of constant apply for NAMELIST input. Logical constants are punched as T or F or .TRUE. or .FALSE., as in the DATA statement. Furthermore, a replication factor can be used, as in the DATA statement, if a particular constant is to be assigned to a succession of elements of an array. For example,

X=2*0.,1.,

could have been used to read values for all three elements of the array X of Example 24.3.

Data items for one NAMELIST data group may be punched on more than one card, but each card must begin with a complete variable or array name or a constant. Column one of each card must be blank. The following illustration shows how the data group for Example 24.3 could have been punched on four cards.

column 2

↓

&INLST
    B(2)=-5.3, Z=(0.,-2.5),
               X=1.,-7.,6.,
  J=11, &END

Now we explain the significance of the header field &INLST. When a READ statement using a NAMELIST name INLST is executed, the next card in the card reader is read and examined. If this card does not contain &INLST in columns 2 to 7, the next card is read, and the process is repeated until a card containing &INLST is found. Then, the items in that data group are used to satisfy the READ request.

There are several other rules that must be followed when using NAMELIST. These are as follows.

(a) A NAMELIST name may appear in a program only in a NAMELIST statement or a READ or WRITE statement.

(b) NAMELIST statements must be placed after any other declaration statements that name variables appearing in the NAMELIST lists.

(c) A subprogram parameter may not be used in a NAMELIST list.

(d) As with the general form of the READ and WRITE statements described in Chapter 20 the unit number may be other than 5 or 6, and may be an integer variable. For example, the statements

    NAMELIST /XYZ/A, B, C
    .
    .
    WRITE(7,XYZ)
    .
    .

may be used in one program to punch a NAMELIST data group to be read by another program.

- 347 -

(e) END and ERR returns may be specified in READ state-
     ments. An example is
              READ(I, INLST, END=107)

24.9   DUMPLIST STATEMENT

The DUMPLIST statement of WATFIV-S was designed especially as a program debugging aid. Here is how it works:

(a) A DUMPLIST statement is essentially a NAMELIST
     statement, except that the word DUMPLIST replaces
     the word NAMELIST. Sample statements are
     DUMPLIST /ABC/X, PVZ, LOGY/LIST1/A, ROVER
     DUMPLIST /HERE/IFOR, ONE, M, KEEN

(b) A DUMPLIST statement has no effect if the program
     in which it appears executes normally.

(c) However, if execution of the program is terminated
     because of an error condition, WATFIV-S will auto-
     matically generate NAMELIST-like output of all
     DUMPLIST lists appearing in program segments which
     have been entered. The values printed are those
     which the variables had when the program was termi-
     nated.

To avoid producing too much output, try to select only a few
key variables when constructing your DUMPLIST statements.
Usually a bug in a program can be spotted by examining the
final values of a few carefully chosen variables.

24.10   ORDERING OF CERTAIN STATEMENTS IN A PROGRAM

WATFIV-S is a one-pass compiler. This means that each
statement of a program is processed only once by the compiler;
any translation to machine-language instructions is done on

this single pass over the program. This is in contrast to some compilers which may process the statements of a program segment two or more times; the program is stored, possibly in a modified form, in the main memory or on peripheral devices such as tapes or discs, so that the compiler can process the program additional times, until the translation is complete.

To simplify the construction of a one-pass compiler, certain restrictions are made on the ordering of statements within a program. The restrictions are:

(a) If a variable name appears in an EQUIVALENCE statement and has not appeared previously in an explicit declaration statement, the variable is assumed to have the standard length and type given by default. If the variable then appears in an explicit declaration statement following the EQUIVALENCE statement, the length of the variable must not be changed. Thus,

```
EQUIVALENCE (I, X), (Z, P)
REAL*8 X
COMPLEX Z
INTEGER P
```

is considered invalid by WATFIV-S. However,

```
COMPLEX Z
REAL*8 X
EQUIVALENCE (I, X), (Z, P)
INTEGER P
```

is acceptable.

(b) If a variable is initialized, the statement in which it is initialized must follow any COMMON or EQUIVALENCE statements which mention the variable. Thus,

```
          INTEGER*2 J/3/, K/4/
          COMMON J
          EQUIVALENCE (K, L)
```
is considered invalid by WATFIV-S, but the sequence
```
          INTEGER*2 J, K
          COMMON J
          EQUIVALENCE (K, L)
          DATA J, K/2,4/
```
is acceptable.

24.11   EXERCISES

24.1   Consider any program you have written which involves
       FORMAT statements.   Remove the FORMAT statements,
       and modify the I/O statements to reference arrays
       which contain execution-time format specifications.
       Initialize these arrays, using DATA statements, so
       that they have the same list of format codes as in
       the original FORMAT statements.   Remember to include
       the parentheses at each end of the list of codes.
       Verify that you have done the job correctly by
       running the program on the computer.

24.2   Exercise 18.2 involves the conversion of binary
       integers to their corresponding decimal equivalents.
       Your work can easily be verified by the computer in
       the following way.

       (a)   Convert the binary integers, by hand, to hexa-
             decimal integers.

       (b)   Write a program which initializes integer vari-
             ables to each of these hexadecimal values.
             Then have the program print the values.

24.3   Exercise 18.3 involves converting a number of hexa-

decimal floating-point constants into their corresponding decimal equivalents. Your work can be
verified as in Exercise 24.2. However, this time
the hexadecimal values must be assigned to real
variables.

24.4 Repeat Exercises 24.2 and 24.3, but instead of
initializing the variables with hexadecimal values,
read these values into the computer from data cards.

24.5 Verify your answers to Exercise 18.5 by reading the
hexadecimal values from data cards, performing the
required calculations, and printing the results.

24.6 Consider any FORTRAN program you have written which
involves integer variables. Declare an integer
array M which has as many elements as there are
integer variables in your program. Then use an
EQUIVALENCE statement to make each integer variable
equivalent to one element of the array M. Now it is
possible to print the current values of all the
integer variables by using the statement

PRINT,M

This can be useful when debugging programs; try it.

Appendix A

FORTRAN BUILT-IN FUNCTIONS

The following table summarizes the built-in functions that are available with FORTRAN processors for IBM computers. Several notational conveniences are used to simplify the table.

The following symbols are used to denote the type of arguments:

    i2   any half-word integer expression
    i4   any full-word integer expression
    r4   any single-precision real expression
    r8   any double-precision real expression
    c8   any complex expression
    c16 any extended-precision complex expression

These symbols are also used to denote the type of result of the functions.

The symbols a, a1, a2, represent arguments in general; a1 and a2 are used specifically to represent first and second arguments. Some functions may be used with an unspecified number of arguments; this is shown by the use of dots (...) with the function name.

MATHEMATICAL SIGNIFICANCE	FUNCTION NAME WITH ARGUMENTS	DEFINITION	TYPE OF RESULT
Square Root	SQRT(r4)	$\sqrt{a}$	r4
	DSQRT(r8)		r8
	CSQRT(c8)		c8
	CDSQRT(c16)		c16
Sine	SIN(r4)	sin a	r4
	DSIN(r8)		r8
	CSIN(c8)		c8
	CDSIN(c16)	a in radians	c16
Cosine	COS(r4)	cos a	r4
	DCOS(r8)		r8
	CCOS(c8)		c8
	CDCOS(c16)	a in radians	c16
Tangent	TAN(r4)	tan a	r4
	DTAN(r8)	a in radians	r8
Cotangent	COTAN(r4)	cot a	r4
	DCOTAN(r8)	a in radians	r8
Arcsine	ARSIN(r4)	$x = \arcsin a$	r4
	DARSIN(r8)	$-\dfrac{\pi}{2} \le x \le \dfrac{\pi}{2}$	r8
Arccosine	ARCOS(r4)	$x = \arccos a$	r4
	DARCOS(r8)	$0 \le x \le \pi$	r8

Arctangent	ATAN (r4) DATAN (r8)	$x = \arctan a$ $-\dfrac{\pi}{2} \le x \le \dfrac{\pi}{2}$	r4 r8
	ATAN2 (r4,r4) DATAN2 (r8,r8)	$x = \arctan (a1/a2)$ $-\pi \le x \le \pi$	r4 r8
Exponential	EXP (r4) DEXP (r8) CEXP (c8) CDEXP (c16)	e^a	r4 r8 c8 c16
Natural Logarithm	ALOG (r4) DLOG (r8) CLOG (c8) CDLOG (c16)	$\log_e a$	r4 r8 c8 c16
Common Logarithm	ALOG10 (r4) DLOG10 (r8)	$\log_{10} a$	r4 r8
Hyperbolic Sine	SINH (r4) DSINH (r8)	$\sinh a$	r4 r8
Hyperbolic Cosine	COSH (r4) DCOSH (r8)	$\cosh a$	r4 r8
Hyperbolic Tangent	TANH (r4) DTANH (r8)	$\tanh a$	r4 r8
Error Function	ERF (r4) DERF (r8)	$\mathrm{erf}(a) = \dfrac{2}{\sqrt{\pi}} \displaystyle\int_0^a e^{-t^2}\, dt$	r4 r8
	ERFC (r4) DERFC (r8)	$1 - \mathrm{erf}(a)$	r4 r8

Gamma Function	GAMMA(r4)	$\Gamma(a)=\int_0^\infty t^{a-1}e^{-t}dt$	r4
	DGAMMA(r8)		r8
	ALGAMA(r4)	$\mathrm{loggamma}(a)=\log_e\Gamma(a)$	r4
	DLGAMA(r8)		r8
Absolute Value	IABS(i4)	$\lvert a\rvert$	i4
	ABS(r4)		r4
	DABS(r8)		r8
	CABS(c8)	$\sqrt{x^2+y^2}$ for x+iy	r4
	CDABS(c16)		r8
Type Conversion	FLOAT(i4)	Convert from integer to real	r4
	DFLOAT(i4)		r8
	IFIX(r4)	Convert from real to integer	i4
	HFIX(r4)		i2
	SNGL(r8)	Most significant part of double-precision value	r4
	DBLE(r4)	Convert single- to double-precision	r8
	CMPLX(r4,r4)	Convert two real values to complex	c8
	DCMPLX(r8,r8)		c16
	REAL(c8)	Obtain real part of complex value	r4
	AIMAG(c8)	Obtain imaginary part to complex value	r4

Complex Conjugate	DONJG(c8) CCONJG(c16)	$\bar{a}=x-iy$ for $a=x+iy$	c8 c16
Transfer of Sign	SIGN(r4,r4) ISIGN(i4,i4) DSIGN(r8,r8)	$\|a1\|sgn(a2)$, where $sgn(a)=\begin{cases} 1 & a>0 \\ 1 & a=0 \\ -1 & a<0 \end{cases}$	r4 i4 r8
Truncation	INT(r4) AINT(r4) IDINT(r8)	$sgn(a)\ \lfloor\|a\|\rfloor$, where $\lfloor x\rfloor$ is the largest integer $\leq x$	i4 r4 i4
Modular Arithmetic	MOD(i4,i4) AMOD(r4,r4) DMOD(r8,r8)	$a1-sgn(x)\ \lfloor\|x\|\rfloor\ a2$ where $x=a1/a2$	i4 r4 r8
Positive Difference	DIM(r4,r4) IDIM(i4,i4)	$a1-min(a1,a2)$	r4 i4
Largest Value	AMAX0(i4,i4,..) AMAX1(r4,r4,..) MAX0(i4,i4,...) MAX1(r4,r4,...) DMAX1(r8,r8,..)	$max(a1,a2,..)$	r4 r4 i4 i4 r8
Smallest Value	AMIN0(i4,i4,..) AMIN1(r4,r4,..) MIN0(i4,i4,...) MIN1(r4,r4,...) DMIN1(r8,r8,..)	$min(a1,a2,..)$	r4 r4 i4 i4 r8

Appendix B

WATFIV-S DIAGNOSTIC MESSAGES

The WATFIV-S FORTRAN compiler has been designed to aid the programmer in the debugging process that is inherent in most programming tasks. To do this, the compiler provides checking of the source program, at compile time, for violations of the rules of the language. An error is indicated by printing a message on the printer listing of the source program, usually following the statement in which the violation occurred. If no serious errors occur, the resulting machine-language program may be executed.

Although WATFIV-S cannot detect errors in the logic of a program, it can continue to check, at execution time, for conditions which indicate an oversight on the part of the programmer. Again, the error is noted by a message on the printed output, and execution of the program is terminated.

At compile time, there are three levels of error message that may appear - Extension, Warning, Error.

An Extension message is meant to indicate that the programmer has used an extension, allowed by WATFIV-S,[1] of the FORTRAN language; the purpose is to warn the programmer that his program will not likely be accepted by any other FORTRAN compiler. For example, the statement

---

[1] Uses of format-free I/O, character variables, and the extended structured programming features are not flagged.

PRINT25, X**2+Y**2

would receive an IO-C extension message.

A warning message indicates that the compiler has made some assumption about the program. For example, the statement

GZORGUMPLATZ = 4.5

would be flagged with a warning message to indicate that WATFIV-S had recognized a variable name longer than six characters, but had proceeded by truncating the name to use only the six farthest-left characters, and had ignored the rest.

An Error message indicates a language violation severe enough to prevent execution.

A complete list of messages that WATFIV-S can produce while diagnosing a program follows in this appendix. A few words should be said about how to interpret these messages. In many cases, some extra information relating to the condition encountered, is printed. It may include, for example, the number of the line[2] or the name of the subprogram in which the condition occurred.

Execution-time messages include a feature which lists all the subprograms involved when an error is found in a subprogram. The trace-back names the calling segment, the segment which calls the calling segment, etc., all the way back to the main program, which is referenced as M/PROG.

WATFIV-S prints the value of an undefined variable as a string of U's. For example, if J is undefined when the statements

---

[2] The line number appears to the left of each statement on the printer listing.

```
I=3
K=2
PRINT,I,J,K
```

are executed, the output appears as

```
3 UUUUUUUUUUUU 2
```

Some printouts include a descriptive phrase which should be read in the context of the message. For example, the statement

```
DO 1 X=1,10     (assume X is real)
```

will be flagged with the message EXPECTING SIMPLE INTEGER VARIABLE OR CONSTANT, BUT X WAS FOUND. In this case the descriptive phrase is "BUT X WAS FOUND". The message should be interpreted as: An invalid DO-parameter, namely, X, has been detected at compile time.

In certain cases the text of the error message may not be printed. This occurs if the installation feels it does not have enough computer memory to store the error message texts. However, a code is printed which can be used to find the appropriate message. The code and messages are included as part of this appendix.

MESSAGES FOR ACCOUNTING
AC-5 THE NUMBER OF STATEMENTS TO BE EXECUTED HAS BEEN EXCEEDED

ASSEMBLER LANGUAGE SUBPROGRAMMES
AL-0 MISSING END CARD ON ASSEMBLY LANGUAGE OBJECT DECK
AL-1 ENTRY-POINT OR CSECT NAME IN AN OBJECT DECK WAS
      PREVIOUSLY DEFINED. FIRST DEFINITION USED

BLOCK DATA STATEMENTS
BD-0 EXECUTABLE STATEMENTS ILLEGAL IN BLOCK DATA SUBPROGRAMS
BD-1 IMPROPER BLOCK DATA STATEMENT

CARD FORMAT AND CONTENTS
CC-0 COLUMNS 1-5 OF CONTINUATION CARD ARE NOT BLANK.
      PROBABLE CAUSE: STATEMENT PUNCHED TO LEFT OF COLUMN 7
CC-1 LIMIT OF 5 CONTINUATION CARDS EXCEEDED
CC-2 INVALID CHARACTER IN FORTRAN STATEMENT. A $ WAS
      INSERTED IN THE SOURCE LISTING
CC-3 FIRST CARD OF A PROGRAM IS A CONTINUATION CARD.
      PROBABLE CAUSE: STATEMENT PUNCHED TO LEFT OF COLUMN 7
CC-4 STATEMENT TOO LONG TO COMPILE (·SCAN-STACK OVERFLOW)
CC-5 A BLANK CARD WAS ENCOUNTERED
CC-6 KEYPUNCH USED DIFFERS FROM KEYPUNCH SPECIFIED ON JOB CARD
CC-7 THE FIRST CHARACTER OF THE STATEMENT WAS NOT ALPHABETIC
CC-8 INVALID CHARACTER(S) CONCATENATED WITH FORTRAN KEYWORD
CC-9 INVALID CHARACTERS IN COLUMNS 1-5.
      STATEMENT NUMBER IGNORED. PROBABLE CAUSE:
      STATEMENT PUNCHED TO LEFT OF COLUMN 7
CC-A CONTROL CARDS MAY NOT BE CONTINUED
CC-B CONTROL CARDS MUST BE IN PROGRAM SEGMENT

COMMON
CM-0 THE VARIABLE IS ALREADY IN COMMON
CM-1 OTHER COMPILERS MAY NOT ALLOW COMMONED VARIABLES TO BE
      INITIALIZED IN OTHER THAN A BLOCK DATA SUBPROGRAM
CM-2 ILLEGAL USE OF A COMMON BLOCK OR NAMELIST NAME

FORTRAN TYPE CONSTANTS
CN-0 MIXED REAL*4, REAL*8 IN COMPLEX CONSTANT; REAL*8 ASSUMED
CN-1 AN INTEGER CONSTANT MAY NOT BE GREATER THAN 2,147,483,647
CN-2 EXPONENT ON A REAL CONSTANT IS GREATER THAN 2 DIGITS
CN-3 A REAL CONSTANT HAS MORE THAN 16 DIGITS. TRUNCATED TO 16
CN-4 INVALID HEXADECIMAL CONSTANT
CN-5 ILLEGAL USE OF A DECIMAL POINT
CN-6 CONSTANT WITH MORE THAN 7 DIGITS BUT E-TYPE EXPONENT,
      ASSUMED TO BE REAL*4
CN-7 CONSTANT OR STATEMENT NUMBER GREATER THAN 99999
CN-8 AN EXPONENT OVERFLOW OR UNDERFLOW OCCURRED WHILE
      CONVERTING A CONSTANT IN A SOURCE STATEMENT

COMPILER ERRORS
CP-0   COMPILER ERROR - LANDR/ARITH
CP-1   COMPILER ERROR. LIKELY CAUSE: MORE THAN 255 DO STATEMENTS
CP-2   COMPILER ERROR
CP-4   COMPILER ERROR-INTERRUPT AT COMPILE TIME,RETURN TO SYSTEM

CHARACTER VARIABLE
CV-0   A CHARACTER VARIABLE IS USED WITH A RELATIONAL OPERATOR
CV-1   LENGTH OF A CHARACTER VALUE ON RIGHT OF EQUAL SIGN
       EXCEEDS THAT ON LEFT. TRUNCATION WILL OCCUR
CV-2   UNFORMATTED CORE-TO-CORE I/O NOT IMPLEMENTED

DATA STATEMENT
DA-0   REPLICATION FACTOR IS 0 OR .GT. 32767 (32767 ASSUMED)
DA-1   MORE VARIABLES THAN CONSTANTS
DA-2   ATTEMPT TO INITIALIZE A SUBPROGRAM PARAMETER IN A
       DATA STATEMENT
DA-3   OTHER COMPILERS MAY NOT ALLOW NON-CONSTANT SUBSCRIPTS
       IN DATA STATEMENTS
DA-4   TYPE OF VARIABLE AND CONSTANT DO NOT AGREE.
       (MESSAGE ISSUED ONCE FOR AN ARRAY)
DA-5   MORE CONSTANTS THAN VARIABLES
DA-6   A VARIABLE WAS PREVIOUSLY INITIALIZED. LATEST VALUE USED
       CHECK COMMONED AND EQUIVALENCED VARIABLES
DA-7   OTHER COMPILERS MAY NOT ALLOW INITIALIZATION OF
       BLANK COMMON
DA-8   A LITERAL CONSTANT HAS BEEN TRUNCATED
DA-9   OTHER COMPILERS MAY NOT ALLOW IMPLIED DO-LOOPS
       IN DATA STATEMENTS
DA-A   MORE THAN 255 CONSTANTS IN A DATA STATEMENT SUBLIST

DEFINE FILE STATEMENTS
DF-0   THE UNIT NUMBER IS MISSING
DF-1   INVALID FORMAT TYPE
DF-2   THE ASSOCIATED VARIABLE IS NOT A SIMPLE INTEGER VARIABLE
DF-3   NUMBER OF RECORDS OR RECORD SIZE IS ZERO OR
       GREATER THAN 32767

DIMENSION STATEMENTS
DM-0   NO DIMENSIONS ARE SPECIFIED FOR A VARIABLE IN A
       DIMENSION STATEMENT
DM-1   THE VARIABLE HAS ALREADY BEEN DIMENSIONED
DM-2   CALL-BY-LOCATION PARAMETERS MAY NOT BE DIMENSIONED
DM-3   THE DECLARED SIZE OF ARRAY EXCEEDS SPACE PROVIDED
       BY CALLING ARGUMENT

DO LOOPS
DO-0   THIS STATEMENT CANNOT BE THE OBJECT OF A DO-LOOP
DO-1   ILLEGAL TRANSFER INTO THE RANGE OF A DO-LOOP
DO-2   THE OBJECT OF THIS DO-LOOP HAS ALREADY APPEARED
DO-3   IMPROPERLY NESTED DO-LOOPS
DO-4   ATTEMPT TO REDEFINE A DO-LOOP PARAMETER WITHIN THE
       RANGE OF THE LOOP
DO-5   INVALID DO-LOOP PARAMETER
DO-6   ILLEGAL TRANSFER TO STATEMENT INSIDE RANGE OF DO
DO-7   A DO-LOOP PARAMETER IS UNDEFINED OR OUT OF RANGE
DO-8   BECAUSE OF ONE OF THE PARAMETERS, THIS DO-LOOP WILL
       TERMINATE AFTER THE FIRST TIME THROUGH
DO-9   A DO-LOOP PARAMETER MAY NOT BE REDEFINED IN AN INPUT LIST
DO-A   OTHER COMPILERS MAY NOT ALLOW THIS STATEMENT TO
       END A DO-LOOP

EQUIVALENCE AND/OR COMMON
EC-0   EQUIVALENCED VARIABLE APPEARS IN A COMMON STATEMENT
EC-1   A COMMON BLOCK HAS A DIFFERENT LENGTH THAN IN A PREVIOUS
       SUBPROGRAM: GREATER LENGTH USED
EC-2   COMMON AND/OR EQUIVALENCE CAUSES INVALID ALIGNMENT.
       EXECUTION SLOWED. REMEDY: ORDER VARIABLES BY
       DECREASING LENGTH
EC-3   EQUIVALENCE EXTENDS COMMON DOWNWARDS
EC-4   SUBPROGRAM PARAMETER APPEARS IN COMMON OR EQUIVALENCE
EC-5   A VARIABLE WAS USED WITH SUBSCRIPTS IN AN EQUIVALENCE
       STATEMENT BUT HAS NOT BEEN PROPERLY DIMENSIONED

END STATEMENTS
EN-0   MISSING END STATEMENT: END STATEMENT GENERATED
EN-1   AN END STATEMENT WAS USED TO TERMINATE EXECUTION
EN-2   END STATEMENT CANNOT HAVE STATEMENT NUMBER (IGNORED)
EN-3   END STATEMENT NOT PRECEDED BY A TRANSFER
EQUAL SIGNS
EQ-0   ILLEGAL QUANTITY ON LEFT OF EQUALS SIGN
EQ-1   ILLEGAL USE OF EQUAL SIGN
EQ-2   OTHER COMPILERS MAY NOT ALLOW MULTIPLE
       ASSIGNMENT STATEMENTS
EQ-3   MULTIPLE ASSIGNMENT IS NOT IMPLEMENTED FOR
       CHARACTER VARIABLES
EQ-4   ILLEGAL QUANTITY ON RIGHT OF EQUALS SIGN

EQUIVALENCE STATEMENTS
EV-0   ATTEMPT TO EQUIVALENCE A VARIABLE TO ITSELF
EV-1   THERE ARE LESS THAN 2 VARIABLES IN AN EQUIVALENCE LIST
EV-2   A MULTI-SUBSCRIPTED EQUIVALENCED VARIABLE HAS BEEN
       INCORRECTLY RE-EQUIVALENCED. REMEDY: DIMENSION THE
       VARIABLE FIRST

POWERS AND EXPONENTIATION
EX-0   ILLEGAL COMPLEX EXPONENTIATION
EX-1   I**J WHERE I=J=0
EX-2   I**J WHERE I=0, J .LT. 0
EX-3   0.0**Y WHERE Y .LE. 0.0
EX-4   0.0**J WHERE J=0
EX-5   0.0**J WHERE J .LT. 0
EX-6   X**Y WHERE X .LT. 0.0, Y IS NOT TYPE INTEGER OR .NE. 0.0

ENTRY STATEMENT
EY-0   ENTRY-POINT NAME WAS PREVIOUSLY DEFINED
EY-1   PREVIOUS DEFINITION OF FUNCTION NAME IN ENTRY IS INCORRECT
EY-2   THE USAGE OF A SUBPROGRAM PARAMETER IS INCONSISTENT WITH
       A PREVIOUS ENTRY-POINT
EY-3   A PARAMETER HAS APPEARED IN A EXECUTABLE STATEMENT BUT
       IS NOT A SUBPROGRAM PARAMETER
EY-4   ENTRY STATEMENTS ARE INVALID IN THE MAIN PROGRAM
EY-5   ENTRY STATEMENT INVALID INSIDE A DO-LOOP

FORMAT
   SOME FORMAT MESSAGES GIVE CHARACTERS IN WHICH ERROR
   WAS DETECTED
FM-0   IMPROPER CHARACTER SEQUENCE OR INVALID CHARACTER IN
       INPUT DATA
FM-1   NO STATEMENT NUMBER ON A FORMAT STATEMENT
FM-2   FORMAT CODE AND DATA TYPE DO NOT MATCH
FM-4   FORMAT PROVIDES NO CONVERSION SPECIFICATION FOR A VALUE
       IN I/O LIST
FM-5   INTEGER IN INPUT DATA IS TOO LARGE. (MAX=2**31-1)
FM-6   A REAL NUMBER IN THE INPUT DATA IS OUT OF MACHINE RANGE
FM-7   UNREFERENCED FORMAT STATEMENT
FT-0   FIRST CHARACTER OF VARIABLE FORMAT IS NOT A PARENTHESIS
FT-1   INVALID CHARACTER ENCOUNTERED IN FORMAT
FT-2   INVALID FORM FOLLOWING A FORMAT CODE
FT-3   INVALID FIELD OR GROUP COUNT
FT-4   A FIELD OR GROUP COUNT GREATER THAN 255
FT-5   NO CLOSING PARENTHESIS ON VARIABLE FORMAT
FT-6   NO CLOSING QUOTE IN A HOLLERITH STRING FIELD
FT-7   INVALID USE OF COMMA
FT-8   FORMAT STATEMENT TOO LONG TO COMPILE (SCAN-STACK OVERFLOW)
FT-9   INVALID USE OF P FORMAT CODE
FT-A   INVALID USE OF PERIOD(.)
FT-B   MORE THAN THREE LEVELS OF PARENTHESES
FT-C   INVALID CHARACTER BEFORE A RIGHT PARENTHESIS
FT-D   MISSING OR ZERO LENGTH HOLLERITH STRING ENCOUNTERED
FT-E   NO CLOSING RIGHT PARENTHESIS
FT-F   CHARACTERS FOLLOW CLOSING RIGHT PARENTHESIS
FT-G   WRONG QUOTE USED FOR KEY-PUNCH SPECIFIED
FT-H   LENGTH OF HOLLERITH STRING EXCEEDS 255
FT-I   EXPECTING COMMA BETWEEN FORMAT ITEMS
FT-J   HOLLERITH STRING EXTENDS BEYOND END OF STATEMENT
FT-K   CHARACTERS FOLLOW CLOSING PARENTHESIS FOR VARIABLE FORMAT

FUNCTIONS AND SUBROUTINES
FN-1 A PARAMETER APPEARS MORE THAN ONCE IN A SUBPROGRAM OR
      STATEMENT FUNCTION DEFINITION
FN-2 SUBSCRIPTS ON RIGHT-HAND SIDE OF STATEMENT FUNCTION.
      PROBABLE CAUSE: VARIABLE TO LEFT OF EQUAL NOT DIMENSIONED
FN-4 ILLEGAL LENGTH MODIFIER
FN-5 INVALID PARAMETER
FN-6 A PARAMETER HAS THE SAME NAME AS THE SUBPROGRAM

GO TO STATEMENTS
GO-0 THIS STATEMENT COULD TRANSFER TO ITSELF
GO-1 THIS STATEMENT TRANSFERS TO A NON-EXECUTABLE STATEMENT
GO-2 ATTEMPT TO DEFINE ASSIGNED GOTO INDEX IN AN
      ARITHMETIC STATEMENT
GO-3 ASSIGNED GOTO INDEX MAY BE USED ONLY IN ASSIGNED GOTO
      AND ASSIGN STATEMENTS
GO-4 INDEX OF AN ASSIGNED GOTO IS UNDEFINED OR OUT OF RANGE,
      OR INDEX OF COMPUTED GOTO OR CASE IS UNDEFINED
GO-5 ASSIGNED GOTO INDEX MAY NOT BE AN INTEGER*2 VARIABLE
GO-Z THE SURGEON-GENERAL WARNS THAT USE OF GO TO IS
      DANGEROUS TO YOUR HEALTH.

HOLLERITH CONSTANTS
HO-0 ZERO LENGTH SPECIFIED FOR H-TYPE HOLLERITH
HO-1 ZERO LENGTH QUOTE-TYPE HOLLERITH
HO-2 NO CLOSING QUOTE OR NEXT CARD NOT A CONTINUATION CARD
HO-3 UNEXPECTED HOLLERITH OR STATEMENT NUMBER CONSTANT

IF STATEMENTS (ARITHMETIC AND LOGICAL)
IF-0 AN INVALID STATEMENT FOLLOWS THE LOGICAL IF OR AT END
IF-1 ARITHMETIC OR INVALID EXPRESSION IN LOGICAL IF OR WHILE
IF-2 LOGICAL, COMPLEX OR INVALID EXPRESSION IN ARITHMETIC IF

IMPLICIT STATEMENT
IM-0 INVALID DATA TYPE
IM-1 INVALID OPTIONAL LENGTH
IM-3 IMPROPER ALPHABETIC SEQUENCE IN CHARACTER RANGE
IM-4 A SPECIFICATION IS NOT A SINGLE CHARACTER. THE FIRST
      CHARACTER IS USED
IM-5 IMPLICIT STATEMENT DOES NOT PRECEDE OTHER
      SPECIFICATION STATEMENTS
IM-6 ATTEMPT TO DECLARE THE TYPE OF A CHARACTER MORE THAN ONCE
IM-7 ONLY ONE IMPLICIT STATEMENT PER PROGRAM SEGMENT ALLOWED.
      THIS ONE IGNORED

INPUT/OUTPUT
IO-0 I/O STATEMENT REFERENCES NON-FORMAT STATEMENT.
      PROBABLE CAUSE: STATEMENT DEFINED AS NON-FORMAT
IO-1 A VARIABLE FORMAT MUST BE AN ARRAY NAME
IO-2 INVALID ELEMENT IN INPUT LIST OR DATA LIST
IO-3 OTHER COMPILERS MAY NOT ALLOW EXPRESSIONS IN OUTPUT LISTS
IO-4 ILLEGAL USE OF END= OR ERR= PARAMETERS
IO-5 INVALID UNIT NUMBER
IO-6 INVALID FORMAT
IO-7 ONLY CONSTANTS, SIMPLE INTEGER*4 VARIABLES, AND CHARACTER
      VARIABLES ARE ALLOWED AS UNIT
IO-8 ATTEMPT TO PERFORM I/O IN A FUNCTION WHICH IS CALLED IN
      AN OUTPUT STATEMENT
IO-9 UNFORMATTED WRITE STATEMENT MUST HAVE A LIST
IO-A EXPECTING STATEMENT TO BE A FORMAT. PREVIOUSLY
      REFERENCED IN I/O STATEMENT

JOB CONTROL CARDS
JB-0 CONTROL CARD ENCOUNTERED DURING COMPILATION;
      PROBABLE CAUSE: MISSING $ENTRY CARD
JB-1 MIS-PUNCHED JOB OPTION

JOB TERMINATION
KO-0 SOURCE ERROR ENCOUNTERED WHILE EXECUTING WITH RUN=FREE
KO-1 LIMIT EXCEEDED FOR FIXED-POINT DIVISION BY ZERO
KO-2 LIMIT EXCEEDED FOR FLOATING-POINT DIVISION BY ZERO
KO-3 EXPONENT OVERFLOW LIMIT EXCEEDED
KO-4 EXPONENT UNDERFLOW LIMIT EXCEEDED
KO-5 FIXED-POINT OVERFLOW LIMIT EXCEEDED
KO-6 JOB-TIME EXCEEDED
KO-7 COMPILER ERROR - EXECUTION TIME: RETURN TO SYSTEM
KO-8 TRACEBACK ERROR. TRACEBACK TERMINATED
KO-9 CANNOT OPEN WATFIV-S ERRTEXTS. RUN TERMINATED
KO-A I/O ERROR ON ERROR TEXT FILE

LOGICAL OPERATIONS
LG-0 .NOT. WAS USED AS A BINARY OPERATOR

LIBRARY ROUTINES
```
LI-0   ARGUMENT OUT OF RANGE DGAMMA OR GAMMA(1.382E-76<X<57.57)
LI-1   ABS(X) .GE. 175.366 FOR SINH,COSH,DSINH OR DCOSH OF X
LI-2   SENSE LIGHT OTHER THAN 0-4 FOR SLITE OR 1-4 FOR SLITET
LI-3   REAL PORTION OF ARGUMENT .GT. 174.673, CEXP OR CDEXP
LI-4   ABS(AIMAG(Z)) > 174.673 FOR CSIN,CCOS,CDSIN OR CDCOS OF Z
LI-5   ABS(REAL(Z)).GE.33.537E15 FOR CSIN,CCOS,CDSIN OR CDCOS OF Z
LI-6   ABS(AIMAG(Z)) .GE. 3.537E15 FOR CEXP OR CDEXP OF Z
LI-7   ARGUMENT .GT. 174.673, EXP OR DEXP
LI-8   ARGUMENT OF CLOG OR CDLOG IS ZERO
LI-9   ARGUMENT IS NEGATIVE OR ZERO, ALOG, ALOG10, DLOG OR DLOG10
LI-A   ABS(X) .GE. 3.537E15 FOR SIN, COS, DSIN OR DCOS OF X
LI-B   ABS(X) .GT. 1,FOR ARSIN,ARCOS,DARSIN,DARCOS OF X
LI-C   ARGUMENT IS NEGATIVE, SQRT OR DSQRT
LI-D   BOTH ARGUMENTS OF DATAN2 OR ATAN2 ARE ZERO
LI-E   ARGUMENT TOO CLOSE TO A SINGULARITY,TAN,COTAN,DTAN,DCOTAN
LI-F   ARGUMENT OUT OF RANGE, DLGAMA OR ALGAMA (0. 0<X<4. 29E73)
LI-G   ABS(X) .GT. 3.537E15-TAN,COTAN,DTAN,DCOTAN OF X
```
MIXED MODE
```
MD-0   RELATIONAL OPERATOR HAS LOGICAL OPERAND
MD-1   RELATIONAL OPERATOR HAS COMPLEX OPERAND
MD-2   MIXED MODE - LOGICAL OR CHARACTER WITH ARITHMETIC
MD-3   OTHER COMPILERS MAY NOT ALLOW SUBSCRIPTS OF TYPE
       COMPLEX, LOGICAL OR CHARACTER
```

MEMORY OVERFLOW
```
MO-0   INSUFFICIENT MEMORY TO COMPILE THIS PROGRAM. REMAINDER
       WILL BE ERROR CHECKED ONLY
MO-1   INSUFFICIENT MEMORY TO ASSIGN ARRAY STORAGE. JOB ABANDONED
MO-2   SYMBOL TABLE EXCEEDS AVAILABLE SPACE, JOB ABANDONED
MO-3   DATA AREA OF SUBPROGRAM EXCEEDS 24K -- SEGMENT SUBPROGRAM
MO-4   INSUFFICIENT MEMORY FOR WORK AREA OR WATLIB BUFFER
MO-5   INSUFFICIENT MEMORY TO PRODUCE CROSS REFERENCE.
```

NAMELIST STATEMENTS
```
NL-0   NAMELIST ENTRY MUST BE A VARIABLE, NOT A SUBPROGRAM
       PARAMETER
NL-1   NAMELIST NAME PREVIOUSLY DEFINED
NL-2   VARIABLE NAME TOO LONG
NL-3   VARIABLE NAME NOT FOUND IN NAMELIST
NL-4   INVALID SYNTAX IN NAMELIST INPUT
NL-6   VARIABLE INCORRECTLY SUBSCRIPTED
NL-7   SUBSCRIPT OUT OF RANGE
NL-8   NESTED BLANKS ARE ILLEGAL IN NAMELIST INPUT
```

PARENTHESES
```
PC-0   UNMATCHED PARENTHESIS
PC-1   INVALID PARENTHESIS NESTING IN I/O LIST
```

PAUSE, STOP STATEMENTS
```
PS-0   OPERATOR MESSAGES NOT ALLOWED: SIMPLE STOP ASSUMED FOR
       STOP, CONTINUE ASSUMED FOR PAUSE
```

RETURN STATEMENT
RE-1   RETURN I, WHERE I IS OUT OF RANGE OR UNDEFINED
RE-2   MULTIPLE RETURN NOT VALID IN FUNCTION SUBPROGRAM
RE-3   VARIABLE IS NOT A SIMPLE INTEGER
RE-4   A MULTIPLE RETURN IS NOT VALID IN THE MAIN PROGRAM

ARITHMETIC AND LOGICAL STATEMENT FUNCTIONS
  (PROBABLE CAUSE - VARIABLE ON LEFT OF = WAS NOT DIMENSIONED)
SF-1   A PREVIOUSLY REFERENCED NUMBER APPEARS ON A STATEMENT
       STATEMENT FUNCTION DEFINITION
SF-2   STATEMENT FUNCTION IS THE OBJECT OF LOGICAL IF STATEMENT
SF-3   RECURSIVE STATEMENT FUNCTION DEFINITION: NAME APPEARS
       ON BOTH SIDES OF EQUAL SIGN. LIKELY CAUSE: VARIABLE NOT
       DIMENSIONED
SF-4   A STATEMENT FUNCTION DEFINITION APPEARS AFTER THE
       FIRST EXECUTABLE STATEMENT
SF-5   ILLEGAL USE OF A STATEMENT FUNCTION NAME

STRUCTURED PROGAMMING FEATURES
SP-0   AT END STATEMENT MUST IMMEDIATELY FOLLOW A READ
SP-1   AT END FOLLOWS CORE TO CORE, DIRECT ACCESS OR INVALID
       READ STATEMENT
SP-2   AT END NOT VALID WHEN END= SPECIFIED IN READ STATEMENT
SP-3   MISSING OR INVALID DO CASE, WHILE, AT END, IF-THEN, LOOP
       GUESS, OR AT END STATEMENT
SP-4   IMPROPER NESTING OF BLOCK OR CONSTRUCT
SP-5   IMPROPER NESTING OF DO-LOOP
SP-6   IMPROPER NESTING WITH DO-LOOP
SP-7   MISSING ENDCASE, ENDWHILE, ENDATEND, ENDIF, ENDLOOP
SP-8   OTHER COMPILERS MAY NOT ALLOW IF-THEN-ELSE, DO CASE,
       STRUCTURED LOOP, OR REMOTE BLOCK STATEMENTS
SP-9   IF NONE BLOCK ALREADY DEFINED FOR CURRENT DO CASE
SP-A   IF NONE BLOCK MUST FOLLOW ALL CASE BLOCKS
SP-B   ATTEMPT TO TRANSFER CONTROL ACROSS REMOTE BLOCK BOUNDARIES
SP-C   REMOTE BLOCK NOT PRECEDED BY A TRANSFER
SP-D   REMOTE BLOCK PREVIOUSLY DEFINED
SP-E   REMOTE BLOCK STATEMENT MISSING OR INVALID
SP-F   LAST REMOTE BLOCK NOT COMPLETED
SP-G   REMOTE BLOCK IS NOT DEFINED
SP-H   REMOTE BLOCK IS NOT REFERENCED
SP-I   ATTEMPT TO NEST REMOTE BLOCK DEFINITIONS
SP-J   MISSING OR INVALID REMOTE BLOCK NAME
SP-K   ATTEMPT TO EXECUTE A REMOTE BLOCK RECURSIVELY
SP-L   NUMBER OF REMOTE BLOCKS EXCEEDS 255
SP-M   RETURN STATEMENTS ARE INVALID WITHIN REMOTE BLOCKS
SP-N   CASE STATEMENT FOR FIRST CASE GENERATED
SP-P   ATTEMPT TO QUIT MORE LEVELS THAN CURRENTLY EXIST
SP-Q   QUIT LEVEL MUST BE A POSITIVE INTEGER

SUBPROGRAMS
SR-0 MISSING SUBPROGRAM
SR-1 SUBPROGRAM REDEFINES A CONSTANT,EXPRESSION,DO-PARAMETER
      OR ASSIGNED GOTO INDEX
SR-2 THE SUBPROGRAM WAS ASSIGNED DIFFERENT TYPES IN DIFFERENT
      PROGRAM SEGMENTS
SR-3 ATTEMPT TO USE A SUBPROGRAM RECURSIVELY
SR-4 INVALID TYPE OF ARGUMENT IN REFERENCE TO A SUBPROGRAM
SR-5 WRONG NUMBER OF ARGUMENTS IN A REFERENCE TO A SUBPROGRAM
SR-6 A SUBPROGRAM PREVIOUSLY DEFINED. FIRST DEFINITION USED
SR-7 NO MAIN PROGRAM
SR-8 ILLEGAL OR MISSING SUBPROGRAM NAME
SR-9 LIBRARY PROGRAM WAS NOT ASSIGNED THE CORRECT TYPE
SR-A METHOD OF ENTERING SUBPROGRAM PRODUCES UNDEFINED VALUE
      FOR CALL-BY-LOCATION PARAMETER
SR-B MAINLINE PROGRAM NOT IN LIBRARY

SUBSCRIPTS
SS-0 ZERO SUBSCRIPT OR DIMENSION NOT ALLOWED
SS-1 ARRAY SUBSCRIPT EXCEEDS DIMENSION
SS-2 INVALID SUBSCRIPT FORM
SS-3 SUBSCRIPT IS OUT OF RANGE
SS-4 SUBSCRIPTS EXCEED BOUNDS OF ACTUAL ARRAY

STATEMENTS AND STATEMENT NUMBERS
ST-0 MISSING STATEMENT NUMBER
ST-1 STATEMENT NUMBER GREATER THAN 99999
ST-2 STATEMENT NUMBER HAS ALREADY BEEN DEFINED
ST-3 UNDECODEABLE STATEMENT
ST-4 UNNUMBERED EXECUTABLE STATEMENT FOLLOWS A TRANSFER
ST-5 STATEMENT NUMBER IN TRANSFER IS NON-EXECUTABLE STATEMENT
ST-6 ONLY CALL STATEMENTS MAY CONTAIN STATEMENT
      NUMBER ARGUMENTS
ST-7 STATEMENT SPECIFIED IN A TRANSFER STATEMENT IS A FORMAT
ST-8 MISSING FORMAT STATEMENT
ST-9 SPECIFICATION STATEMENT DOES NOT PRECEDE STATEMENT
      FUNCTION DEFINITIONS OR EXECUTABLE STATEMENTS
ST-A UNREFERENCED STATEMENT FOLLOWS A TRANSFER
ST-B STATEMENT NUMBER MUST END WITH COLON. NUMBER WAS IGNORED

SUBSCRIPTED VARIABLES
SV-0 WRONG NUMBER OF SUBSCRIPTS WERE SPECIFIED FOR A VARIABLE
SV-1 ARRAY OR SUBPROGRAM NAME USED INCORRECTLY WITHOUT A LIST
SV-2 MORE THAN 7 DIMENSIONS ARE NOT ALLOWED
SV-3 DIMENSION OR SUBSCRIPT TOO LARGE (MAXIMUM 10**8-1)
SV-4 A VARIABLE USED WITH VARIABLE DIMENSIONS IS NOT A
      SUBPROGRAM PARAMETER
SV-5 A VARIABLE DIMENSION IS NOT ONE OF SIMPLE INTEGER
      VARIABLE, SUBPROGRAM PARAMETER, IN COMMON
SV-6 CRYPTO VARIABLE DIMENSIONING ASSUMED FOR ARRAY

SYNTAX ERRORS
SX-0 MISSING OPERATOR
SX-1 EXPECTING OPERATOR
SX-2 EXPECTING SYMBOL
SX-3 EXPECTING SYMBOL OR OPERATOR
SX-4 EXPECTING CONSTANT
SX-5 EXPECTING SYMBOL OR CONSTANT
SX-6 EXPECTING STATEMENT NUMBER
SX-7 EXPECTING SIMPLE INTEGER VARIABLE
SX-8 EXPECTING SIMPLE INTEGER VARIABLE OR CONSTANT
SX-9 ILLEGAL SEQUENCE OF OPERATORS IN EXPRESSION
SX-A EXPECTING END-OF-STATEMENT
SX-B SYNTAX ERROR
SX-C EXPECTING (OR END-OF-STATEMENT

TYPE STATEMENTS
TY-0 THE VARIABLE HAS ALREADY BEEN EXPLICITLY TYPED
TY-1 LENGTH OF THE EQUIVALENCED VARIABLE MAY NOT BE CHANGED.
      REMEDY: INTERCHANGE TYPE AND EQUIVALENCE STATEMENTS

I/O OPERATIONS
UN-0 CONTROL CARD ENCOUNTERED ON UNIT 5 AT EXECUTION.
      PROBABLE CAUSE: MISSING DATA OR INCORRECT FORMAT
UN-1 END OF FILE ENCOUNTERED (IBM CODE IHC217)
UN-2 I/O ERROR (IBM CODE IHC218)
UN-3 NO DD STATEMENT WAS SUPPLIED (IBM CODE IHC219)
UN-4 REWIND, ENDFILE, BACKSPACE REFERENCES UNIT 5, 6 OR 7
UN-5 ATTEMPT TO READ ON UNIT 5 AFTER IT HAS HAD END-OF-FILE
UN-6 AN INVALID VARIABLE UNIT NUMBER (IBM CODE IHC220)
UN-7 PAGE LIMIT EXCEEDED
UN-8 ATTEMPT TO DO DIRECT ACCESS I/O ON A SEQUENTIAL FILE OR
      VICE VERSA.
      POSSIBLE MISSING DEFINE FILE STATEMENT (IBM CODE IHC231)
UN-9 WRITE REFERENCES 5 OR READ REFERENCES 6 OR 7
UN-A DEFINE FILE REFERENCES A UNIT PREVIOUSLY USED FOR
      SEQUENTIAL I/O (IBM CODE IHC235)
UN-B RECORD SIZE FOR UNIT EXCEEDS 32767,OR DIFFERS FROM DD
      STATEMENT SPECIFICATION (IBM CODES IHC233,IHC237)
UN-C FOR DIRECT ACCESS I/O THE RELATIVE RECORD POSITION IS
      NEGATIVE, ZERO, OR TOO LARGE (IBM CODE IHC232)
UN-D ATTEMPT TO READ MORE INFORMATION THAN LOGICAL RECORD
      CONTAINS (IBM CODE IHC213)
UN-E FORMATTED LINE EXCEEDS BUFFER LENGTH (IBM CODE IHC212)
UN-F I/O ERROR - SEARCHING LIBRARY DIRECTORY
UN-G I/O ERROR - READING LIBRARY
UN-H ATTEMPT TO DEFINE THE OBJECT ERROR FILE AS A DIRECT
      ACCESS FILE (IBM CODE IHC234)

```
UN-I   RECFM IS NOT V(B)S FOR I/O WITHOUT FORMAT CONTROL
       (IBM CODE IHC214)
UN-J   MISSING DD CARD FOR WATLIB. NO LIBRARY ASSUMED
UN-K   ATTEMPT TO READ OR WRITE PAST THE END OF CHARACTER
       VARIABLE BUFFER
UN-L   ATTEMPT TO READ AN UNCREATED DIRECT ACCESS FILE (IHC236)
UN-M   DIRECT ACCESS SPACE EXCEEDED
UN-N   UNABLE TO OPEN WATLIB (I/O ERROR); NO LIBRARY ASSUMED
UN-P   ATTEMPT TO WRITE ON A READ-ONLY FILE
UN-Q   DIRECT ACCESS UNAVAILABLE IN DEBUG MODE
UN-R   NAME ON C$COPY CARD NOT FOUND IN LIBRARY
UN-S   MISSING OR INVALID NAME ON C$COPY CARD
UN-T   C$COPY CONTROL CARD OR PGM= OPTION FOUND IN LIBRARY
UN-U   ATTEMPT TO DO UNFORMATTED (BINARY) I/O ON READER,
       PRINTER, OR PUNCH
UNDEFINED VARIABLES
UV-0   VARIABLE IS UNDEFINED
UV-3   SUBSCRIPT IS UNDEFINED
UV-4   SUBPROGRAM IS UNDEFINED
UV-5   ARGUMENT IS UNDEFINED
UV-6   UNDECODABLE CHARACTERS IN VARIABLE FORMAT
UV-7   VARIABLE UNIT NUMBER IS UNDEFINED

VARIABLE NAMES
VA-0   A NAME IS TOO LONG. IT HAS BEEN TRUNCATED TO SIX CHARACTER
VA-1   ATTEMPT TO USE AN ASSIGNED OR INITIALIZED VARIABLE OR
       DO-PARAMETER IN A SPECIFICATION STATEMENT
VA-2   ILLEGAL USE OF A SUBROUTINE NAME
VA-3   ILLEGAL USE OF A VARIABLE NAME
VA-4   ATTEMPT TO USE THE PREVIOUSLY DEFINED NAME AS A FUNCTION
       OR AN ARRAY
VA-5   ATTEMPT TO USE A PREVIOUSLY DEFINED NAME AS A SUBROUTINE
VA-6   ATTEMPT TO USE A PREVIOUSLY DEFINED NAME AS A SUBPROGRAM
VA-7   ATTEMPT TO USE A PREVIOUSLY DEFINED NAME AS A COMMON BLOCK
VA-8   ATTEMPT TO USE A FUNCTION NAME AS A VARIABLE
VA-9   ATTEMPT TO USE A PREVIOUSLY DEFINED NAME AS A VARIABLE
VA-A   ILLEGAL USE OF A PREVIOUSLY DEFINED NAME
```

Appendix C

ADDITIONAL CONTROL STATEMENTS IN FORTRAN IV

There are a number of control statements available in FORTRAN, but these are rarely used when writing structured programs with WATFIV-S. To provide a complete presentation of the FORTRAN language, we have included this material in this Appendix.

C.1 UNCONDITIONAL GO TO

The GO TO statement permits the programmer to cause an unconditional transfer of control to any executable statement in a program. This is illustrated in Example C.1 which is an alternate method of programming Example 1.2.

```
C EXAMPLE  C.1
      X = 4.
12    Y = X*X
      PRINT, X, Y
      X = X + 1.0
      GO TO 12
      END
```

The statement GO TO 12 causes a transfer of control back to the statement with statement number 12. Thus the program will continue looping endlessly, as was the case with Example 1.2.

Example C.2 illustrates how the GO TO can be used with the logical IF to terminate the looping when X exceeds 9.0.

```
C EXAMPLE  C.2
      X = 4.0
12    Y = X*X
      PRINT, X, Y
      X = X + 1.0
      IF (X .LE. 9.0) GO TO 12
      STOP
      END
```

When X has been incremented to 10.0 the logical expression

$$X \ .LE. \ 9.0$$

is no longer "true", and control proceeds to the STOP statement.

Consider Example C.3, which shows some common errors that can be made with a statement as simple as the GO TO statement.

```
C EXAMPLE  C.3 - IMPROPER USE OF GO TO
2     INTEGER X, SUM
      SUM = 0
      READ, X
      SUM = SUM + X
      GO TO 2
      PRINT, SUM
      STOP
      END
```

Here, the GO TO attempts to transfer control to a non-executable statement; transfer must always be made to executable statements. Notice also that it is impossible to get to the unnumbered PRINT statement since it immediately follows the GO TO; thus, to ensure that the PRINT statement may be executed, the statement following the GO TO should be assigned a number, and some means of transferring control to this statement should be provided.

C.2 GOING TO A DO

It is not valid, to attempt to transfer into the range of a DO from outside the range. In short, the only way to get into the range of a DO is to enter through the controlling DO statement itself. An example which violates this rule follows:

```
                    GO TO 12
                    DO 3 J=1,25
        12          ISQ = I*J
        3           CONTINUE
```

It is perfectly valid to transfer within the range of a DO, provided the statement transferring control is also with the same range.

It is possible to exit from a DO-loop before it is satisified. However, in this case, the value of of the index is to be considered indefinite (see Rule 6 in Chapter 8).

C.3 IF STATEMENTS

There are two kinds of IF statements in FORTRAN - logical IF and arithemetic IF. Both are examples of conditional control statements, since they allow the programmer the facility of making tests at execution time and possibly altering control within the program, depending on the results of the tests.

In essence, the logical IF statement allows us a two-way choice - do something or do not do something - based on a test performed at execution time. The arithmetic IF statement is somewhat different, in that it allows a possibility of a three-way choice. Suppose it is desired to read in values of X, positive and negative, but to sum only the positive values. The program is to print the sum and terminate when a zero value is read. Example C.4 illustrates the use of the arithmetic IF to solve this problem.

```
C EXAMPLE  C.4 - USE OF ARITHMETIC IF
          INTEGER X, SUM
          SUM = 0
62        READ, X
          IF (X) 62, 5, 133
133       SUM = SUM + X
          GO TO 62
5         PRINT, SUM
          STOP
          END
```

The arithmetic IF statement in the program, namely

IF (X) 62, 5, 133

works in the following fashion; a test is performed on X and, if X is negative, control transfers to the statement numbered 62; if X is zero, control transfers to the statement numbered 5; if X is positive, control transfers to the statement numbered 133.

Actually, what appears between the parentheses of the arithmetic IF statement may be any real- or integer-valued expression. Consider the next example, which is a program to tabulate the function

$$y = \frac{x^2 - 3x + 2}{x - 3}$$

for x = 0, 1, 2, 3, 4, ..., 10,

but skips the value where the denominator vanishes.

Notice that, even when we are interested in only a two-way choice for the result of the test on the value of the expression, three statement numbers of executable statements must be provided following the closing parenthesis of the IF; they always correspond to a negative result, a zero result, or

```
C EXAMPLE   C.5 - USE OF ARITHMETIC IF
      X = 0.
7     IF (X-3.) 12, 2, 12
12    Y = (X*X-3.*X+2.) / (X-3.)
      PRINT, X, Y
2     X = X + 1.
      IF (X-20.) 7, 7, 85
85    STOP
      END
```

a positive result, from left to right.   Control will transfer
from the arithmetic IF to a statement which is numbered by one
of the three statement numbers.   For this reason, the next
executable statement following an arithmetic IF should be
numbered, since otherwise there is no way that control can
ever pass to that statement.   Example C.6 illustrates this
possibility; the statement PRINT, X can never be executed.

```
C EXAMPLE   C.6 - FAULTY STATEMENT NUMBERING
3     READ, X
      IF ((X-5.)*(X+3.)) 1, 2, 3
      PRINT, X
1     Y = X*X - 13.2*X
      PRINT, Y
      GO TO 3
2     STOP
      END
```

    The question might be asked: When does one use a logical
IF, and when does one use an arithmetic IF?   Usually this will
be answered by experience.   The logical IF statement is often
easier to understand, is more descriptive because of its
structure, and is very natural to write when coding a program;
but the arithmetic IF is sometimes convenient because it
allows the three-way choice.   Historically, earlier versions
of the FORTRAN language did not have logical IF statements.

C.4   COMPUTED GO TO

The computed GO TO statement is a conditional control statement that allows a many-way choice for transfer of control. This feature is often convenient when different calculations must be performed on some values depending on a code or a "key" that can be associated with the values.

To illustrate this, suppose the height of each student in a school is punched on a separate data card along with a code specifying the sex of the student: 1 for male, 2 for female. A card with a code of 3 is used to indicate the end of the data. Example C.7 is a program to calculate the average height of males and females in the school.

The computed GO TO

                GO TO (14, 29, 17), SEX

transfers control to one of the statements numbered 14, 29, or 17 depending on the value read for the code variable SEX. If the value of SEX is 1, control transfers to statement 14 to perform the calculations for a male student; if the value of SEX is 2, control transfers to statement 29 to process the data for a female. The last data card has a value of 3 for SEX, and control transfers to statement 17 to print the averages. (Note that the last card must contain a dummy value for HEIGHT to satisfy the read list.)

This example has shown a three-way choice for transfer of control, since only three statement numbers were included. Computed GO TO statements may have any number of choices as the following sample statements show.

                GO TO (16, 3, 3, 8, 14, 16),JACK
                GO TO (1, 2, 3, 4, 5, 5, 4, 3, 2, 2), K
                GO TO (99, 28), LPT

```
C EXAMPLE   C.7 - AVERAGE HEIGHT
            INTEGER SEX, FEMALE, MALE
            REAL HMALE, HFEMAL
            HMALE = HFEMAL = FEMALE = MALE = 0
3           READ, HEIGHT, SEX
            GO TO (14, 29, 17), SEX
14          HMALE = HMALE + HEIGHT
            MALE = MALE + 1
            GO TO 3
29          HFEMAL = HFEMAL + HEIGHT
            FEMALE = FEMALE + 1
            GO TO 3
17          PRINT, HMALE/MALE, HFEMAL/FEMALE
            STOP
            END
```

If the first statement were executed, control would pass to statement number 16, if the value of JACK, called the index, had the value one; similarly if JACK had the value 2, control would pass to statement 3; if JACK had the value 4, control would pass to statement 8; and so forth.

There are only a few simple rules to remember about the use of the computed GO TO, and these are:

(a)   The index must be a simple integer variable
        e.g.,   GO TO(12, 2, 63), 2*I+1
      is invalid.

(b)   If the value of the index exceeds the number of statement numbers in the GO TO control passes to the next executable statement following the GO TO. For example, control would pass to statement 5 if the following were executed:
            I = 99
            GO TO (3, 17, 4), I
        5   SUM = SUM + 1

(c)   All the statement numbers in the list must be numbers of executable statements.

A common error when using computed GO TO's is to forget the comma following the parenthesized list of statement numbers.

Another use of computed GO TO's is that of a <u>switch</u>, as illustrated in Example C.8.

```
C EXAMPLE   C.8 - COMPUTED GO TO AS A SWITCH
        INTEGER SWITCH
        SWITCH = 1
16      READ, X
        GO TO(3, 5), SWITCH
3       SWITCH = 2
        SUM = -X
        GO TO 16
5       SUM = SUM + X
        IF (X .NE. 0.) GO TO 16
        PRINT, SUM
        STOP
        END
```

Note that the statement numbered 3 and the two statements following it are executed only once.

C.5   ASSIGN AND ASSIGNED GO TO STATEMENTS

The assigned GO TO statement is very much like the computed GO TO statement in that it allows a many-way choice for transfer of control. However, the choice of statement to which control is transferred depends on the previous execution of a special statement called the ASSIGN statement. To see what these statements look like and how they work together, suppose the following statements were executed sequentially in a program:

```
ASSIGN 15 TO IX3
GO TO IX3, (3, 7, 15, 8)
```

As a result of executing the GO TO, control will be transferred to the statement numbered 15 since the previous execution of the ASSIGN statement associated that statement number with the variable IX3 mentioned in the GO TO. The numbers appearing in the GO TO statement are a list of statement numbers which are potential targets for transfer of control from the GO TO.

Example C.9 shows that different statement numbers may be associated with a variable, thus allowing a many-way branch.

```
C EXAMPLE   C.9
        ASSIGN 3 TO JUMP
5       GO TO JUMP, (7, 3, 6)
6       PRINT, 999999
7       STOP
3       PRINT, 888888
        ASSIGN 6 TO JUMP
        GO TO 5
        END
```

The output for this program consists of the following two lines:

888888

999999

The assigned GO TO can be used in much the same way as the computed GO TO, that is, as a switch which can transfer control to one of many points in a program, depending on the most recent assignment of a statement number to the integer variable associated with the GO TO. It has the advantage that, when reading over a program, the effect of the assigned GO TO is easier to follow, particularly where the equivalent computed GO TO has a very long list of statement numbers. Also, the assigned GO TO usually takes less time to execute on a computer than the equivalent computed GO TO. However, the computed GO TO is quite useful when transfer of control can be made to depend on some code or key.

The rules for the ASSIGN statement and the assigned GO TO statement are quite simple, namely,

(a)   The variable used in these statements must be an integer variable of length 4.

(b)   This integer variable should not be used for any other purpose in a program since this could lead to

troubles at execution time. For example, the
following two statements appearing in a program
would be considered invalid.

ASSIGN 5 TO JUMP

JUMP = JUMP + 3

(c) The statement to which an assigned GO TO transfers
control <u>must</u> be one of the statements numbered in
the list of the GO TO. Thus, although any executable statement's number may be mentioned in an
ASSIGN statement, when an assigned GO TO is
executed, a previously-executed ASSIGN statement
must have assigned one of the numbers in the list
to the variable of the GO TO. Failure to do this
results in an error.

Finally, one must not forget that the forms of
the computed and assigned GO TO are slightly
different:

Computed GO TO   GO TO (26, 3, 35, 8), K

Assigned GO TO   GO TO JUMP, (4, 7, 57, 22)

C.6   STOP STATEMENT

A STOP statement has appeared in almost every program; it
is a control statement that has an obvious meaning. However,
it should be made clear that the STOP statement does not actually stop the operation of the computer; its effect is to
terminate execution of the program, thus freeing the computer
to start working on some other person's program. It might be
added that, in earlier versions of FORTRAN used on smaller
computers, the STOP statement did bring the computer to a
halt, thus requiring some sort of operator action before the
computer could be started up on another program.

There is an additional form of the STOP statement which consists of the word STOP followed by a constant of up to five digits, e.g., STOP 673. It has the same effect as the simple STOP, but in addition the constant is displayed on the computer operator's console (usually a typewriter connected to the computer). This gives a record of the STOP statement which terminated execution of the program. Since it is usually the case, in present-day large computer installations, that the programmer does not have access to the operator's console output, this form of the STOP statement is of limited usefulness and, in some installations, it is not allowed. In this case, WATFIV-S treats such a STOP statement like a simple STOP.

Note that a program may have any number of STOP statements; the first one encountered at execution time terminates program execution. Note also that the first executable statement following a STOP statement should have a statement number; otherwise, there is no possibility of its being executed.

C.7   PAUSE STATEMENT

The PAUSE statement is another control statement which, when encountered, involves the computer operator and thus, because of its limited usefulness and potential nuisance value, is not permitted at some installations.

There are three forms:

(a)   simple PAUSE, e.g., PAUSE

(b)   PAUSE with a constant, e.g., PAUSE 125

(c)   PAUSE with a message, e.g., PAUSE 'MOUNT TAPE 25'

When a PAUSE statement is executed, a message is displayed on the operator console and further execution of the program is temporarily suspended until the operator responds, usually by typing something on the console. Control then proceeds to the next statement following the PAUSE statement. The message the operator receives is the constant in the statement (00000 for simple PAUSE) or the actual letters between the quote marks.

Thus the PAUSE statement would be used only if the program had encountered some special problem which involved operator assistance, e.g., mounting a special data tape at a certain point in the program's execution.

C.8 STATEMENT RESTRICTIONS

FORTRAN places certain restrictions on the use of control statements presented in this appendix.

(a) Logical IF - In the general form of the logical IF namely, IF(e)s, the statement s may not be a DO or another logical IF.

(b) DO statement - The object of a DO may not be a STOP, PAUSE, RETURN, another DO, an arithmetic IF, any GO TO, or a logical IF containing any of these.

Appendix D

CHARACTER MANIPULATION USING STANDARD FORTRAN IV

Character variables and constants have been introduced in Chapter 11 and have been used extensively throughout this text. There is an alternative means of handling character information in WATFIV-S. This involves the use of the other variable types to optionally store character data. Standard FORTRAN IV uses this latter technique, and it is introduced in this appendix to round out the character handling facilities in WATFIV-S. Normally however, the programmer will find it easier to use Character variables.

Some of the information in this appendix repeats material introduced in previous discussions about character handling. It is included to permit the reader to directly compare the two techniques, and to consolidate the concepts into a single location.

D.1   CHARACTER STRINGS

Each byte of the computer's memory is capable of storing one character. Hence, four characters can occupy the space used by an integer variable. In fact, one way of storing character strings is as values assigned to integer variables. Then the name of the variable becomes the name of the string of four characters.

Let us consider the following declaration statement:

        INTEGER A/'JOKE'/, X/2568/

Here the variables A and X are declared to be of integer type. The variable X is initialized to have the value 2568; the variable A is initialized so that it contains the character string JOKE. Note that this would completely fill the full word, with J as the first byte, O as the second, K as the third, and E as the last. The extremities of the character string are delimited using quote symbols. These symbols, as is usually the case with Hollerith strings, are not part of the string itself.

Suppose the string were longer than four characters, as is the case for CHARLIE. This could be stored using two integer variables as follows:

        INTEGER A/'CHAR'/, B/'LIE'/

Here B has assigned to it a character string LIE, which is not long enough to fill the full word. In cases like this, blank characters are automatically inserted on the right, as necessary.

At this point consider Example D.1.

```
C EXAMPLE D.1
        INTEGER A/'CHAR'/, B/'LIE'/
        INTEGER X/2568/, Y/'2568'/
        PRINT, A, B, X, Y
        STOP
        END
```

The output for the example would be

    -1010253351   -741751488   2568   -218761480

which might not be what the reader would have expected. This is because the computer has no way of identifying that A, B, and Y, contain character strings when it encounters the statement

They are treated as integer variables, and hence are assumed to represent integer values. Consequently, apparently meaningless integer values are printed. In a later section, we will see how these variables can be more appropriately printed using the A format code.

The example also emphasizes the fact that the integer constant 2568 takes on quite a different appearance when represented as a character string.

Character strings can also be stored in the other types of variables. For example, a string of sixteen characters can be stored as the value of an extended-precision complex variable or in an integer array of four elements.

We are now in a position to describe the various possibilities in detail.

D.2   STORING CHARACTER DATA

Characters may be stored using any of four types of variables - real, integer, complex, or logical. As seen previously, each integer variable can store a maximum of four characters, whereas each extended-precision complex variable can store a maximum of sixteen characters. Figure D.1 is a table which shows the number of characters that can be stored for each of the various types of variables. The length specification of the type of variable indicates the maximum number of characters which can be stored in it.

Variable Type	Number of Characters
INTEGER*2	2
INTEGER*4 or INTEGER	4
REAL*4 or REAL	4
REAL*8 or DOUBLE PRECISION	8
COMPLEX*8 or COMPLEX	8
COMPLEX*16	16
LOGICAL*4 or LOGICAL	4
LOGICAL*1	1

Figure D.1

D.3   DEFINING CHARACTER DATA IN DECLARATION STATEMENTS

Declaration statements may be used to initialize character variables prior to execution time. The following examples further demonstrate how character strings can be formed.

    (a)   INTEGER A/'LIFE'/, B/'DOGS'/

    (b)   REAL*8 X/8HABCDEFGH/

    (c)   REAL XX(3)/'SUBC', 'OMMI', 'TTEE'/

    (d)   LOGICAL*1 Z(5)/'A', 'B', 'C', 'D', 'E'/

    (e)   INTEGER N/'AB'/

    (f)   REAL*8 Q/'HORSE'/, W/'ABCDEFGHIJK'/

    (g)   REAL X(4)/4*'AB'/, Y(4)/'AB', 'AB', 'AB', 'AB'/

Example (a) assigns the character strings LIFE and DOGS
to the integer variables A and B respectively.

Example (b) illustrates the use of the H-type Hollerith
constant. Usually the quote-type constant is more convenient
to use.

Example (c) illustrates how a relatively large amount of character data can be stored using consecutive elements of an array. Here, the word SUBCOMMITTEE is segmented into three strings of four letters each, and they are assigned to the three elements of the array XX. It is important to note that the character data must be subdivided into strings of length less than or equal to the length of the elements in the array. Thus, the following statement would not produce the desired results.

REAL XX(3)/'SUBCOMMITTEE'/

It would cause an error message to be produced, and is another example of the rule that there must be one piece of data for every element in an array which is being initialized.

Example (d) declares Z to be a logical array with five elements. Each of the elements occupies one byte; the five elements are initialized to the character data A, B, C, D, and E respectively.

In Example (e), we have a situation where there are only two characters in the string, whereas the integer variable N is capable of storing four characters. As has been stated in Section D.1, two blanks are inserted on the right. In Example (f), we have the opposite situation; the string has eleven characters, and the variable can store only eight. In such cases, the string is truncated, and the farthest-right characters, in this case the letters IJK, are lost.

Example (g) illustrates the use of a replication factor. Here the character string AB, padded on the right with two blanks, will be repeated four times, once for each of the elements of the array X. The array Y will be initialized to exactly the same data, but this time no replication factor is used.

We have seen how to initialize variables with character data. If we wish to print the values of these variables and have them appear as characters, we must use the A format code. Consider Example D.2.

```
          C EXAMPLE D.2
                INTEGER A/'CHAR'/, B/'LIE'/
                INTEGER X/2568/, Y/'2568'/
                PRINT 6, A, B, X, Y
          6     FORMAT('0', A4, A4, 3X, I4, 3X, A4)
                STOP
                END
```

The following line would be printed, after double spacing.

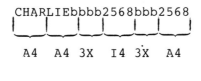

```
          A   B    X    Y
```

The format code Aw assumes that character data is stored in the variable being printed. This data is printed right-justified in a field of width w. Thus the letters CHAR are printed in the first four print positions, followed by LIEb in the next four print positions. Three blanks are inserted because of the 3X code, and the integer value for X is printed using the I format code. Finally, three more spaces are left, and the character string 2568 is printed using format code A4.

It would be instructive to consider the effect of replacing the FORMAT statement in Example D.2 with the following statement:

```
          6     FORMAT('0', A3, A6, 3X, I4, 3X, A2)
```

In this case the line printed would be

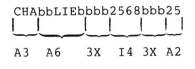

```
CHAbbLIEbbbb2568bbb25
| |  |   |  | |  | |
A3  A6   3X  I4 3X A2
```

                    A   B   X   Y

Here the format code A3 is used to print A. Since the field
width is three, only the three farthest-left characters stored
in A are printed; the fourth character is ignored. Thus,
whenever the field width w is less than the number of characters in the string, only the w farthest-left characters are
printed, and the remainder are ignored.

The format code for B is A6, which means that the field
width has two more character positions than the string stored
in B. Thus, the output is right-justified in the field, with
two blanks padded on the left.

The variable Y is printed under format A2, and once again
only the farthest-left characters are printed, as was the case
for the variable A.

The A format code is also used for input. Suppose the
following sequence of statements was executed.

                    INTEGER A, B, C,
                    READ 4, A, B, C,
          4   FORMAT(A4,A4,A4)

A card would be read, and the first four columns would be
assigned to A as character data, because of the A4 format
code. Similarly, the characters in columns 5 to 8 would be
stored in B, and the characters in columns 9 to 12 would be
stored in C. Thus, if the input data card contained the
following characters in columns 1 to 12 inclusive,

                    X$*AB123+9Z@

then the integer variables A, B, and C would have assigned to
them the character strings X$*A, B123 and +9Z@ respectively.

Suppose that the FORMAT statement were replaced by

4   FORMAT(A6, A2, A4)

and the same input data card were read. In this case, the first six columns are considered as the field associated with the integer variable A; since A can store only four characters, the four farthest-right characters in the field are assigned. Thus A has assigned to it the character string *AB1.

The integer variable B has its input controlled by the format code A2. Only a two-column field is involved, namely, the contents of columns 7 and 8; however, the integer variable B is capable of storing four characters. In this case, the two characters are stored left-justified, and blanks are inserted on the right. Thus, B has assigned to it the character string 23bb.

Example D.3 illustrates the use of the A format code with both input and output. The example is designed to read a deck of 50 cards, one at a time, and output their contents on the printer.

```
      C EXAMPLE D.3
            INTEGER CARD(20)
            DO 13 I=1,50
               READ 21, CARD
               PRINT 22, CARD
      13    CONTINUE
            STOP
      22    FORMAT('0', 20A4)
      21    FORMAT(20A4)
            END
```

The integer array CARD has 20 elements, and each of these has assigned to it the characters contained in four consecutive columns of the input data card. The characters in columns 1 to 4 are stored in CARD(1), the characters in columns 5 to 8 are stored in CARD(2), etc. Note that the format code A4 has a field count of 20 to satisfy the requirements of the whole array.

For each card read, a line is printed. This line contains the entire contents of the vector CARD, printed using the A format code. Exactly 80 print positions are used, with the result that the contents of all 80 columns of each of the previously read input cards are printed.

It would be appropriate to summarize the rules for using the Aw format code.

(a) On output, if the number of characters stored in the string being printed is less than the field width w, the field is padded on the left with blanks. If the number of characters in the string exceeds the field width, only the w farthest-left characters are printed to fill out the field.

(b) On input, if w exceeds the length specification, s, of the variable which is to store the string, only the s farthest-right characters in the field are stored. If w is less than s, the entire field is stored left-justified in the variable, and blanks are inserted on the right.

D.5 COMPARISON OF CHARACTER STRINGS

The previous sections were concerned with the assignment and printing of character strings. It is important to be able to do comparisons with character strings, as illustrated in Example D.4.

Example D.4 reads a single data card which contains an English sentence, beginning in column one. The individual words in the sentence may have any length, up to a maximum of ten characters. The words are separated by single blanks, with a period terminating the sentence. The program determines the number of words having one letter, the number of words having two letters, and so on up to words having ten letters.

```
C EXAMPLE D.4
      INTEGER BLANK/' '/,  DOT/'.'/
      INTEGER CHAR(80), COUNT(10)
      READ 22, CHAR
      DO 1 I=1,10
          COUNT(I) = 0
1     CONTINUE
      NUMBER = 0
      I = 1
      LOOP
          IF (CHAR(I) .EQ. DOT) QUIT
          IF (CHAR(I) .EQ. BLANK) THEN
              COUNT(NUMBER) = COUNT(NUMBER) + 1
              NUMBER = 0
          ELSE
              NUMBER = NUMBER + 1
          ENDIF
          I = I + 1
      ENDLOOP
      COUNT(NUMBER) = COUNT(NUMBER) + 1
      PRINT 23, CHAR
      PRINT 24, (COUNT(I), I, I=1,10)
      STOP
24    FORMAT(' ', I3, 'WORDS OF LENGTH', I3)
23    FORMAT(' ', 80A1)
22    FORMAT(80A1)
      END
```

The program reads the data card, and places each character of the sentence in a separate element of the vector CHAR. The elements of the array COUNT are used as word length counters, and NUMBER is used as the character counter. All of these counters are initialized to the value zero. A DO-loop is used to control the scanning of the characters. The scan consists of testing for a period or blank. For each character in a word, unity is added to NUMBER. Each time a blank is encountered, the appropriate element of the array COUNT is increased by one, using the current value of NUMBER as a subscript. Similarly, when the period is encountered, the appropriate element of the array COUNT is increased by one. The original sentence and counts are then printed.

This example is useful to illustrate several points.

The statements

```
        IF (CHAR(I) .EQ. DOT) QUIT
        IF (CHAR(I) .EQ. BLANK) THEN
```

utilize the comparison of character strings. This is accomplished by treating the character string which is assigned to an integer variable as if it were an integer value; these integer variables may then be used in arithmetic expressions and assignment statements. Thus if CHAR(13) has the character string .bbb assigned to it, there will be a true result for the logical expression

```
        CHAR(13) .EQ. DOT
```

since the integer variable DOT has been initialized to the character string .bbb.

Memory space could have been saved if all variables used were declared with the INTEGER*2 statement. However, note that the program would not work if the variables were declared with either of the LOGICAL or LOGICAL*1 declaration statements. This is because the expressions

```
        CHAR(I) .EQ. DOT
        CHAR(I) .EQ. BLANK
```

would not be legal expressions, since logical expressions may not be used as operands with relational operators.

Could we have declared the variables to be of any other type, such as REAL? The answer is yes for Example D.4. However, if the example were slightly different, trouble could arise in certain relatively rare circumstances. This is because of the nature of normalized floating-point numbers. A random assignment of data as a character string could result in an unnormalized floating-point number.

Consequently, as a general rule, it is advisable to use integer variables to store character strings whenever these variables are to be used in comparisons or other arithmetic computations.

If a program requires no such operations, any type of variable is suitable. For example, it is usually more convenient to use variables of type COMPLEX*16 when lengthy strings are involved. For instance, the statement

COMPLEX*16 C/'THIS IS THE DATA'/

is easier to formulate and key-punch than is

INTEGER*4 N(4)/'THIS', ' IS ', 'THE ', 'DATA'/

D.6 ALPHABETIC SORTING OF CHARACTER STRINGS

Consider the following two statements

INTEGER X/'AAAA'/, Y/'AAAB'/
PRINT, X, Y

The values printed for X and Y would be -1944266559 and -1044266558, respectively. If the two character strings are compared, we have the condition that X is less than Y. This is as we would like it, since AAAA precedes AAAB in alphabetical order. The character representations for all the letters have been chosen in such a way that alphabetic sequence is always reflected in such comparisons. Thus, if the integer variables X and Y each contain character data, the expression

X .LT. Y

will have the value .TRUE. if and only if the character string stored in X precedes, in alphabetical order, the character string stored in Y.

The program in Example D.5 reads one hundred data cards, each containing a word which consists of four letters, and stores them in the vector WORD. Then it arranges them in alphabetical order.

```
C EXAMPLE D.5
      INTEGER WORD(100)
      LOGICAL SWT
      DO 1 I=1,100
          READ 2, WORD(I)
1     CONTINUE
      N = 99
      DO 3 I=1,99
          SWT = .FALSE.
          DO 4 J=1,N
              IF (WORD(J) .GT. WORD(J+1)) THEN
                  ITEMP = WORD(J)
                  WORD(J) = WORD(J+1)
                  WORD(J+1) = ITEMP
                  SWT = .TRUE.
              ENDIF
4         CONTINUE·
          IF (.NOT.SWT) QUIT
          N = N - 1
3     CONTINUE
      PRINT 7, WORD
      STOP
7     FORMAT('0', 10A6)
2     FORMAT(A4)
      END
```

The method used compares successive pairs of four-letter
words. Two successive words are interchanged in the vector if
they are not in alphabetical order, i.e., the first is not
"less than" the second. After the entire vector has been
processed, the last word in alphabetical order has been "shuffled" to the end of the vector. The vector is processed
again, and, as a result, the "second-largest" word appears in
the second-last position. After at most ninety-nine passes
over the data in the vector, the words are arranged in the
required order. The reader might determine the purpose served
by the logical variable SWT.

As a final note, consider Example D.6, which illustrates
that mixed-mode comparisons produce unexpected results.
The value printed for L is F, representing false. Since A is
an integer variable, its value is converted to a real number
before the comparison with the real variable B occurs. Thus,

- 395 -

```
C EXAMPLE D.6
      LOGICAL L
      INTEGER A/'ABCD'/
      REAL B/'ABCD'/
      L = A .EQ. B
      PRINT, L
      STOP
      END
```

even though the original character strings are identical, one
of them is changed before the comparison is made. Hence they
are not recognized as equal.

INDEX

```
  one-dimensional,91                 Unlabelled common - see
  two-dimensional,99                             blank common
  multi-dimensional,106
  names,91                           Variables,2
  I/O,96,103                           character,138
  use of,92                           complex,221
  storage order,103,107               double-precision,211
  summary,107                         integer,54
Supervisor,5                          logical,194
Symbolic name,9                       real,42
Syntax,8                            Variable dimensions - see
                                               object-time
                                               dimensions
T format,281                        Variable format,293,303
Tape - see magnetic tape            Vector,88,98
THEN,30                               see subscripted variable
Type declaration statements
  rules,246                         WATFIV,preface
  initialization in,244             WATFOR,preface
Type FUNCTION,253                   WHILE,23
                                    Words half, full, double,234
Unary minus,43,55                   WRITE statement,264,267,
Undefined variable,12                             293,308
  see Appendix B                      with format,274,311
Underflow,44                          without format,268,316
  exponent,238
  floating point,44                 X format,122,131
Unit number,264,308
  standard,264                      Z format,280
```